LORD of the DANCE

MICHAEL FLATLEY has performed his electrifying brand of Irish dancing all over the world to audiences of millions. His most recent show, *Celtic Tiger*, is currently touring the world.

DOUGLAS THOMPSON is the bestselling author of more than twenty books. A biographer, broadcaster and international journalist, he is a regular contributor to major newspapers and magazines worldwide. His books, published in a dozen languages, included the television-based anthology *Hollywood People* and top-ten biographies. His next book, *The Hustlers*, will be published by Sidgwick & Jackson. He divides his time between Los Angeles and London.

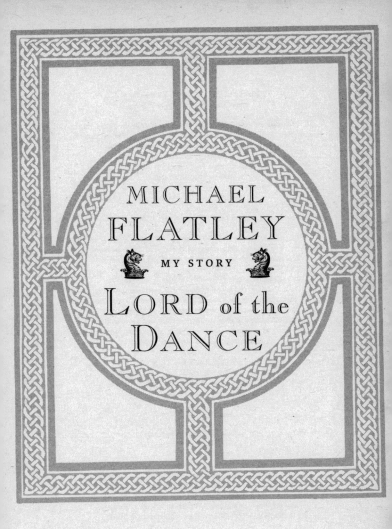

MICHAEL FLATLEY

MY STORY

LORD of the DANCE

PAN BOOKS

First published 2006 by Sidgwick & Jackson
and simultaneously in paperback

This edition first published in paperback 2007 by Pan Books
an imprint of Pan Macmillan, a division of Macmillan Publishers Limited
Pan Macmillan, 20 New Wharf Road, London N1 9RR
Basingstoke and Oxford
Associated companies throughout the world
www.panmacmillan.com

ISBN 978-0-330-44540-5

3 5 7 9 8 6 4 2

A CIP catalogue record for this book is available from
the British Library.

Designed by Elliott Beard

Printed and bound in Great Britain by
CPI Mackays, Chatham ME5 8TD

Nothing is impossible. Follow your dreams.

MICHAEL FLATLEY

The world needs more people like Michael Flatley.

NELSON MANDELA,
September 2003

Michael Flatley is an Irish-American treasure.

BILL CLINTON,
March 2001

Michael Flatley is not only Irish by descent, he is Irish through his convictions. Born in the United States, he had the opportunity to follow any avenue which he chose. It was his love of Irish culture that drew him back to his Irish roots, and in particular to Irish dance. The story of his success is very well known. But we should not forget the years of endless astonishing practice, patience and perseverance that contributed to his success. Dance is incredibly demanding and punishing physically. It requires enormous determination and stamina. Michael has those qualities, as well as a great stage presence and business acumen.

I salute Michael for what he has achieved for himself as well as for the encouragement, and the possibilities which his work has proved for others.

TAOISEACH BERTIE AHERN,
February 2006

To my mother and father and my family

To the people of Ireland,
whose support has been inexhaustible

And to my late grandmother "Hannah"

Acknowledgments

I wish to thank the following people for their help in writing this book: Douglas Thompson, Rachel Krantz, Ingrid Connell, all the friends and colleagues who took the time to be interviewed, David Zedeck and the team at CAA, and Martin Flitton and the rest of my amazing team.

My thanks to Brian McEvoy for so many of the wonderful photographs in the book.

CONTENTS

Act Four

FEET OF FLAMES

Act Five

CELTIC TIGER

Encore

INTRODUCTION

Looking for Michael Flatley

There are two ways of spreading light:
to be the candle or the mirror that reflects it.

EDITH WHARTON

Michael Flatley wants to take on the world. Then he wants to have sex with it. And then he wants to do its accounts. Irish dancer, flautist, champion boxer, multi-millionaire businessman with a genius IQ , Flatley is one of the highest paid stage performers in the world. His personal glamour and fanatical careerism have made him the most significant figure in Irish dancing–an art he's helped transform from a stiff-armed stamping that Dublin schoolchildren are forced to learn at school into a massively lucrative global industry.

MATTHEW SWEET,
The Independent, London, November 24, 1996

MICHAEL FLATLEY is one of the most successful men alive. He has created an entertainment empire totally through his own endeavor. Today he stands at the crest of his achievements and has only a more astonishing future ahead of him. Among the highest paid performers in the world–known as The Billion-Dollar Dancer–he is a showman of grand ideas.

He is that rare and so very potent phenomenon, a dreamer and a doer, a world-winner in the grand tradition of American enterprise.

The eldest son of Irish immigrants who settled in the United States a little more than half a century ago, Michael Flatley has become one of history's most popular and distinguished superstars.

He is also a complex human being who has had to make difficult choices and sacrifices during his trip to the top. His life has been packed, on and off stage, with a turbulent extravaganza of romance and drama.

For the past two years I have been seeking the untold story of his past and present. His life is continually thrusting new challenges in his path. In fact, the only thing predictable about his future is that it's not.

I have talked to scores of people who have touched his life, including his most intimate friends and lovers. I've also spoken to many whose lives have been enriched by him, including his troupes of dancers and a tremendous number of his fans worldwide. I have interviewed those who were with him during his early days, as well as those involved in his roller-coaster triumphs with *Riverdance* and *Lord of the Dance*, and as an international businessman.

Everyone feels strongly about Michael Flatley–he's that sort of man, one who arouses passions. There is no place in his life for the middle road. And that remarkable depth of feeling has dominated his life. Like any person of stature, he has detractors and critics as well as cheerleaders.

The stories are legion, the raw material of my work, along with a heady mix of reality and legend. It's impossible to live for months at a time with an idea of someone and not develop your own picture. But that picture remains a personal snapshot, incomplete no matter how many people you speak to who have known, liked, hated, and loved him.

Typically, Michael Flatley has devised something new to give us an autobiographical picture of the man we want to know. While most superstars prefer to remain puzzles wrapped in enigmas, Michael has done everything he can to reveal his innermost self by inviting many of the people who've been instrumental in his life to offer their own views–sometimes contradictory–of his life and work. These added voices make Michael Flatley's fearless autobiography even richer and more meaningful.

I say "fearless" with careful intent. It was a brave step for Michael Flatley to encourage me to interview people on three continents with no assurances of what they might choose to say about him. Most reported that, like me, they'd found in Michael a man who was larger than life and hugely driven, a man given to the great thought and the grand gesture.

Like me, most of the people I spoke with were enormously fond of Michael, even if they'd been annoyed or angry with him in the past. They described a man who exudes a remarkable energy that inspires countless others: audiences, dancers, producers, directors, writers, costume makers and set designers, collaborators and composers, friends and lovers, and even foes. Some are even a bit critical of his enthusiasm.

In my experience, when that's over, he's ready for his encore. He's always ready, alert.

Reality often pales in comparison to legend. Not this time. I went looking for the man behind the myth and found an astonishing story. And a friend.

Legends, I've found, are often exhausted. Michael Flatley is more alive than anyone I've ever met. This is a man who would ban "pastime" from the dictionary. He only wants to *use* time. And he does.

From humble beginnings in a poor Chicago neighborhood he has soared to become an international superstar. Along the way he has established himself as a person of standards and morals and work ethic, in so many ways an old-fashioned man. He has returned to his own Celtic past, surveyed the history of his ancestors, and become the catalyst for a marvelous, marketable metamorphosis of a centuries-old discipline.

More surprising still, he made Irish dancing sexy. He made it fast and furious. He made it exciting and entertaining. He took something that has often been relegated to drafty, dusty church halls and tiny theaters and turned it into twenty-first-century rock 'n' roll.

Almost everyone says Irish dancing changed on the evening of Eurovision and yes, it did. But look at the DVDs or videos: the dancers have their arms by their sides in the traditional way—it's Michael Flatley who's flying. Many months earlier he'd had a standing ovation from 18,000 people at the Hollywood Bowl with just one similar dance performance with the Chieftains. The Eurovision show, *Riverdance*, *Lord of the Dance*, *Feet of Flames* and *Celtic Tiger*, which sold out in eight minutes in Dublin, were all to follow.

Now Michael sits at the top of his world, seeing not the horizon, but beyond it. For Michael Flatley, arguably the most famous Irish-American since JFK, this first half-century is only the end of the beginning.

His dancing years gave him an astonishing ability to open his mind up like a channel. He would come offstage, feeling that his heart was pumping outside his body, and begin the long process of coming down from yet another epic performance. Yet his mind was on fire as well, full of creative ideas, and the thoughts would multiply into the small hours. Yes, some would be discarded, but he'd retain the best of his inspiration and take action upon it; he believes that more is lost with indecision than with a wrong decision. The alchemy of his inspiration and energy and drive creates new treasure troves of gold each day.

As a Chicago schoolboy he was the classic dreamer: his textbook open but ignored, he gazed intently out of the window, imagining what might be. By flashlight he'd work into the night on his model ships, carefully crafting the intricate sails, creating and building what was valuable and available to him.

He is protective of what he values and, understandably, most of all with his family. When talking about them he was reticent about speaking in detail. Instead, he would point to his mother's family crest, which dictates death before dishonor.

He believed as a child, as he does now, in the arithmetic of dreams; that the more you build on your dreams, the more certain it is that they will come true. He's the proof, the architect of his own miracles.

Look at *Lord of the Dance*, of which he is still very much the hands-on creative director, working on every detail of one of the most successful shows in history. He leads from the top, his sleeves rolled up. He has suffered, and survived some harsh lessons on his bumpy road to the highest heights in the entertainment business–and learned from them.

What other creation has played such a wide range of venues: the Kremlin Palace and Radio City Music Hall? Beirut and Euro-Disney? London and Helsinki? Dublin and Sydney?

Michael's success might look like happenstance. After thirty-five years of grueling work, he seems to have become a star overnight. Yet, he has been a champion all his life. Which, arguably, is why, when the moments of truth have challenged him, he has walked away the winner. He's dictated his own terms to be center stage rather than allowing himself to be outmaneuvered by those with big names, small ideas, and narrow vision.

His drive has taken him to where he is today, at the top of the world.

DOUGLAS THOMPSON
Los Angeles/Las Vegas/Chicago/New York/Nice/London/Dublin, 2006
www.dougiethompson.com
review@michaelflatley.com

The Curtain Rises

I Didn't Come This Far to Finish Second

I'M SITTING ON THE PORCH of Castlehyde, staring into the depths of the Blackwater River as it flows past me.

I've agreed to tell the story of my life, and I'm thinking of how it should begin.

For sure, I'm not a perfect man. I'm a workaholic. I'm a taskmaster. I'm probably too fond of the ladies and the Irish whiskey. I hate the way I look in the mirror and on TV.

I like taking chances. I love living on the edge. I'm a deep-sea fisherman and a big-game hunter. I love boxing, ice hockey, and football. I have a wicked temper but a long fuse.

I know who I am and how good I am because I've done the work. Some people might confuse that with ego, but that's their problem, not mine.

I love life. I live every day as if it's the last. I never play defense—only offense. I thank God every day for what I have and I love to share. Giving is far better than receiving. (I've never understood why so many people fail to see that!)

I appreciate everything, and I love beauty, romance, and art. If more people took the time to notice all the beauty around them, they wouldn't have time left for hate or violence.

Like anyone else who's done the rags-to-riches thing, I've gone a bit crazy at times–but I've no regrets. Yes, I plead guilty to partying to excess. There are many hotel suites around the world that I've had to refurnish after too many late-night parties with the dancers. I've had my share of bathtubs full of champagne and naked women, and for several years, I think I added handsomely to the profits of the Guinness brewery. No stranger to Irish whiskey and the odd fistfight, I've lived my life to the fullest–and I think people who look down their noses at that part of my story might be secretly a little jealous that they never let go themselves.

I've swum with the dolphins, and I've swum with the sharks–literally. I've woken up in bed between fiddle players and leading ladies. I love fine art, fine wine, great whiskey, and beautiful women. Like all foolish young first-comers, I bought a chain of houses and fast cars when I first got rich–and I'm glad I did. I wouldn't be human if I didn't try the things I grew up dreaming about. If this makes me a bad person, that's a knock I'm willing to live with. As I see it, working sixteen-hour days and dancing to exhaustion, I deserve to enjoy whatever bit of time off I have, even if I come out looking a little foolish in the process.

I'm probably the luckiest man I know–I do what I love, and I've had the opportunity to share my passion with millions of people around the globe. But from the time I was a young man, I've had to fight my way up in the world, whether it was walking to school and fighting bullies, or digging ditches and trying to make a better life for myself. Whenever I thought I had achieved something, I found myself having to win it again, and again–and again. It almost felt as though God was testing me. To see if I'd stay down? Or to make me stronger?

When I started touring with the Chieftains–those world-renowned performers of Irish music–I thought I had it made. But even working with such a famous group, I couldn't support myself. We'd finish a tour–and I'd come home to dig ditches. The contrast was unbearable.

Finally I got my big break with *Riverdance*. I can't tell you all that happened with the show, but anyone who knows me knows the history. And everyone knows the truth. *Riverdance* was a team project. Bill Whelan created the magical music. Moya Doherty and John McColgan raised the money to produce the show. They were all major contributions. Together we created a masterpiece. The show is called *RiverDANCE*. So, when you see the line of dancers at the front of the stage in perfect precision, that was my work, my artistic endeavor. Suddenly, I was at the top of the world. I was breaking new ground in Irish dance, working with terrific people, and making fifty grand a week. For a guy who'd been broke and struggling to find a place in the dance world, it seemed like a dream come true. Then I got fired unceremoniously the night before the big London run–and again I found myself on my back.

I had to get back up and fight again, this time against my own show. A lifetime of struggle had prepared me for this battle, I suppose, but it was probably the most painful fight of all–and the one whose victory was sweetest. Instead of bringing *Riverdance* down, I went for the positive. I opened my own show and a new life rose out of the ashes.

So here is my story as I remember it.

And what have I learned from it all? I learned the importance of believing in myself and my dream. If those of you reading this book remember only one thing about my life story, let this be it: *Nothing is impossible. The whole world can be yours, if you want it badly enough. But you've got to follow your dream.*

Act One

Dreaming of the Dance

Of the living speak only truth,
Of the dead speak only well.

Inscription on the Castlehyde Crest

Chapter One

Playing It by Ear

I LOVE THE FLUTE because it's the one instrument in the world where you can feel your own breath. When I play, I can feel my breath with my fingers. It's as if I'm speaking from my soul.

Today, most people know me as a dancer and choreographer, the star and artistic creator of the world-famous *Riverdance* and *Lord of the Dance.* Not everyone remembers that I'm also a musician, winner of two All-Ireland Flute Championships, and creator of two flute albums that include some of my own original melodies.

My road to becoming a professional flautist had some rocky patches, however. The story begins, like so many other good things in my life, with my father.

My father is a big, broad-shouldered man with a heart as huge as a lion's. He's from County Sligo in western Ireland, a miraculous area with an absolute wealth of musical tradition. He was always whistling the old Irish tunes–he seemed to know every single one. He never had a formal lesson in his life but he had an ear for the music. At home, he'd play one old LP after another, Tommy Makem and the Clancy Brothers, Sligo music, flutes and fiddlers, Seamus

Tansey, Kevin Henry, Matt Molloy—the musicians who are still my heroes, even after all these years.

I listened and learned and fell in love with the music. It was the flute that took my fancy. I loved the sound of it. Maybe, too, I wanted to make my dad proud. I knew how much he loved the music. And he knew how enthusiastic I was about learning to play—but we didn't have the money to buy me an instrument.

Somehow, though, my father got hold of an old wooden flute, the kind they must have used in the old country where everybody was too poor to buy proper instruments. To have a wooden flute to play! It was absolutely everything to me. I can't ever explain how happy my father's gift made me.

My father didn't see the difference between that wooden flute and the shiny silver ones they used on the record albums—and neither did I. But my father did know that the only way to learn to play properly was to be able to read music. "That's how you get to be good," he told me. And I wanted to make him proud.

Since we didn't have money for lessons, I started working at it on my own. Every chance I got, I'd blow on that little wooden flute, sometimes for hours at a time. My poor mother, God bless her, trying to raise five kids on very little money, didn't share my enthusiasm for what must have been a dreadful noise. "Mickey," she'd snap at me, "will you stop blowing your brains out through that flute!"

Maybe, I thought, I would sound better with some lessons. I knew there was a music shop called Q and F on Seventy-ninth Street in our southwest Chicago neighborhood where you could find teachers. I started saving all the nickels, dimes, and quarters I got for doing chores. It seemed to take the longest time but finally I'd saved up what seemed to me a huge amount of money—almost nine dollars. Surely that would be enough.

One Sunday afternoon I decided to go over there and find out what my nine dollars could buy. I took hold of my precious wooden flute and set off. We didn't exactly live in the best neighborhood back then, and my journey took me through some even worse ones. Past Damon Avenue. Over to Western. It was a blazing hot day, and I was getting really thirsty. How long had I been walking now–an hour? Two hours? Every few minutes I had to cross another big busy street, and while I'd've died rather than admit it, I was scared.

I remember one kind lady who stopped me to ask if I was all right. I must have been quite a sight–a little eight-year-old kid clutching his wooden flute for dear life.

"Are you lost?" she asked me. No, I told her, I knew exactly where I was headed–the Q and F music store. In fact, I assured her, I was almost there.

"Oh, no, it's much further on," she told me, and pointed out the way. There was nothing for it but to keep going.

Finally, I found the shop. By now my face was all runny with sweat and I would've killed for a cold drink. But it would all be worth it, I thought, when I got my proper lessons. I'd be able to read music. And my father would be so proud.

I walked into the shop and looked around shyly. I hadn't expected such a crowd, and what was left of my courage seemed to evaporate. What was I doing in such a fancy store? Up at the counter, a young girl with braces and frizzy hair was standing there like she owned the place, while her mother arranged to get her lessons on the guitar.

Then I noticed the huge glass case to one side. It was full of beautiful silver flutes. I stared at it in awe. One day, I thought, I'd have a flute like that.

Somehow I found my way into the line of customers and waited patiently until it was my turn. "Yes? Can I help you?" asked the large woman behind the counter. I was too nervous to answer her. "Can I help you?" she repeated.

"Yes," I finally answered. "I want to take flute lessons."

"Where's your mom and dad?" she asked.

I didn't have an answer for that question. "I want to take flute lessons," I repeated.

"Well, first," she said in a quick, impatient way, "*normally*, you're supposed to start with piano lessons. You have to learn the whole scale and understand music and octaves, and then we go on to the flute."

"I just want to learn to play the flute," I answered. "I don't want to learn the piano because we couldn't fit one in our house."

Everyone stared at me. In the back, a customer laughed.

"Well," said the counterwoman. "How many lessons? When do you want to start? How many times a week?" She rattled off the questions really fast, as though she was angry with me. But I was ecstatic. Finally, I thought, we were getting somewhere.

"At least once a week to begin with," I said proudly. "Then we can go for more."

My answer seemed to make her angrier than ever. "Who's going to pay for this, son?"

"I will."

Her anger disappeared in a flash as she started to laugh. It seemed as though everyone in the store was laughing, too.

"Well," I made myself ask, "how much are they?"

"Oh, son," she said. "They're eight dollars an hour. Five dollars for half an hour."

All of a sudden I couldn't breathe. Everyone was still looking at me.

"Do you even have a flute?" she asked me. I swallowed nervously. "Sonny boy, please make up your mind," she said. "There's people behind you."

Did I already guess what was coming? I took out my flute, the gift from my dad, and showed it to her. The whole shop roared with laughter.

"That's not a flute," she told me, pointing to the glass case. "*These* are flutes!"

I'm nearly crying writing about it. I was such a little kid. I thought it was going to be the best day in my life and it turned out to be my worst nightmare.

I felt my face getting red. My whole body got hot. She looked at me for the longest minute in my life. Then she said, "Next in line, please."

I couldn't get out of that store fast enough. I ran all the way home, hotter, thirstier, and more out of breath than ever. When I burst in through the front door, there was my dad, sitting on the couch.

"Mick. Mick. Where the hell did you go to? Why don't you play a tune for me? I've just got home from work. Come on. Make Daddy happy, play a tune for me on your flute."

I looked at him and ran straight up the stairs. "What's the matter with Mick?" I could hear him saying.

I ran into my room and I flung the flute under the bed. I didn't play it for six months. I couldn't even look under the bed. If anyone asked me, I said the flute music was stupid and I didn't want to play it again.

Ever.

Months later my dad put on an LP of Irish tunes.

I don't know what was different about that day. My heart was crying but for some reason, my determination kicked in. "I can play that," I thought. "I can." And I went to get my flute from under the bed. It was the hardest thing I'd ever done, but I knew I had to do it. I held the wooden object in my hand, staring at it for a moment. Then I put it to my lips and blew my first note. Even to my own ears, it sounded dreadful–sour and flat–but I carried on. That day and the next and the one after that. By the end of the week, I had done it. I taught myself how to play an Irish tune–by ear.

To this day, I can't read a note of music. But I can bloody well play the flute.

Dancer Kevin McCormac, talking in Dublin in February 2004, recalled an evening a decade earlier: "One night we all went to The Ferryman pub where they play traditional music, and Michael brought his flute along, and some others brought their instruments, and a regular Saturday session was on. By the end of the night, Michael was leading the session. He played the tunes and everyone else was following. It was the first time we heard Michael play music, and he is an amazing musician."

When I won the All-Ireland Concert Flute Championships in 1975, at the age of seventeen, I used a silver flute. That victory was sweet—but something was missing. So the next year, I entered the contest using an old wooden flute, just like the one I'd first learned to play. It brought me my second All-Ireland championship.

Today, I own a vast selection of flutes, including a rare nineteenth-century Rudall and Rose. I can have my pick of any type of flute I want. But when I recorded my second album in 2003—playing my own music—I decided again to use my old wooden flute.

I love the flute—and apparently, I'm not the only one. In March 2004, I put my flute composition "Barbados Blues" on my Web site, www.MichaelFlatley.com. Within a month, the melody had gotten more than two million hits. I like to think that maybe some of them were the same people who laughed at that scared little kid in the Q and F music shop, all those years ago.

Chapter Two

The Dance of the High Kings

If you want to make God laugh, just tell him your plans.

Folk saying

THE DANCE is there in my very first memory.

I was four years old. A woman who seemed very old to me then—but still beautiful—held my hand as she patiently performed the steps for me. She showed me how they went, over and over, smiling all the while. "You can do it, Michael," she'd whisper. "Come on now. Practice makes perfect. And you can be perfect—you can."

I learned my first dance steps in my grandmother's kitchen. Hannah Ryan was a Leinster champion dancer and the closest thing to Irish royalty. She was born in Brownsford Castle in Kilkenny and later lived in Carlow where she raised her daughter—my mother—to be a champion as well. Now it was my turn.

My grandmother taught me more than just the dance. She told me you could get everything you wanted if only you concentrated and worked hard. She explained that we were descendants of the High Kings of Ireland and that it was in my blood to be a great leader. She said that one day I would be famous—and more than that.

"You will be the King of Ireland some day, Michael," she told me. "You'll live in a castle. You must work hard and believe in yourself and your bloodline." I'm sure most Irish grandmothers say such things, but as a little child I truly believed her.

I remember walking with her around her fields as she told me how important the land was, how much she loved it, how she hated to leave it, even for a holiday in America. Lucky for both of us, I traveled a lot as a kid, back and forth between our tough Chicago neighborhood and my grandmother's beautiful farm.

Although my grandmother died in 1993—just a few weeks before I got my big chance as a dancer—she remains one of the most important influences in my life. I always felt I would see her again, and I can feel her spirit looking after me still. Every time I'm away from home, my grandmother sends me a signal by turning off or dimming the lights. She's done it in dressing rooms and hotels around the world. Oh, she's with me—definitely. To this day, whenever I perform I always leave an empty seat for her in the audience.

Even after all her teachings, I still wasn't ready to set off on the path she saw for me. Back in Chicago, when my mother gave the command, my sister Annie had to drag me by the ears from a baseball game over to the Irish community church hall where the dancing was taught. That first class was a disaster, and I hated it. I still had to learn to fall in love with dancing.

Liza, Michael's sister, remembers her brother's early love of dance: "I remember my parents going out, and Mike would do these choreographies with us. He'd put things over the lampshades, and put us around the furniture and was coaching us, even as a little kid. I was only about six or seven. He was already doing that kind of thing. I remember Mom and Dad pulling up and everybody grabbing the things from the lampshades. He was always creative that way.

"When I look back on it you could almost see his future. It seemed so obvious this is what he was born to do."

I had my first proper dance lesson at age eleven, which anyone who knows Irish dancing will tell you is almost too late to start. I was half a dozen years older than the other students in my class, and like most boys my age, I was mortified to be stuck with a bunch of little kids. I was sports mad in those days and admired all the sport stars–great boxers like Muhammad Ali and Roberto Duran, and the Chicago Black Hawks hockey player Bobby Hull. For myself, I loved ice hockey (I played goalie), football, and street fighting–not a traditional sport, to be sure, but in our neighborhood, it should have had Olympics status. I always wanted to play hurling and Gaelic football, but I never got the chance.

I'd learned to fight in self-defense. The tough part of Chicago where my folks could afford to live was full of street gangs who didn't like my Irish accent and thought I was an easy number. I tried to avoid trouble, but the more I attempted to keep out of it, the more it seemed to happen. When after one too many bloody noses my father realized how much fighting was going on, he took my younger brother Patrick and me to boxing classes at a local gym. All my friends were doing the same, and we all loved boxing. It gave us a bit of confidence, and we sorely needed that.

Now I'd say that my education as a dancer continued at that gym, for the foundation of great boxing, like that of great dancing, is discipline. From the first day my dad took me to learn the sport, I never went off to the park to play or hang out. I went to the gym.

Of course, back then I didn't know where my days of boxing practice would take me. I only knew that I was tired of being picked on. But I quickly learned what discipline can bring you when I got into a scrap with this one big bully who'd often picked on me on my way to school. He was huge, husky kid, and I never saw him without half a dozen of his friends, who I knew would gang up on me the moment something started. He used to try to start a fight with me, and then he and his friends would laugh when I got scared and ran away. But when I complained about it to my dad, he only shook his head. "A hero dies once, Mickey," he told me. "A coward dies a thousand times." God help me, I thought he'd made that up himself.

So after a few weeks of boxing lessons, I went looking for my nemesis. Maybe my dad was right, because just taking matters into my own hands made me feel a bit braver. But when I saw the big bully, my legs started to shake and I had to force myself to stand my ground.

When my enemy saw I wasn't running scared, he came running after me. I stood my ground, pulled back my right hand—and knocked him on his ass. I don't know which of us was more surprised. But I was even more astonished when this kid, who had to be at least twice my size, got up and ran from me. I expected a real scrap with his swaggering friends, but they ran for it, too. I decided that day that no matter whatever frightened me, I would always stand my ground. My dad was right—you couldn't get anywhere if you didn't.

The boxing began as self-defense, but as time went on I became good enough to fight in tournaments. I wasn't nearly as good as my dad and my uncle had been—they were real fighters—and even my brother Pat was better than I was. Still, I had a big heart and a powerful right hand. And I learned that whenever I got knocked down, I had to get up again. It's a habit I still have.

So you can see why I was less than thrilled when my sister dragged me to my first dance lesson. Sports were the thing—not Irish dancing. It didn't help that the teacher sent me home from my first class because he thought I was too old to start.

But my competitive spirit had been engaged. Before I quit, I wanted to prove I could catch up with the class. I'd go to the house of other students I knew and get them to show me the steps they'd been taught. Then I'd do them my way. I don't know what it was, but from that very first class, I could never do the steps like anyone else—not even like the teacher. I always had to put my own spin on things. I got my dad to leave his car out of our garage so I could practice for hours, but I had no idea if I was any good. Then my dad put up a broken mirror for me and my whole world changed. Suddenly, I could see myself dance. And I started to think I might someday be good at this.

Easy as the dance came to me, it was still hard work. I had to learn four steps a week to my classmates' one if I was ever going to catch up. But the more I learned, the better I got. Pretty soon I'd gotten past the point where I could study with anyone else, so I began to teach myself.

It didn't help my confidence, though. I was still a shy little kid, and lots of times when people would talk to me, I would hardly talk back. They probably thought I was stuck-up. But really, I was just afraid of looking stupid.

Patrick: "Mike had a vision going on in his mind for years. He came up with so many of the movements used today when we were young. He tried so many different things: he'd do a spin and then do a click, all at the same time. He was really into doing his own thing all the time.

"If the teacher–and he was a great teacher–gave Mike a step, it wouldn't be the same step at all by the next week. He would have to change it. He'd have his own totally different thing.

"The teacher liked him and gave him the freedom, let him run with the ball a little bit. I was a little bit more traditional than Mike.

"He had a real stage presence. I think I was a lot . . . quieter when it came down to performing. Even though we did a lot of shows together, it was pretty easy to see who the real star was in the family."

Michael Flatley, Senior: "Mike had only been dancing for five weeks when the teacher came over to me and said, 'You've an unusual kid here. I've never seen a guy with feet who can dance like that.'"

By 2004, Marge Dennehy had moved her School of Irish Dance to the Chicago suburb of Mount Greenwood. But she still remembers teaching Michael Flatley in her city school: "Someone like Michael Flatley walks into your school once in a lifetime. Fortunately, he chose us. He would have been great no matter who he studied with. He was always brilliant."

Chapter Three

Coming to America

Both my parents have a remarkable heritage–hard work, strong families, and, in my mother's case, a bedrock love of Irish dance. My mother–a dance champion in her own right–was lucky enough to learn from her own mother, my grandmother Hannah Ryan.

My father was born and raised in an old thatched house on a small farm in Sligo, west Ireland. His mother, Mary Ann Henry, was what they call "black Irish." She was a beautiful woman who had that blue-black hair, tumbles of it–there must have been a spot of Spanish blood in her. She was certainly feisty: for years, she was a member of *Cumann na mBan*, the women's group that carried supplies and messages for the fighting men of the IRA.

Dad learned to work hard in Ireland, for sure. From the time he was small he left the house at five o'clock each morning to work and never got home again until after dark. His family lived on credit from the local grocery, which let them run credit for three or four months until they could sell their cattle and pay up. There was barely enough food and no cash, and Dad never even made it to Dublin more than three times–the last time, in 1946, to get his visa for America.

Each of my parents came over from Ireland in 1947. They met in Detroit, where a friendly priest from County Kerry married them on August 25, 1956. In those days, you couldn't have a church wedding on a Friday; otherwise, they would have married on August 24, my mother's birthday.

Life in Detroit was wicked. After a boom during the war years, the city was struggling with a growing depression as industry after industry closed its doors and moved away. For working people like my parents, just surviving day to day was a struggle. To say they were poor was an understatement–they never knew where their next meal was coming from. They shared a one-room apartment with my mother's parents–and times got even harder when my older sister and I were born.

Then my mother got sick, and they knew it was time for a change. When I was two months old, the family moved to Chicago, to the southwest side of the city.

Dad wanted to get ahead and he was willing to work all hours to do so. He worked as a bricklayer but that was only seasonal work. Next, he tried plastering. Then he found his way into a plumbing business, figuring that he'd never want for work. After all, plumbing goes wrong around the clock, all year long, including Christmas Day. I know. I worked plenty of Christmases side by side with my dad, grateful for the income but resenting the time away from our family celebration.

To this day, even though I was mostly raised in America, I speak with my dad's Sligo brogue, just because I was around him so much as a kid. I wouldn't change my accent if I could–it was part of him, and now it's part of me.

Despite his long hours, Dad's progress was slow. He built up his bank account dollar by dollar, wringing the money out of long weeks made up of endless, backbreaking days.

* * *

Today, Michael Flatley, Senior, and his wife Eilish live in a splendid r ambling house set on four acres, about an hour's drive from central Chicago. No matter where he is in the world, Michael calls them every Sunday.

Eilish remembers how hard it was getting started in America: "I didn't find it easy at all. It was very difficult, very hard to get by. Nobody had money. After World War II that was just the way it was. If people had five or ten pounds (Irish), it was a lot of money. We all came on the boat, five days on the boat. My parents came with me. I didn't have any other family."

Michael, Senior: "I always had that drive to make life a little bit better. We certainly stayed on the bottom rung for a long time as I was working at construction because I didn't have a trade. I couldn't get a union job . . . and it was sixty cents a hour for a wage. When the union arrived it went from sixty cents to a dollar-sixty and that was good money; overtime was time and a half for the first two hours and then you went on double time after that. That's where you made the money.

"I was awful greedy coming from Ireland. When one job was finished, the superintendent said to me: 'I can tell one thing about you, Flatley. You're the only one to put in the same hours as I did.' He was there all the time.

"They always say in America, 'If you're not lazy, you can get ahead.' It's so true. If you want to work you can get ahead. It's always been a great country to me."

Eilish: "Yet, when we lived in Detroit, Motor City–Motown–the car industry went down and the economy was a mess. . . . We had to come to Chicago.

"In those days people just had children. I had five in the first seven years. We did the best we could. You don't worry about the separate lives. You do what you have to do. We got the business up and running and we built our houses, invested into the land."

Michael, Senior: "When I had a great deal of work on I'd offer guys two hundred dollars a day, a whole week's wages, and they'd say no as it was their day off to drink and watch the ball game. The average guy is just not ambitious. Give him forty hours and that's all he wants even though he'd get double time if he'd work on a Saturday and Sunday. I'd always tell the boys if you try and work hard enough, you'll get there."

Eilish: "Dad always thought that way, to get a better house and improve his business for his family, his wife and children. I had the kids to look after."

We first settled near Seventy-ninth Street and Ashland Avenue. It wasn't easy for me, growing up in America. I was just a little kid when President Kennedy was assassinated–an event that devastated the Irish-American community. The older generation, especially, had felt so proud of having an Irishman in the White House. His sudden, tragic death made everyone feel vulnerable.

The killings of Bobby Kennedy and Martin Luther King, Junior, were also hard to deal with. The America that everyone had looked to for opportunity and freedom now seemed a dangerous place–full of anger, fear, and violence.

Our neighborhood in those days was an ethnic rainbow–Irish, Greek, Mexican, German, Italian, Puerto Rican, and African American. Sometimes we got along; sometimes we were split along ethnic lines. The great equalizer, of course, was that everybody was poor.

What made all the difference to me were my brothers and sisters: older sister Annie, little brother Patrick, middle sister Liza, and Thomasina, the baby of the family. Although I know it wasn't easy for my folks, raising and caring for us all, I feel like the luckiest guy in the world to have such a wonderful, loving family. You can't really understand me without understanding them, so let me introduce them to you.

Annie is an elegant lady, beautiful in the extreme. She is almost too nice for this world–and I'm always telling her so. She has that something special that so few have, a kind of goodness that can't be faked or expressed halfheartedly. Whenever I need cheering, it's Annie I turn to. A couple of good CDs and a bottle of red, and we can always solve the problems of the world.

Liza is the family movie star. Glamorous and gorgeous with the voice of an angel, Liza is the life of the party. If you're looking to laugh and laugh till your sides hurt, she's your girl. For my money, she's more talented than any of today's singers, but she's chosen another life, taking care of her family.

Thoma is the businesswoman of the house. Maybe that comes from being the youngest and seeing the folly of all us older kids. Our little Thomasina learned fast to tell it like it is–no nonsense, no BS. I have so much respect for her. Since she got her first job, she's never stopped working, and any success she's had, she's won on her own. The winner of more first-place trophies than any other woman in Irish dancing, she's quite simply one of the best female dancers America has ever had. As if that weren't enough, she's a great drinking buddy!

Patrick may be my little brother, but he's also my best friend. He's the handsome one in the family–gorgeous and full of muscles. Honest and loyal and soft as butter, he's got a great sense of humor and the best left hook next to Joe Frazier. Like me, Pat went from boxing to dancing, and he's done very well in the World Championships. If you ask me, I think Pat should have been the star. He's the best brother in the world.

We were a lively bunch of kids. And we had a great heritage.

Today, Patrick Flatley lives with his wife and three children in a beautiful home only fifteen minutes away from his parents. He too recalls hard times growing up: "When we were young, Dad was starting in business for himself and things were tough. They were young and they always did their best, although we didn't have much money at the time. . . .

"Dad was muscular, really well built. Mom's father was in the Guinness Book of World Records. *He used to throw the hammer and*

won lots of trophies although he was just a little fellow. It was all down to his style and determination.

"And Mike always had–and has–that champion's attitude. He always believed. I can see him now, riding around in Dad's truck, playing the flute. He never lost a chance to practice. And before that, in Dad's van, when we were just little, little kids, he'd be playing the tin whistle. . . ."

Michael Flatley's sister Thomasina is married with three daughters–two of them Irish dancers–and runs a restaurant in Chicago. In February 2004, she recalled fondly, "Michael had a wicked sense of humor."

In November 2004, Annie Flatley remembered a time when, as an adult, her brother had helped pull her out of a deep depression. "I thought my whole world was crashing down around me–I'd never felt worse in my life. Michael came over and he said to me, 'Come, let's go for a walk.'

"I said to him, 'Are you out of your feckin' mind? Have you been outside? It's freezing. Look, Mike, I'm not going for walk. You can go for a walk, have a nice time. Come back when you're done.'

"He said: 'No, no, I have to talk to you. I can't breathe in here because of the cat.' That was his excuse, but he is allergic to cats.

"Finally, he convinced me. Actually, he went to the closet and got my coat, put it on me. We went out and walked in the forest for at least three hours. My hands and feet were so numb with the cold.

"But we talked, and Mike helped me see that life wasn't so bad, and for the first time in months I felt better. It was a combination, of course, of just us having a really heartfelt and shared time and conversation together. It was a great service to me. I really have to fully appreciate that I owe that to Mike. That was a very important lesson for me and the beginning of a wonderful healing process at that time.

"When we have these times together, they're very important. . . . We have a good way of sidestepping all the nonsense and getting right to the core.

"He was around with me when my youngest daughter was born,

Devon. Michael and Devon are very connected because of that. He held her before I did in the hospital. . . ."

In November 2004 in Chicago, Liza Flatley remembered how her big brother Mike had taken care of her as a child: "I begged my Mom in the grocery store to buy this Little Golden Book, *but I didn't know how to read. There were all these pictures, and little birds were making this thatched roof on this house for these little animals that lived in the forest. Nobody had time to read it to me, except for Mike.*

"I used to go to Mike—we all called him Mikey when he was little—and I used to go, 'Mikey, would you read it to me?' and he would always take the time to read me my book. It meant the world to me. That's one of my fondest things about Mike when we were little.

"Mike was just the coolest guy. Everybody wanted to hang out with Mike. He's a great guy. He was destined for greatness, I think. Sometimes I look back, and I think it's amazing to see how much a person can accomplish in one lifetime. I can't believe it. But if you knew him as a child, now you can look back and see, even in the photographs, there's something about him. He was always special, you know.

"I'm just so proud of Mike. As a family we're really proud of him. We love him."

Chapter Four

Christmas Is For Kids

The boy is the father of the man.

Chinese proverb

"It's time to grow up—there is no Santa Claus!

"Come downstairs and help me put together these toys.

"Mickey, Christmas is for kids! It's almost morning and I haven't got these toys together. The kids'll be up any minute, please help."

That was my mother shouting at me in frustration.

I was a little boy, seven years old, and it was Christmas Eve. My little brother Paddy and I had fallen asleep looking at the snow out of the window of our shared room. As we'd tried to keep our eyes open, waiting for Santa Claus to come, I'd tricked myself into thinking I could hear the sleigh bells.

Pretty soon, Paddy was asleep with his hands on the window. I couldn't keep my eyes open any longer, either.

Then I felt somebody shaking my shoulder. It was my mother.

"Is Santa Claus here?" I asked sleepily.

She gave my shoulder another shake. "There is no Santa Claus."

I stared at her in disbelief.

"It's time for you to grow up," she snapped. "Now come downstairs and help me."

She was in a terrible humor, I could see, for my father hadn't come home yet, even though it was very late. He was probably just having a few beers with the guys, but my mother was mad. Quietly I sat down in the living room and got the toys sorted–all secondhand stuff, the way it always was.

Just as I was finishing, my sisters came rushing down from the room they shared. Paddy was following them, nearly stumbling on the stairs in his eagerness to see what Santa had brought. He got a plastic model of the Creature of the Black Lagoon, I remember, and a Frankenstein's monster. He loved them–he was always such a happy little kid–and he started in playing with them right away.

Then he stopped. "Mickey," he said to me, "why aren't you opening your presents? Don't you want to see what Santa brought?"

Santa hadn't brought me anything, I wanted to tell him. I wrapped my presents myself. I couldn't even remember what they were–and I couldn't have cared less.

But I couldn't bring myself to spoil my brother's Christmas, too. "Sure, Paddy," I told him. As he went back to his happy game, I knew that something had changed forever. Overnight, I'd gone from being one of the kids to the father figure, the one my mother turned to when she needed help. I was the second child–but the oldest boy. Now I had to be a man as well. Maybe my mother was right. Christmas was for kids–and it was time for me to grow up.

For the first few years of my life I was close to my mother. I was a pale little Irish kid in what was a very tough neighborhood, and let me tell you, it was scary out there. People did not cut you a lot of space. There wasn't much room at home, either. Our house on Seventy-fifth Street had two stories and three bedrooms–one for my parents, one for the boys, and one for the girls. They were tiny little rooms, but we didn't mind sharing.

Even before I turned seven my mother relied on me a lot. I was the kid who ran to the store, the guy who kept my head down and walked fast through the neighborhood and carried the groceries until my arms were falling off. Determined as I was, the grocery bags would burst, spilling packets and cans into the street. I'd have to scuffle around to pick them up.

One day on my way home an elderly couple called me over to their front door. They told me they had watched me cope with the grocery run for months and said I was too small to be carting around so much shopping on my own. They presented me with a red wagon so I could put the groceries in it and pull it along behind me.

It could have been a Rolls-Royce, I was so proud of that wagon. But it didn't last long–it got stolen, the way all my bikes did.

My mother and I got on well. I did all the jobs she gave me and was rewarded by her love. I was her little tin soldier. I was her little prince.

My mother is a great woman–highly intelligent, deeply sensitive, and extremely highly strung. She's got radar like the Nautilus. She has one particular talent that she passed on to my sister Thoma and me: She can carry on a full conversation while hearing everybody else's conversation in the room and still watch TV, play chess, and be planning the rest of her day in her head. She's a brave woman whom I love and admire and always will.

My dad always had time for me. I admired him, too. He's got guts, and he believed that with hard work and diligence you could make it. Not that he didn't also believe in having his share of fun. Most nights he went to McNamara's Pub to drink with his mates at the bar–a bottle of Bud and a shot of VO. He had done his day's labor and felt that was his due.

I don't blame my dad for wanting a bit of time off. But my mother seemed to have decided that his role should fall to me. From that Christmas on, whenever there was a problem, my mother would ask, "What are we going to do, Michael?"

"Don't worry, Liz," I'd answer her. "I'll take care of everything." I grew up fast because I had to. And from then on, I used her first name, just as if I really had been head of the house. That Christmas was the last time I ever called her "Mom."

Michael Flatley's friend and tour manager Martin Flitton said, "His mother always had a way of winding Michael up, saying, 'Ah, River-dance, *I've seen a commercial on TV. Haven't seen one of* your *ads.'*

"Why does she do it? Why does she wind him up? I stopped talking to her. I couldn't do it."

Kelley Byrne was a dancer who worked with Michael and also had a long romantic relationship with him. She recalls, "His mother is a typical fiery redhead. I like her. I don't think she understands everything that's going on. She says things, I suppose all mothers do it a bit, and maybe they rub each other up the wrong way. He's got all these skills, and she would talk about 'so-and-so is doing so well,' and it would hurt. He's very generous with his family and looks after them as best as he can even if they do upset him.

"He didn't have an easy childhood. He was told, 'Stop wasting your time with your dancing. Stop wasting your time with the flute.' There were ups and downs–and nice stories, too. It wasn't all bad.

"He was on his little bicycle when he was six years old, and he had to go and pay the rent, and he was given an envelope full of money and lost the envelope on the way. He was frightened to death to go home and sat in a little doorway with his bike, and when it was dark his dad came out and found him. Michael thought he would get beaten and his dad said, 'Mikey, it's okay, it doesn't matter.' He was so worried. There was no rent for the month. That was OK.

"There were five kids. He was the eldest boy and maybe he's looking for love and looking for affection, which he didn't get from his mother."

I was the family leader. Yet I was still a shy kid. Even today, I may enjoy being on stage, but I'll still be very shy in a lot of situations. When it comes to meeting new people or getting to know new places, I like to take my time.

As a child, I was even more tentative–everybody noticed that and commented on it. I think I spent a lot of time inside my own head.

I certainly wasn't a big mixer at the Little Flower Grammar School, which was about a mile's walk from our house. I wasn't a big child–often I was the smallest boy in the class. I was usually pretty quiet. It seemed safer that way.

All the time, I got into trouble for my dreamy ways. Of course, sometimes I really was half asleep. I used to stay up till three in the morning, building model ships by flashlight. I'd hand-paint them and use little knots to create the rigging for the masts. I loved building those models, maybe because I made them alone. It gave me a feeling of accomplishment.

But sometimes, I was dreaming about the life I wanted. Although it annoyed my teachers, I think my daydreams were actually more useful to me than homework. Because you're too young to know any better, you dream what is truly the truth, things you can refer back to for the whole rest of your life. God wouldn't give you that desire–that need and yearning, that passion–unless He was giving you an equal amount of opportunity to be successful. The dreams you have as a child can become a blueprint for an entire life.

Mike's sister Annie: "I love Mike with all my heart. He's a very complicated, eccentric, genius in his talent. But he's also a very vulnerable, gentle artist that has a very soft side and spends a lot of time making sure that we don't see it, or at least that he's protecting it. He's extremely vulnerable and sensitive.

"He's been a fantastic brother to me. A wonderful inspiration to me. A confidant."

Chapter Five

Digging for Gold

"COME ON, Mick, let's go to work."

God, how I hated hearing those words.

"Get in the ditch."

That was my dad greeting me after school. I wasn't a kid any longer. I was a teenager, and I was expected to do my share in my dad's construction business. Of course, Dad made sure I never missed school and always did my homework. But I was the oldest son and he needed my help. And there were lots of long days.

Now, I'm not ashamed of digging ditches. Any man who does that kind of work can hold his head up. I'm proud of what my dad and I accomplished. When I dug ditches after I graduated, I earned a living and I kept my body fit.

But I won't lie to you: Most of the time I hated that work with a passion, especially as a young boy. I couldn't wait for the job to be over so I could go off to a school dance, or practice my own dancing, or just hang out with my mates.

Dad was having none of that, though. He had a family to support, and work came first.

When I was a little kid, my father worked for other men. I wonder sometimes what my life would have been like if he'd continued on that way, if he'd never gone off and started his own business. The last place he worked was a plumbing and sewer company. Things were fine enough, I suppose, until they shafted him: They told him one day that there was little work and he had to be laid off.

Dad understood that, hard as it was on the family. Then one Sunday by sheer chance we drove by the company headquarters and there were men working on a weekend afternoon. I don't have to spell it out for you. It was the first time I saw my father get really mad, really lose-his-temper mad. I was used to my mother being always at it, but this was the first time I saw Dad really going off the deep end. He was furious.

Then he made a decision. He didn't talk about it. He just did it. He started his own business and said "F.U." to all those guys who had betrayed him.

I can honestly say for the next ten years, I never saw my dad take another beer. Within a few years he had built us the nicest house in the best neighborhood in Illinois. He had his own business, and he was determined at all costs to make a go of it. So he worked all hours, and my mother worked too, building the business with him. She was "the office," and though she never put her hands to a shovel, I believe she worked as hard as he did.

I'll never forget how I felt when I saw that Dad hadn't taken his betrayal lying down. He followed that big rule he always taught me: *It's not how many times you go down, it's how many times you get up.* That's in my blood, now; you can take a lot of things away from me, but you can't take that. It's probably the most valuable thing I've got, and I learned it from watching my dad.

From that day on, though, our life was on a murderous schedule. Dad didn't miss a working day in ten years, and whenever I wasn't at school, I worked with him. The Flatleys worked on birthdays, Thanksgiving Day, Christmas Eve, Christmas Day, New Year's Eve, and New Year's Day. We worked in 110 degrees with humidity, the mosquitoes crawling on our backs. We worked at forty degrees below zero when we had to move furiously just to feel the blood flow in our fingers. No job was too much trouble or too much work.

Those were hard times for everyone, the 1960s in Chicago. The city was troubled, and our neighborhood got some of the worst of it, a racial melting pot that would sometimes boil over. The tension was like a tightrope stretched across the streets, and you always expected it to snap at any second. Going out to work in such an atmosphere made a hard job even harder. But Dad just kept on going, all discipline and determination. And I was right there beside him in the ditch.

"Dad," I used to ask, "why do we have to work every Sunday?"

He'd always smile. "So when you grow up you won't have to."

He used to pick me up after school when I was still a tiny boy, just big enough to pass him the hammer and the wrench. On Saturdays, I'd do a quick tidy-up for him, so I learned every fitting in the truck. At first, he'd ask me for a tool and I'd find it instantly. Then it got to the point when he didn't even have to tell me what he needed–I'd have it waiting. That's how well we understood each other.

I hated digging ditches, and though I never complained, Dad could always tell how I felt. He'd laugh and say, "Don't worry, Mickey, we're going to be rich some day!"

I knew he'd never asked me to do anything he wouldn't do himself for twice as long. But I was just a kid, and I wanted to have fun. "Dad," I would say, "there's a party I'd like to go to–can't you let me off a bit early?"

"I'll try and get you to the party, Mickey," he'd always answer, " but we've got to finish the job, so let's see what we can do." Then he'd put his back into it even more so I could go and have fun. He was a reasonable man, but business was business, and that's just the way it was.

Anyone who's ever been in business for himself knows that the hardest part of the job is when people don't pay what they promise.

There we'd be, working for someone on a Sunday afternoon, a rush job and a dirty one, and they'd promised us the world to get us to come over. Then, when the job was done, they'd say they had no money. Sometimes they'd just laugh at us.

My dad would never turn down a job, though. I'd say, "Dad, it's a bad neighborhood, you know some people don't pay."

And he'd say, "Mickey, we have to do our best–you never know what might come of it."

Sometimes, it was my dad who wouldn't take the money. I remember one old black lady who lived in a really tough neighborhood, a frail woman with snow-white hair. Her pipes used to freeze and she couldn't get the water going. Every time she had trouble she'd call my dad, asking him politely in her funny high-pitched voice if he could possibly make the time for her.

One Christmas Eve when we were all dressed up eating our holiday meal, she called us. I could hear my dad take the call. "Yes, I understand. You can't have your dinner. The Lord save us. This is a terrible thing." He put down the phone and said, "Mickey, it'll only take us fifteen minutes to help that woman."

"Dad!" I protested. "It's an hour to drive over there."

"Ah, Mickey," he replied. "It'll only take fifteen minutes. She can't have her dinner."

I wanted to say, Dad, it's Christmas Eve. And what if she doesn't pay you? But of course, I kept silent. I just changed into my work clothes and went with my dad to fix the pipes.

That nice old lady couldn't stop thanking him. She tried to give him five dollars–a lot of money in those days–but no way; my dad wouldn't take a penny. He would always help that lady for free. There were a few he never asked for the money because he knew they didn't have it. Maybe somehow that helped balance the ones who lied to us, the ones who had the money but didn't pay up. Hard as iron, soft as butter–that's my dad. I'm not ashamed to say that he'll always be my hero.

CHAPTER SIX

Becoming a Champion

BY THIS POINT, I've won so many dance championships–more than a hundred–you'd think I'd take it for granted. But I don't. I remember every single time I came in second. In some ways, the second-place contests are a bigger part of my memory than the big wins. It was coming in second that really honed my competitive edge, made me work harder, made me even more determined to do better and make it to the top. Don't get me wrong: I believe in winning. But sometimes you learn even more from losing.

When I was growing up, Irish dancing was a massive underground world that very few people knew about. Yet thousands of people were involved in it, people addicted to Irish music and dance.

Everything begins in class, where your teacher chooses the handful of people who are good enough to represent the school in a citywide competition. Each contest has its own set of rules and trophies, though usually they're organized by sex (boys against boys; girls against girls) and level (beginners, advanced beginners, intermediate, and open). When I was a boy, there were competitions all across America, not only the East Coast but also the Midwest and the industrial heartland: Chicago, Detroit, Cleveland, Youngstown, Pittsburgh.

As you start to win some citywide trophies, you move up to the regional contests: Midwest, East Coast, or West Coast. Once you get very good, you might attempt to compete in America's national dance championship. If you're good enough to take first, second, or third place in America, you're eligible to compete for the top prize of all, the World Championship, held each year in Dublin.

The whole spirit of the contests was quite competitive–but I've got to tell you, the parents were far more obsessed with winning than the kids. I'd imagine it's like ice skating or the Olympics or any other sport where children are involved. The kids are all friendly with one another–with a healthy competitive spirit, to be sure, and certainly a great deal of rivalry–but nothing like the parents. For the parents, it was live or die: *my kid must win.* They might be smiling when they shook hands, but underneath there was a different feeling, and all of us kids knew it.

The father of one of my friends went so far as to beat his son–even in public–whenever he didn't win, or even when he was just misbehaving. It was so ugly, yet no one ever talked about it. One night over a couple of beers that we shouldn't have been having, because we were not yet fifteen, my buddy started crying and told me the whole story. So to say parents took the competitions seriously would be an understatement.

Having said that, these weekends were tremendous fun and held a lot of excitement, and we all looked forward to them with great eagerness. Certainly, in the early years, dancing came far second to the fun! And my buddies and I only wanted to get the dancing and the competitive part out of the way, so we could go chat up all the Canadian girls in their tight blue jeans and high heels.

Although I didn't start dancing until I was eleven (most kids started by the time they were five), I was lucky enough to be chosen to compete soon thereafter. My first contest was in Detroit, of all places —quite a journey for a young boy from Chicago. As I walked into the conference hall, I remember thinking how confusing it all was. There were so many stages with dancers performing on them, and so many people, all taking in Irish accents. It was exciting, but really a bit scary for a little kid.

My nervousness probably held me back a bit. I danced my very best, but I only came second. I knew from the very beginning I didn't like that feeling. So I went home and practiced harder.

The next weekend, we went off to another competition in a different town. Again, I got second place. Now I was more determined than ever, and I practiced even harder.

Finally, at my third competition, I came in first. Something went off inside of me, a little spark bursting into flame. Even at this very early stage in my career, I began to recognize that hard work pays.

I noticed, too, that people seemed to look at me differently, talk to me differently. Being chosen as "the best" seemed to change everything just that little bit, even way back then.

The officials must have thought I was good, because they had me skip a few stages, moving me straight up from beginners to the open division, where dancers did all the hard steps. I was very much looking forward to it—competition was in my blood now, and I was hungry for each new challenge.

Back I went to Detroit, where I had to dance against this terrific young kid in three different categories: the reel, the jig, and the hornpipe. He got three first places—and I got three seconds.

I was fascinated by this guy who seemed to have beaten me so easily. He appeared to be very comfortable in his dancing, and very sure of himself, having won so many times at his young age. His steps fit him like the old shoes he wore, because he'd done them to perfection so many times. I could see the difference between his comfort level and my own. He knew he would win before he danced. I, on the other hand, was trying much too hard; I lacked the confidence and faith in myself that he seemed to wear so easily. Some people saw his confidence as ego. I saw it as the heart of a champion.

So when I got back home, I began to try to build that sort of confidence in myself. I was determined to defeat this new rival–to come in first from now on–and I put my mind as well as my body to work. I didn't want to believe that this other kid was a better dancer than I was, and beating him in a competition was the only way I knew to prove he wasn't.

But he kept winning. I must have gotten half a dozen firsts when I wasn't competing against him–and maybe the same number of seconds when I was.

So I kept working. My goal was to match my rival's level of confidence, till my own steps, too, felt as comfortable as my beaten, worn old shoes. I trained my body harder and harder, so that the muscles in my legs did all the work and there was no strain or tension in my upper posture. Then I added the secret magic ingredient that would always bring a touch of intrigue into my stage presence (and my life!): I added confidence. My confidence, too, has been misconstrued many times as ego, but my rival's successes taught me not to see it that way. It wasn't ego, but rather a clear understanding of who we were and what we could do, a calm trust in our own abilities.

You don't get that kind of confidence for free. Back I went to the garage, day after day, several hours at a time, burning with a fierce devotion. All I wanted was never to get beaten again.

The odd part about it was, I really liked that other guy, even though he didn't always treat me so well. The very first time he beat me, I went over to shake his hand, but he ignored me, brushing me aside so he could go on chatting up the girls.

When I finally defeated him, it was a different story. Then he was the first one to come over and put out his hand. And yes, I shook it immediately. And yes–we both went right out and starting chatting up the girls! From that point on, we were great mates.

* * *

I rarely lost after that. Soon I'd won enough firsts to move up into the Championship Division, competing against dancers from the entire Midwest. And once again, I found myself coming in second, third, fourth. It took several attempts before I was victorious.

At this point, something very interesting had begun to happen in my dance practice. I wasn't only learning the steps my teachers had given me. I had started creating steps of my own–steps that were far more difficult than those of the other dancers.

I had wonderful teachers at this time, Dennis Dennehy and his wife, Margie. They'd worked hard with me in the beginning years, trying to teach me the style that all Irish dancers used at that time. The Irish dance world was extremely traditional back then, and everybody was expected to dance the same way. But as I grew older, I began to develop my own style, and then to create my own steps to complement it. That, too, took hours of practice in the garage.

The Dennehys were very lenient with me, though I know I must have been a right pain in the ass at times. But even then, I felt that I was doing quality stuff, and I'm glad I did it.

And so, at the championship level, I began to raise some eyebrows, both because people began to think I was good–and because they'd never before seen anyone dance quite like I did. Meanwhile, my own ambition was growing. Once I'd won all the city and regional titles in the Midwest, I thought it was time to try the Big Leagues.

I knew it wouldn't be easy. Word of good dancers spreads quickly in the Irish dance world, and we in the Midwest had heard plenty about two guys on the East Coast who were fast becoming Irish dance royalty. If I went into the National Championships, I'd be up against them.

The competition was being held north of New York City, which was intimidating in itself–the very definition of the Big Time. To make the whole thing even more exciting–and scarier–I was traveling there alone. My folks had scrimped and saved to pay for my plane fare and hotel room, but there was nothing left for anyone else to come, even if they could have afforded to take so much time off from work. So when I flew into New York to have a shot at the best there was, I was just fifteen years old, and on my own.

The contest was held at Yonkers Raceway, and the huge space was crowded with thousands of people. These were the hard-core fans, the ones who followed every up and down of the Irish dance world. Nobody had even heard of me, but everybody expected that those two East Coast champions would be battling it out, so there was mad excitement about who was going to win.

I was intimidated by them, I'll admit, but they couldn't have cared less. To them, I was just this guy who'd gotten lucky in the Midwest.

To everyone's surprise, neither favorite took the crown. At the championship level, you get three judges rating the contestants. They're allowed to vote different ways, and it's rare that all three judges will award the First to the same person. But this time they all agreed upon a single champion–me.

Now the war was on. People were asking, "Who *is* this kid? Where the hell did he come from?" They'd never heard of me, yet I had defeated their gods–me, the guy who came out of nowhere.

From that time on, I won almost every American contest I ever danced in, racking up about a hundred championships in my career. But do you know what I remember? The five times I lost. I didn't lose to better dancers, either–they were just better on the day. I lost, I realized, whenever I got too cocky. That was a valuable lesson.

And in case I didn't remember to stay humble, I could always count on being brought down to earth back home. I'd get up the morning after a contest, my trophy in its place beside the others on my shelf, and my father would say quietly, "All right, Mickey, forget all the dancing now. Let's get in the truck . . ."

* * *

Eilish Flatley: "It became an enormous burden to always be with Michael. He would go to about thirty big competitions a year. We had to take the children and then come home and run a business and do all the practices and the schools and the hockey and whatever else. There was no way we could afford to fly abroad with him [when he entered the Irish championships later on].

"He never slowed up. He always went alone. . . . When he won the World [Dance Championships in Ireland], he won alone."

Seamus Tansey is an internationally renowned flautist and a musical influence on the young Michael Flatley. He spoke in Belfast in March, 2005: "The first time we met was in 1972 when he was a little boy about thirteen or fourteen years of age. I was with a band touring the United States and we were in Chicago and this couple came to see us. They invited us to their home the following evening for music and for dinner. That was Michael's father and mother.

"Now Michael's whole family can dance and at a very high standard at that. That evening it was very good dancing and we played with them. We didn't notice anything, until Michael was called to follow.

"This young lad took the floor and he started dancing the hornpipe. Although we had seen Irish dancers before, this was something else. He was like a ball, he could jump off his feet into the air and come down feet away–his feet were absolutely spot on, the timing was absolutely outstanding and we were all looking at him as we were playing.

"There was this small little fella in the band, he was a cousin of mine, a very philosophical little fella he was. He said: 'I'm making a prophecy here today. There will be more about that young fella yet. That fella will be famous. That fella is special.' That's what he said and we agreed with him."

Chapter Seven

School Days

In spite of my preoccupation with dancing, school was a big part of my daily life. As I was finishing eighth grade, I took a special exam to get into the all-boys Brother Rice High School, a parochial school run by the Christian Brothers. In elementary school, I was able to get by with all my dreaming and still make good grades, but those Christian Brothers were tough. They expected you to work to your fullest, and they weren't shy about correcting you if they thought you were slacking off.

A lot of people think that going to a religious school is somehow easier than a regular high school, but let me tell you, the monks and priests at my school were no soft touch. They were disciplinarians. If I was wrong, they found a way of drawing my attention to it so that even I, a stupid teenager, could not fail to understand.

People are shocked when they hear about it today, but I think getting strict discipline from my teachers was the best bloody thing that ever happened to me. Today's world is too politically correct, and it makes me sick. When some of those Irish teachers gave me a belt to the side of the head, I remembered it, surely—but I never hated them. Instead, I respected them. I was honored to go to that school. There's such a thing as too much freedom, in my opinion—we could use a bit more discipline in today's world.

Still, I was never really focused at school because I wasn't interested in most of my classes. I got great marks in art studies and science, and horrible grades in just about everything else. I couldn't stand them talking on and on about all that stuff, and even a whipping couldn't make me pay attention for very long.

Years later, I found out that I had a high IQ and that my real problem at school was that I'd been bored. But that wasn't my teachers' fault. It was mine.

Meanwhile, I enjoyed the social part of school. During my junior year, we all hung out in the cafeteria. Every day of my school life, I had the same lunch: a ham sandwich with mayonnaise on white bread, a bag of potato chips, a Twinkie, and a little carton of chocolate milk. I remember using my pen to pierce a hole through the milk carton so I could put the straw down through.

The cafeteria was our social center. One table was for the big muscle-bound jocks. Another was for the "heads," long-haired guys who smoked pot all the time. A third table was for the bookworms, and so on. You had to know who you wanted your friends to be, because a guy who didn't have a regular table to sit at was dead, socially.

The guys at my table were a good mix, mainly athletes, but also some other guys. We had Tom, my locker partner, a six-foot-six jock with muscles in places where I didn't even have places. Everyone called him "Slick." He was a nice enough guy underneath it all. We also had Mark, another Irish-American whose father played the flute; plus a guy from the track team and a baseball player. And me. I played hockey and boxed.

One Monday morning one of the Brothers came into the cafeteria and announced that they were starting Crusader Clouts, a boxing tournament. Who was going to fight whom?

I remembered back to what my parents taught me as a kid: Keep your head low. Don't show off. And just mind your own business. Much as I wanted to join the club, I decided to steer clear.

Later that week Mark sat down next to me and dropped his head into his hands. He looked despairing, but he wouldn't say why. Then this muscle-bound guy called Jack Love came over. Jackie was the school hero. On every corridor and every wall, you would see his picture, mainly because he was the wrestling champion. He'd won every title that there was, which I guess made him the champion of champions.

It turned out that when Mark was a little drunk, he had agreed to fight Jack Love. Nobody else would have agreed to such a dumb thing, drunk or sober, and now Love was making the most of it.

Mark couldn't look up. I felt sorry for him, actually. He was the guy who sang Irish songs at parties and boasted of his heritage. Sure, he should have kept his mouth shut. But Love and his mates were scary.

Mark decided he had to pull out of the fight. When I asked him why, he said, "I'm scared to death of that guy." I looked at Mark—an ordinary-sized boy, nothing like Jack the Tough Guy—and I thought, "Good choice." But I couldn't tell him that. We still had the problem of who was going to fight the school champ. I decided then and there that I was going to fight Jack Love.

Love was a world-class wrestler but I knew that one clean right hand would take care of the guy. No one at the school knew I was a boxer. To them I was just the skinny kid with the Irish accent. They didn't have a clue that my father was a fighter, my uncle was a fighter, my mother's father was a fighter, my brother was a fighter. They didn't realize that fighting was in my blood.

In fairness, I was only an amateur boxer who'd won a couple of local titles in Chicago. Nothing to brag about, and I was certainly no pro. But I had confidence and I convinced myself I could defeat this guy, even though Love was intimidating. I responded by visualizing the entire fight, imagining in vivid detail how I'd win my victory. I worked hard to prepare—but I kept silent about it. I learned another lesson that week, for the more silent I was, the more respect I got.

On the night of the fight, the auditorium was packed with people. Everyone was there to cheer for Jack Love; the only two fans on my side were my father and my brother. I could not point to another living soul who thought I had a chance—and that really hurt me. When I'd stood in the dressing room, lacing up my boots, Mark had come in and said, "Flatley, just keep your gloves up, do the best you can. Stay away from Jackie, Dance Man, stay away."

I said, "Is that it? That's all you've got to say to me?"

He said, "You should probably know, even your buddy Tom bet against you."

That was my locker partner, one of my best friends. So then, not one of the two thousand people in that hall other than my father and brother believed in me? That really hurt.

Of course, I believed in myself. But my heart still sank when I heard the enormous roar of approval for Love, the school champion, as he stepped into the ring.

He got in my face and started telling me he was going to kill me. I still wouldn't speak. Then the bell rang for the first round. Jack ran straight at me and started throwing punches in all directions. He'd obviously boxed before. I kept my gloves high. He was very strong, a real warrior.

He just went crazy and I let him. He kept on punching and punching, just hitting my gloves. Then he took a step back to catch his breath and I knew he was tired already.

I was looking for an opening and just before the first round ended, I found it. Jack made another charge, and I threw my right. Bang! His nose was broken. I could hear a big "Oooh," from the crowd. He staggered all over the ring until finally he was saved by the bell.

Then the second round began. This time I didn't wait for him to start punching: I landed a right before he could get his own hands into position. I heard him grunt, and that was all the encouragement I needed. I landed about ten or fifteen unanswered punches to his body and his head, going and going, until finally, the referee stepped in twenty seconds later and stopped the fight.

Jack staggered back to his corner. He could barely stand up. He was a much better athlete than I was, and I know he should have won. But I beat the odds because I believed I could.

The auditorium was dead silent. I thought I heard maybe two people clapping–my brother and my dad.

Believe it or not, at my twenty-fifth high school reunion in 2003, when I was inducted into the school's Hall of Fame, the first person who came over to congratulate me was Jack Love. He gave me a big hug and a lot of compliments and as the night wore on, we shared a few beers. He's a good guy–a real competitor–and someone whom I've come to really like. He told me that everything in his life changed that day. As I looked into his eyes again, I wondered what he meant by that. I couldn't help feeling the same was true for me. I gained enormous respect at school–and one last proof that I should always stand up for myself, no matter what anyone thought about it. Determination and grit will win out over sheer weight, any day of the week.

Patrick Flatley: "Mike . . . had the most deceiving right hand. I know because Mike and I used to spar. I always said in all the times that I used to box, all the fights that I used to have, the hardest punch I ever took was from my own brother. It was a straight one, right in on the jaw. He was so deceiving and he got me right there. It was the closest I ever came to getting knocked out from one punch. . . .

"Mike and I always took our boxing seriously. We went with my dad to the Scottsdale Boxing Gym, and I was set up against a talented fighter

called Danny Estrada. He was older than me and a two-time Golden Gloves champion, but I considered myself a beast. I would normally beat up everybody.

"As much as I was a great technical fighter, this kid was a real pro. My back was against the rope and we just started to trade punches. Mike is such a beautiful boxer, fast as lightning. He would never get conned into trading with a puncher but I took the bait and slugged it with him.

"I just remember having my back to the rope. . . . I was hanging on for dear life after taking five beauties. The coach came in and said: 'That's enough, Pat. Don't worry—this kid is too tough. I shouldn't have put you in there anyway.'

"Then they put Mike in the ring directly after me. I came out and Mike came in and I knew just to look into his eyes that it was: 'Leave it to me!'

"You could see it in his face. He was pissed royal at what had happened to me. My face was all red and bruised and I sat down next to Dad as Mike went in the ring.

"He was the exact opposite to me. You couldn't stop Mike. You just couldn't. He was so fast. He never missed, and it was all over within the first round.

"Mike was determined to win so he did."

Henry Coyle is a renowned boxing trainer and expert in Chicago. In November 2004 he recalled the young Michael Flatley in the ring: "The first time he went to the gym, really, you could tell that there was something special about him. He was absolutely lovely. The way with Michael Flatley, whatever he did really he was good at. He was exceptional. You knew he was a boxer, really, because he was just like the same as the dancing, he was just natural.

"The first time he boxed here there was something about him. He was just very very talented and won the Golden Gloves the first time he tried it. . . . It was an exceptional feat that the first time he competed he won it. The first year he started boxing. . . . Amazing.

"He was talented. He could really have made it in boxing in that weight, which was a very tough weight. . . . To win the Golden Gloves at that time was very, very hard. . . . He could have made it really big in boxing, we all know that. It's not just me saying that. He was willing to listen and learn. Then he brought in his own moves. He was good on his feet, but you'd expect that, wouldn't you?"

Mike Tyson said in Beverly Hills on March 3, 2004: "That fucking Flatley! That fucking Flatley, what a stud.

"Me? I think he's the best dancer in the world–and one of the world's greatest athletes. And I'm not just talking about sex!"

Boxing champion brothers Vitali and Wladimir Klitschko are big fans of Michael Flatley. In Los Angeles in December 2004, Vitali said, "He's been a great supporter of ours. He's a really knowledgeable man on boxing–he knows all the history. And can talk tactics too."

Wladimir said, "He's one of the men you want in your corner."

Irish boxing champion Wayne "Pocket Rocket" McCullough, who has fought more than fifty times for Ireland, is based in Las Vegas, where he has his own training gym. He said there in December 2004: "I've known Michael since a fight in Dublin in 1994, and he was a great supporter. When I fought Naseem Hamed in 1998, he was part of my entourage–he walked to the ring with me. If you watch the fight, you'll see him walk into the ring at the start of the fight. That's when we became really good friends. . . . We've stayed in touch ever since.

"About two months ago he was here in Las Vegas and came out to the gym and we did a little sparring. He used to box–he was a Golden Gloves guy. He loves boxing–I often see him at the fights. He was here for the Klitschko brothers.

"He knows his stuff. He has a whole boxing library of fights. New fights, old fights. Some day I'd love to go in and watch the old fights. I love the old fighters.

"Michael loves boxing. He supports the game, especially Irish fighters. He enjoys the fights and I'm sure he'd love to try and get back in there!

"He's in good shape. I told him that the next time he's in Vegas– because I've got my own boxing ring and gym here . . . I told him I'd come up and give him a boxing workout. He said he'd love it. It's just getting the time. He's on the go."

Famed photographer Bob Carlos Clarke recalled in London a moment Michael Flatley went into the ring–for charity: "Michael was a really good sport and generous with his time. I was photographing a Powergen calendar in aid of the British Red Cross, and I photographed Michael in a gym in south London. It takes time to get such an image, but he gave it all he had.

"The bonus is that it's a great image of him."

Chapter Eight

Irish Dancer

The good dancer kept the body rigid, moving only from the hips down and with arms extended straight at the side.

Breandán Breathnach,
Folk Music and Dances of Ireland

I'D HAD A VERY GOOD RUN in competitions in America as an Irish dancer. As I said, I'd won most, lost a few.

But I'd not found success in Ireland. That was where most Irish-Americans felt the best dancers were. The Irish kids, as I soon found out, eat, drink, and sleep step dancing–it's part of their heritage and they're way ahead of everyone else. So if I wanted to take myself seriously as an Irish dancer, that was where I had to triumph.

Irish dancing first took an organized form in 1893, when Douglas Hyde, the first President of Ireland, formed the Gaelic League, an Irish cultural group that helped keep traditional Irish dancing alive. But it wasn't until 1969 that the World Irish Dancing Championships–the Irish dance Olympics–were established. I was able to dance in that competition four years after its founding, in 1974–and I was sure I'd win.

But I hadn't realized that I was now dancing at a completely different level. To my disappointment, I took only fourth place.

Maybe I should have been proud of my partial success, but all I could feel was the pain of my failure. I hadn't taken anything less than first in such a long time. What I hadn't realized was that Ireland was a very different world, with unique and steadfast dance traditions. By now, I'd gone a long way toward developing my own personal style. Years later, when I went on to create *Riverdance* and *Lord of the Dance*, that style would be credited by people like the award-winning Irish author Frank McCourt with bringing sex into Irish dancing. But in the 1970s, it was no go. The Irish wanted that traditional stiff-armed style, and anyone who danced as freely as I did–no matter how skillfully–was sure to be penalized.

I loved putting my own individual mark on every single move. But I also wanted to win. And if I wanted to take first place in the World Championships, I had to think like an Irishman. They danced with their arms held tight, their shoulders never moving. Their faces never moved, either. I did the fancy stuff, but they did very conservative steps. I'd been thinking too bloody American, that was my problem.

But how could I get into their Irish shoes? If I was going to play their game, I decided, I'd play it with the best of them. So I flew to Ireland to take private dance lessons from Kevin Massey, one of the greatest traditional Irish dancers ever.

I loved Kevin dearly and I learned a lot from him. Tragically, he's dead now. He was a quiet, gentle man who had a brilliant gift and was a fantastic teacher, patient, persistent, and exact–precisely what I wanted. If anyone could get me to follow the rules, he could.

I was used to working at fever pitch, but Kevin held me back. Whenever the temperature got too hot and my steps got too racy for what the Dublin judges would accept, Kevin corrected me. "Remember, remember, remember," he kept saying. "Rules, rules, rules." I'd never been one to follow the rules–but the Irish did, and now I had to learn how to think as they did.

Keeping myself from dancing my own way was one of the toughest things I ever did. I was longing to "dance outside the lines," to try something different, and I didn't want anybody telling me that I couldn't do it. I'll admit it–I was a huge pain in the ass. But because I respected Kevin so much, I listened to him. I adapted, and I found a way to perform at a level I could accept.

I went back to Chicago totally pumped up, more enthusiastic than I'd ever been. At the time, I was still digging ditches for my dad, but my father wanted me to win the Irish crown almost as much as I did, so he gave me time off to dance in the garage–a huge sacrifice, but one he made gladly, almost eagerly, in the hopes that I would do the family proud. I worked eight hours a day, sweating through four or five T-shirts at every practice. I was so thrilled to have the time to do nothing except dance–and I knew, if I practiced long enough, I could win.

Kevin was the only person in the dance world who believed that, though. I'd been told point-blank, "An American can never win the World Irish Dancing Championships. No American has. All the winners have come from Europe. And you in particular can never win: You dance too flamboyantly, do too many fancy things. It can't happen. It's out of the question. No chance."

Here's what trying for the Irish crown taught me: Some people are true champions. No matter how different they might seem, the people who get to the top of the world all have one thing in common: They're willing to endure the pain, even to embrace it. That's what separates them from the ones who come in second. In the end, the differences between me and the Irish champions turned out not to matter so much. As long as we all had the will to dance on through the pain, we all ended up in the same place.

So why not dream big? So many of us lose our dreams simply because we're afraid of setting super goals, of being ridiculed for having confidence in our own abilities. But why not go ahead and dream? Who cares what anyone else tells you?

So I went to the 1975 Irish championships in Dublin, and I danced the best I could. I can still recall perfectly how I stood up on a balcony waiting for the results. When I was announced the winner, there was a big roar that floated up from below, surrounding me in a huge cloud of deafening noise. I forced myself to turn away, to walk down the empty staircase that led into the main hall where I would receive my trophy. But just before I entered the main hall, I stopped, and stood alone in the empty corridor, just listening. I couldn't believe that all these people were clapping for me. And I swear I heard the voice of God talking to me, the universe sending me a message, telling me never to doubt myself again.

I remember thinking of Kevin and all our hopes, all our hard work. "Thank you, Kevin," I found myself saying. "Thank you, God." I could feel the spirits there with me, an enormous power flooding that little hallway.

Thank you, Kevin Massey, a hundred thousand times. You helped me stick to the rules while I stayed my own man. You're the greatest.

During the 1970s, Michael's honors included seven consecutive years as North American Dance Champion (1972–78); five consecutive years as Canadian Dance Champion (1973–77); and two separate Irish dance titles, the Priceless Madame Markievicz Chalice (1974–76) and the Aer Lingus Award for the Greatest Performance Overseas (1973–77).

Eileen Lally, MBE, had by 2004 taught Irish dancing in northwest England for more than forty-five years: "I was one of the panel of judges when Michael Flatley won the World Championship in 1975. When his career soared, I could not keep up with the demand of people who wanted to be taught Irish dancing. For the first time in my memory we had to have waiting lists for classes. Waiting lists! Who would have imagined that?"

Seamus O'Shea (O'Se), with his wife Aine, runs the O'Shea School of Irish Dancing in Dublin. A vice-president of the Commission of Irish Dancing

(An Coimisiún le Rinci Gaelacha), he attended the World Championships in 1975. He recalls, "Most people didn't know who this person Michael Flatley was. I met him as a young fellow when he came to Ireland in 1975, and there was a great big buzz. I don't know what it was about Michael Flatley, but people were talking about him coming over to dance at the World Championship. There was an aura and a buzz going on about the place.

"He came out to dance, and he was wearing this green kilt with a snow-white jacket. The other guys might have had satin or something, but it's what Michael was wearing that I remember.

"This guy came out with a 'Look at the splendor of this' attitude, and he just took the place by storm. He won the World Championship. He was quite brilliant."

Edward Sullivan competed against Michael when Michael made one of his last competitive appearances at Gurteen on the west coast of Ireland in 1977. On July 25, 1996, Sullivan published a recollection of the event in the London newspaper, the Evening Standard. *Here's an excerpt:*

"There are people who are favoured by fate: born with star quality, the will to win, and the charisma to carry off the entire package. Michael Flatley is one of those people.

"It was apparent when I competed against him. In 1977 he was a world champion dancer who lived in Chicago and travelled to Britain and Ireland on the Feis circuit, a series of Irish dancing competitions.

"We were both in a world of distinct amateurs, a world where you retired at twenty, and then found nothing to do with your talent other than teach others.

"I was bumbling around from one competition to another trying to find one that I could win. I arrived in Gurteen confident of victory in that town's championship. But my plans were thwarted by the arrival of Michael Flatley.

"He had returned, Messiah-like, to his native roots and the whole

town had turned out to see him. His pedigree was so strong in this area that tractors, pubs and post offices carried his family name.

"There was something about him. In the extremely sociable world of the Irish dancing competition circuit, he had the sort of starriness that manifested itself by turning up at the last possible moment to do the job of winning.

"I had won a couple of individual dances and had great hopes of the big event. By a quirk of organizational rules the championship age groups were reorganized which meant that I was pitched unfairly and unsquarely against the great Michael Flatley.

"The wait to take the floor is always a nervous one, exacerbated only by the fact that you are sharing the stage with a World Champion whom everyone in the room adores.

"His stage presence was such that nobody else in the room knew I existed, including the judge.

"The crowd cheered him as we walked on stage, he moved around quicker, higher, faster, lighter than I did and his shoes seemed to have microphone attachments which drowned out my timid attempts.

"The results were announced, the crowd cheered loudly and there was a ripple of applause for the runner-up, yours truly.

"It was clear then that Flatley was destined for something greater than amateur competition.

"Neither do I have any doubt that it is he who has created this professional entertainment phenomenon.

"There can hardly be an Irish dancer, current or past, that isn't applauding him for what he has done. He has provided hope for youngsters who want to make a living from their art."

Eilish Flatley: "The Irish dance officials called Michael's dancing avant-garde. They said there really wasn't a category to fit it into. They only had 'Choreography,' but no 'Dance Drama,' which they introduced later.

"There was no way we could all afford to fly to the World Championships, so we sent him. He went from there and won the West of

Ireland Championship and other competitions. What he wanted to do was phenomenal."

Michael Flatley, Senior: "The thing we found out . . . was that it was awful hard to bring the championship out of Ireland. They all tried desperately to keep it in Ireland, but Mike went back for it again and again. He never gave up and I don't suppose he ever would have.

"He'd still be after it today if he hadn't won it, the first American. It was also the first time the trophy ever left Ireland."

Chapter Nine

Dead End

I FELT TRIUMPHANT. I had played their game and won. And although I'd taken the championship only by giving up the use of my arms—bowing to the restraint of traditional Irish dance—I knew that the time would come when I'd be dancing with my arms, my face, my whole being.

I've always believed in spirituality—that there are powers and influences out there. That's probably why I am so intrigued by the myths and mysteries of Ireland. I know it sounds crazy, but I believe that much of the work I've created has been within me for hundreds of years. Some of it I dreamed of when I was seven years old.

Now, another dream had come true. And in that same year of 1975, I won the All-Ireland Concert Flute Championship in Donegal. But none of that was enough to pay the rent. Irish music and dance had not yet become recognized commercial forms, and I had no idea how I could make a living from them. But although I had my bad moments, I never got really disheartened, certainly not enough to give up the dream.

When I ask myself why I never even came close to giving up, I've got to credit my grandma Hannah Ryan. She visited me in Chicago once during an ice-cold winter when I was working odd jobs for a few dollars an hour, dreaming up dance routines. My body may have been in the ditch, but my mind was in Madison Square Garden. My grandmother saw my sad reality–but she also saw my dreams. She talked to me for hours, painting the path for success. At the times of my greatest troubles–and also during my biggest triumphs–my grandmother has always been there in body or spirit.

In those days, Irish dance was definitely the poor stepcousin to Irish music. I toured with a few little Irish bands, but the focus was always on the musicians, never on the dancers. Still, I could always hear my grandmother's encouraging voice in my ear. And my dad's words were constantly with me as well. "Never do anything unless you are going to do it properly," he'd always told me. "And once you begin to do something, never give in. If you're not being successful, there's only one reason–you're not trying hard enough."

So I kept trying harder. I even opened an Irish dance school on the northwest side of Chicago. It isn't easy making a school pay, especially if you're young and inexperienced. But I had the advantage of being a world champion and that was better than an advertising campaign. On the opening evening, hundreds of kids and their parents were lined up to study with me. Soon I was taking down a fortune in cash. Finally–success! But even more rewarding was our competition successes. I also taught music and my three bands all won first place in their sections.

Patrick Flatley: "When Mike opened up the school, he cleaned out half the other schools of their pupils, who wanted to go to a great teacher and a great dancer. The first night you couldn't get in the door.

"It was a really terrific business, but you need other teachers. Mike couldn't teach them all, especially when he had seven or eight hundred in the very first week. As soon as he opened up there was an unmerciful following going to Mike's school."

Ah, success! There was just one problem: I was miserable.

First of all, I wanted to dance, not teach. Dreaming of the great choreography I knew was in me, I had trouble focusing on the baby steps that my students were ready for.

The bigger problem, though, was that so many of the kids I was teaching didn't really want to learn. Mainly, it was their parents who wanted them to dance. The kids themselves couldn't have cared less.

It takes a special kind of patience to teach someone who doesn't want to learn, especially if the student is only a little kid. I had pupils as young as six years old, whose mothers and fathers dreamed of raising a champion dancer. To see their little darlings balk at dancing when I loved it so much was hard for me. And longing for greatness so much myself, I found it hard to work with anyone whose dedication did not match mine.

I did have some great students, of course, as well as some students who had been dancing for years, even winning competitions. But the truly dedicated ones were few and far between. Eileen Mulhern O'Kane was one of my star pupils. I confess I had feelings for her when we were young. In fact, I've loved her for twenty years. She's the one that got away, as they say. She's happily married now, with her own family.

Yet once again, fate took charge. Running my school was the first opportunity I'd really had to choreograph work for large groups: dance dramas, lineups, and other big numbers. Years later I realized that this experience, so frustrating at the time, was a training ground for me as much as for any of my students. Lord knows what I'd've done without the valuable experience I got there, the opportunities to experiment, with my students and myself. It was while I was teaching that I invented different types of heel clicks, hitting my heels together in mid-air—the back clicks, side clicks, double-clicks, and triples. I taught a lot of these steps to my students, but I'm still the only dancer in the world who can do seven clicks of my heels without touching the ground. And my school was where I first taught people to tell stories in their dancing, where I first created the long lines of dancers that would eventually become my trademark.

Still, I wasn't cut out to be a teacher—I found it too frustrating, even with the best pupils. No matter how good my students were, I couldn't bear that they were performing, not I. I'd choreograph their routines, dance out their steps in front of them, inspire them, sweet-talk them, and give them beautiful costumes to wear. But when they got on stage in front of the judges, I couldn't dance for them—and that was hell for me. The one rule I had made for myself was always to do everything myself. But as a teacher, I could only stand and watch while my pupils succeeded or failed on their own merits. It made me feel helpless, and I hated that feeling.

My students were winning lots of awards. And I was making a decent living. But the daily frustration was too high a price. Finally, at the Midwest Dance Championship (my last), my school won nine first-place trophies, and I retired from teaching on a high. There were lots of tears from the pupils that day.

Eileen Mulhern O'Kane is married and lives in Chicago. She has two children who are Irish dancers. She was a pupil of Michael Flatley and remained his friend. In 2004, she recalled: "We got to know Michael in 1980 . . . as a teacher and as someone we thought was the most amazing thing out there. That he had won the world championship was wonderful, so when he opened up his school he had quite a following. Most of us who had gone to him were quite established already but it was exciting to be taught by him.

"He was a legend before his time.

"Of course, I didn't realize that as a child. We just had a ball. He made

everyone feel like you were next world champion; he instilled that level of confidence in you. 'You are the best. You can be the best.' He did that for himself; he had that drive and he wanted everyone to have it. If you didn't have that naturally, he at least made you believe you did. Even if you didn't realize you did, he brought it out. He helped you develop it.

"As a teacher, he kind of broke the rules. He was kind of ahead of himself in so many ways with just the solo dancing creativity as well as the group dancing.

"We danced what was then called 'The Choreography'–that was the name of the competition–and Michael put together something that was very, very creative to a point where we were disqualified because he introduced things they had never seen before. The officials felt it was beyond what was acceptable for the competition.

"As a result, a whole new category was created. They created a new drama category, because what we did was so cutting edge it didn't quite fit the normal dancing with your hands at your sides.

"[But the first time,] we won first place and then they took it away. They disqualified us an hour later and we ended up getting nothing. But in our hearts we knew we were the winners and we didn't care that they took the trophies away from us. We had won. We knew we were head and shoulders above anything anyone had ever seen.

"It was just the top of the day. Even then, Michael was lining up the dancers in a chorus line, way ahead of everyone else.

"I guess what I think of when I think of Michael is someone very kind, very giving. He wanted everyone in the class, whether you had natural ability or not, to be a winner. He was always saying, 'You are an excellent dancer,' and 'Keep it up,' and he made everyone feel one hundred and ten percent.

"I'm sure inside he thought, 'Oh, my God, what in heck am I doing here?'

"No one had what he had. He's a good, nice man. I had an opportunity to see him and spend some time with him when he was in Chicago in

2004, and I thought he would say 'Eileen Who?' I thought he'd hardly remember, but he remembered the very small details of the past.

"He wanted to know what I was up to, curious about where I've gone and what I've done. Michael's lifestyle is very different than any of his family would be living, but then it's different from all our lifestyles. He's quite established now, but he still loves his family and maybe yearns for a little of what they have.

"He said to me, something like, 'Tell me about your life.'

"I said, 'I guess it's fairly normal.'

"He said, 'Gosh, I yearn for simple. I yearn for normal.'

"As much as he has, I think he would love to have that. But who am I to say that my life is normal? What's normal?

"We were like ships that sail past each other in the night. I'll never know what might have been between us."

Chapter Ten

Dream Dancing

He would have gone to the moon if he could.

Paddy Moloney of the Chieftains
talking to *The Times*, London, October 25, 1997,
about the young Michael Flatley

When the telephone rang, I was actually annoyed. I'd had a long, hard day—I was back to digging ditches again. How was I to know that this was the call that would change my life?

Of course, my life wasn't so bad. I'd finally managed to walk away from the dance school—from my reluctant pupils and their eager parents—with enough profit to work on an album of flute music. I recorded it at the Pumpklin Studio in Oak Lawn in Chicago in 1981, with my brother Pat on the bodhran and a great Belfast-born guy called Wallace Hood on guitar and bouzouki. It was truly *my* album: I had creative control; I wrote three of the tracks; and I directed, arranged, and co-mixed the music. Without reading a note of music, I'd become a successful musician.

But I was still digging ditches with my father, even though I was also getting quite a lot of dancing work, including a 1981–1982 tour through America and Canada with the Dublin-based group Comhaltus Ceoltori in Hearin. I loved dancing full-time—which made it all the harder to go back to the grime and the graft.

And that's when when I took the telephone call. It was Chieftains manager Joe Whitston. Calling me.

I knew well that the Chieftains—Paddy Moloney, Martin Faye, Sean Keane, Derek Bell, Kevin Conneff, and Matt Malloy—were probably the most famous traditional Irish band in the world. As far as I can tell, they still are. They've played more big-name concert halls than I could count and won a string of Grammy awards in the process. So when Joe identified himself, I was thunderstruck.

The lads, he told me, had seen me dance in New York and been impressed. They wanted me to tour with them. Was I interested?

I didn't have the words to tell him just how interested I was. At that point, the Chieftains were the only band playing traditional Irish music on the international stage. Their offer was to make me the first ever professional Irish dancer.

My first night out, I got a standing ovation. I came off the stage, breathing heavily as I made my way to my tiny, beat-up dressing room. I looked into the cloudy mirror and thought, "This is it. I'm never going back. This is what I want to do."

Traveling with the Chieftains was the most fun I could imagine: getting one standing ovation after another, seeing cities around the world, doing what I loved with guys who would become lifelong friends. Matt Malloy is still one of my best friends in the world. Listening to him play the flute night after night was like getting a master's degree in music.

There was just one problem. My kind of dancing was not the Irish dancing that An Coimisiún le Rinci Gaelacha would endorse. At first, I was hardly aware of the way that traditional dancers viewed me. How could I notice anything negative?—I was in seventh heaven. The Chieftains were giving me audiences to work with, people who could see the steps I'd come up with, the heel clicks and waving arms, the sexuality and the flash. And they loved it. It was like having a live laboratory out there in the concert halls. No more judges marking me down for coming up with my own steps, my own style. No more worry about who was taking first place and who was stuck coming in second. Whatever didn't work one night, I could simply change by the next. Finally, I could experiment without fear of consequences. For the first time in my life, I had the freedom to express what I felt.

The Chieftains couldn't have been more encouraging. And I'd been waiting for this chance so long, which made it even more precious. My newfound freedom was a release, a drug to which I'd become addicted. I wanted more and more and more–and the audiences kept cheering me on.

More and more often, now, I was using my arms and my body to be more expressive. I couldn't use my arms like a tap dancer. Or like a ballet dancer–that would be too soft. I couldn't use them like a flamenco dancer–although what I created was probably closer to flamenco than to any other existing style. But I was looking for a new way to dance–my own brand. It had to be less formal than traditional Irish dancing–strong and powerful and confident. The further out I went, the more the audiences yelled and screamed.

One stage effect got more attention and caused more controversy than any dance step I ever created. It all came about by accident. Remember, I was traveling with a bunch of guys–no wife or girlfriend to help me out–and I was a hopeless bachelor on the domestic front. One night I couldn't find my shirt, though I thought it was probably under the bed somewhere. Even if I rooted it out, I thought, it would be dirty and wrinkled–an embarrassment.

So I appeared on stage with just a jacket–and no shirt. The audience went nuts.

Irish traditionalists were enraged. But the Chieftains couldn't have been happier. Still, in some ways, I was too far out even for them. "What you're doing is brilliant," Moloney told me once. "But hold on, we've got to meld you into the band. I can't make a new planet for you."

Now I realize I must have been a right pain in the ass. The Chieftains were the real stars–they had worked with Van Morrison and Mick Jagger and scores of other names–and here I was turning out to be the pin-up boy. They couldn't have been nicer about it, though, and they never showed a moment's irritation.

As for me, I knew this was the main chance, and I grabbed for it with both hands. Every night that we got a standing ovation, every time the audience stomped its feet and whistled and cheered, I knew I was doing something right. It wasn't just the audiences, either. The critics were praising us all–with special notice for what they saw as my exciting new style.

The ladies were a bonus. There was always a bunch of women around after the shows, and after all that dancing, I was generally in good form, to say the least.

Still, no matter how encouraging the Chieftains wanted to be, they couldn't make me a full-time dancer. The most they could offer was a few tours here and there. I was so frustrated, especially knowing that the audiences were out there, waiting, eager. I was dancing, they were screaming, the girls were willing–and then once again, I'd find myself at 7 a.m. sitting at the back of a cheap flight on my way home to Chicago.

I could hear the fans shouting. And the next voice shouting would be the real-life voice of my boss: "Let's go, let's go, let's go! Move it, Michael, move it!" From the stage at Carnegie Hall to the bottom of a ditch in twenty-four hours. That's show business for you!

A dancer's life doesn't last forever. If you don't make it while you're young, there's not much hope for you. And my dreams were becoming bigger, more urgent, the shows I was continually conjuring up in my head becoming more and more elaborate.

I needed money, I decided, and I just wouldn't make enough if I kept on with Dad and Patrick. So I left the family construction business and founded my own business.

Everyone who worked for me was told to arrive at the job on time looking clean and neat, to do good work, and to leave the work area spotlessly clean. I'd learned that much from my dad, and I knew that it would always be a winning formula.

Meanwhile, I kept working with the Chieftains, who were finally getting the recognition they deserved. They too had been working all their lives, from playing Irish music in local pubs to prestigious concerts at the Great Wall of China, Rome's Villa Milanese, the Sydney Opera House, and New York's Carnegie Hall. They offered me a new tour whose highlight was a summer 1985 performance at London's Royal Albert Hall—one of the world's great locations. I said yes—and experienced another life-changing moment. Because while I was dancing in London, I was to meet the woman who became my wife.

Chapter Eleven

Foreign Affairs

Michael is the love of my life.

Beata Flatley,
interviewed in Chicago, February 12, 2004

I'd just come offstage, sweaty and exhilarated from another standing ovation. I was tired but excited as I made my way to my dressing room—not the tiny, cramped space I'd had on my first tour, but a luxurious room befitting the splendor of the Royal Albert Hall.

There was a woman standing in the reception area—the most beautiful person I'd ever seen, surrounded by an incredible aura that pulled me toward her. From the moment I laid eyes on her, I was hooked. She had everything that anyone could ever want—class, sophistication, and elegance. Her name was Beata Dziaba, and she was the first woman I ever wanted to marry.

As soon as I saw her, I knew I couldn't let her get away. After all the small talk, I walked her home. We couldn't stop talking—somehow, we needed three hours to take a twenty-minute walk. She told me she was from Poland but that she and her parents now lived in Germany. We spoke about our impressions of London and I told her about my life in America. The conversation was easy, like old friends catching up. There wasn't even a good-night kiss, simply a promise to talk the next day.

For our second meeting, I dressed to the nines. I was waiting anxiously outside the stage door when my best mate Matt Malloy appeared.

"Hey," he greeted me. "You're all dressed up."

"Yeah, I'm waiting for my date."

He looked me up and down, taking in how smart I'd got myself turned out.

"I think she's the one," I told him.

He looked me over again and shook his head. "Look," he said, "get lost. Go out and get drunk. Get sick all over your shirt, wet your pants, and turn up five or six hours late–stone drunk. If she still loves you after all that, then she *is* the one."

Now you know why Matt is one of my best mates! Later in life, I would learn how good his advice had been. But that night I only listened and laughed. And I stayed right where I was.

I felt I had known Beata all my life, that she had been handpicked just for me. Can you fall in love in a moment? The second I saw her, in the summer of 1985, I knew she'd be my wife. She was pure. Our love was magical. But alas, my life was not a movie script.

I had to return to America and back to my construction business, which had taken off. Excited by my quick success, I'd raced ahead with building my little enterprise–maybe too fast. I'd opened up a second new location–and then a third, and then a fourth. The men in green uniforms, wearing our badges, became familiar figures on the Greater Chicago landscape. But success is a double-edged sword. You can't neglect a successful business; it demands your time and attention. If you don't focus on it, sooner or later, it will fail, no matter how successful it once was.

So I worked the way I always had—all the time. Now my hard work wasn't just for me but for Beata, too.

It was hard for both of us being apart, even though we talked on the phone all the time. Finally, in late 1985, I took another trip back to London.

Beata came to meet me at Heathrow Airport. The terminal was mobbed, but I'd been smart—I'd only brought hand luggage—so I made my way through customs pretty quickly. I caught sight of her there on the concourse, her face freeze-framed against the crowd—and it simply stopped me cold. I stood there, glued to the ground. On the plane, I'd wondered if my feelings had really survived our long separation. Now I knew they had.

I rushed over and took Beata in my arms. I had been planning to take her out to dinner, but something made me look over at the departure board. "Want to go to Paris?" I asked her. We flew there straight from Heathrow, walking the romantic side streets of Paris, and down the Champs Elysées. We were both caught up in the mood of the city, and after a couple of glasses of red, I pulled her by the arm through the screaming traffic around the Arc de Triomphe, went down on one knee, and asked her to marry me.

Beata said *yes*, and we went all out for a wonderful time in Paris. Then I had to get back to America, to my business. *Our* business.

Working day and night, I saved enough to make the down payment on a house for myself and my future bride. I wrote her every week. I'm not much of a poet, but I did my best in those weekly letters. And I sent her roses every chance I got: a dozen red with two white ones in the center. She had to know how much I loved her.

Still, as so often happened, I faced a seemingly insurmountable problem: How was I going to get Beata into America? She was a Polish citizen with no American visa. If we told customs officials that she was my fiancée, they'd be suspicious: Lots of women marry guys just to get U.S. passports.

My first step was getting back to Europe. Beata was still living in Hanover, Germany, with her parents, although her father, a professor of veterinary medicine, had been spending a few weeks in Hamburg, where he was giving a series of lectures.

I took the cheapest flights I could: Chicago to Reykjavik to Luxembourg, where a blizzard was causing trouble. It was Christmas Eve, 1985, and I was a man in love. I never even thought about letting Beata know I was on my way. Instead, I went to the airport's cheapest car-rental place and made arrangements to take their last car, a little Renault. It had no luxuries–like snow chains. I drove off in that blizzard on blind chance, making my slow and painful way through the snowy German countryside. It took forever!

When I finally made it to Hanover, I went into the nearest bar. The bartender was a lovely blonde girl wearing just her brassiere on top, which was all the go in those days, the real cool look. I ordered myself a shot of whiskey and a cold beer. I lit a little cigar, threw back the shot, and then, hoping I hadn't been too impulsive, called Beata.

I didn't even know if she was at home. She and her mother might have gone to Hamburg to join her father for Christmas. But no, she answered the phone and soon she was joyously on her way to meet me.

"Mikey," I heard her say. I turned round and saw her standing beside a big, young man. My stomach did a somersault before I realized that he was only her brother Robert. Then all my attention was on her.

We were both desperate for her to come back to Chicago with me. But the British authorities had told us that to get Beata into America, we had to be married, not just engaged. At the American Embassy, we heard the same story but a nice young woman also told us, "As soon as you're married, come back and see me."

Getting married in a hurry–sounds simple, right? Not on your life–we couldn't do it anywhere. In Paris, you had to be a resident for six months to tie the knot. In Germany, there were other rules, and in London, likewise.

Then, we discovered Copenhagen, where only a seven-day residency was required. Finally, we were home free!

No again. Now we needed a wedding ring, and we couldn't find one in Copenhagen for love nor money: It was the week after Christmas and nothing was open. Finally, we braved the snow once again and took a ferry across to Malmö, Sweden.

It was freezing cold, and the two of us were huddled together for warmth. At first it didn't look as though we were having any better luck in Sweden than we had in Denmark. But when we had almost given up, we found one tiny shop down a little side street, whose owner—crippled by arthritis that made it painful for him to work—was just about to close his store for good. We must have been the last customers of his life.

Any other time, I'd've been sympathetic. Now I was simply desperate. We urgently needed two 24-carat gold wedding bands. Could he please, please help us?

The old man looked from me to Beata and smiled.

"I'll make them," he told us. "It will be a pleasure for my last task."

The rings were absolutely gorgeous. I still have mine. And on January 6, 1986, in the beautiful city of Copenhagen, Beata and I were finally able to wear those rings as husband and wife.

We had lots of love but not much cash, and we still had to get back to Chicago. After the wedding, we managed to get tickets out of Luxembourg to London, where I arranged to get money transferred from my American bank via Western Union. We used the funds to get a small room so we could set about getting back home. But our problems weren't over.

At the U.S. Embassy, we asked for the young woman who had been so encouraging. "She doesn't want to come out and see you," snarled the British official at the front desk.

"What?" I exclaimed. "Why not?"

The man gave me a superior glare as only the British can do. "Well, she's busy, isn't she, mate?"

We had to wait all day. That stuck-up guy kept us there until scores of people had come and gone. When we were the last ones left in the office and he was laughing with a friend on the phone, we went up to him and said, "Please, can't we see her?"

"No," he snapped. "She's gone for the day. Sorry, you've missed her."

We were in despair. I watched the man sort through some papers. "Come back in six weeks," he said without looking up, "and you'll have your visa."

Six weeks? We didn't have enough money to last the weekend.

We walked outside, and Beata cried. But if I hadn't given up before, I would surely not do so now. I recalled that the year before, I'd played a youth festival with the Chieftains in Kingston, Jamaica. There, Miss Doris offered space in her cottages–right on the beach–for only fifteen dollars a night. I steered Beata to the nearest travel agent, hoping that our little bit of money would stretch to two plane tickets and a room with Miss Doris.

Miss Doris, may I tell you, was the most cantankerous old hairpin that ever walked the planet, although at ninety years of age, perhaps she was entitled. Anyway, for fifteen bucks a night, who could complain? The price was per room, not per person.

So Beata and I flew to Jamaica and waited out our six weeks. We got so hungry I used to go to the neighboring Treehouse Hotel and steal tomatoes from their kitchen. Then I'd wait for the bread van. If my luck was in, we'd have tomato sandwiches. On unlucky days, we'd settle for plain tomatoes and the little bits of fish that the generous Jamaicans gave us to celebrate our "honeymoon."

Still, it was a glorious, carefree time in its way. After all, there was nothing for the two of us to do but get to know each other. We felt like castaways–just the sun and the sea and the two of us. Our love made it a brilliant honeymoon.

Then it was back to London for a fast reality fix. After another dogfight with the embassy and another few days' wait, we finally got Beata's visa–but now I was completely out of cash. We came out of the building in Grosvenor Square and sank down onto the embassy steps. (This was before they had all those concrete security blocks there.) I hugged my new wife and thought of our future together–growing old, having children and grandchildren, fulfilling our dreams.

Then I remembered that the immediate future didn't look so bright. I didn't have a penny, my credit card was over the limit, and the prospects of getting back to America at that moment seemed daunting.

Reluctantly, I phoned my bank, asking them to send me the last of my "rainy day" money. But though I'd given clear instructions for them to wire the money to Gatwick Airport, the money never turned up. There were Beata and I, at the airport, praying for the dollars.

I was even more upset when I called home. Apparently the bank had called my father–they had no contact information for me–and told him that they refused to transfer my money. I had to be there in person for them to release the funds.

Beata sat surrounded by all her worldly possessions, the suitcases that she'd planned to take to America to begin her new life. I kept walking back and forth between her and the Western Union office, compulsively checking for my money, although by now I knew that the bank hadn't sent it. But I had to do something, and I couldn't bear to face Beata. Then, on my fifth visit to the money exchange window, I looked back and saw my wife burst into tears.

Slowly I walked over to comfort her. What would we do? Where would we sleep? We didn't have a penny left.

Then I heard an announcement over the loudspeakers. "Last call for People Express to Chicago!"

"Oh God," I told Beata. "If only that was for us."

I felt a sudden jolt in my brain, as though someone had given me a sharp mental kick. "Wait a second," I thought. "People Express, the no-frills airline. That's when you pay on board—*with your credit card*."

My card was maxed out, of course, but once you're on board, what are they going to do, turn the plane around? I booked two last-minute seats. In no time at all our bags were on the plane—and so were we. I was embarrassed to give them my card—it would probably explode in the machine!—but if there was any problem, I was ready to argue about it. After all, I had the funds waiting for me in Chicago.

The stewardess walked towards me. My heart was in my mouth. She opened her lips—to yell at me? To threaten me with arrest?

Her soft voice broke in on my worrying. "Thank you very much, Mr. Flatley. Have a nice flight."

A few seconds later another flight attendant showed up with a nice cold beer. "Mikey," Beata said, "we made it!"

She fell asleep before I took my first sip. Hours later, I had to wake her so she could see the lights of Chicago's Midway airport.

Beata blinked sleepily, her face a beautiful picture. "Mikey, are we really in America?"

"Yes, love. This is it."

The picture grinned. We were finally home.

"MICHAEL FLATLEY IS FAST BECOMING A STEPPING LEGEND," read the headline on an article by David Prescott in the Chicago Tribune *on December 8, 1985. Prescott wrote, "Michael Flatley has one blue eye and one green eye (a condition known as heterochromia) and if you think that's extraordinary you ought to see him dance."*

And the Los Angeles Herald-Examiner *lauded Flatley as "the Rudolf Nureyev of Irish dance."*

Matt Malloy of the Chieftains is a longtime friend of Michael Flatley and in April, 2005, spoke at his home on the west coast of Ireland about the beginnings of their friendship: "It was the mid-70s when I met him first when I was first in Chicago with The Bothy Band. The connections were there–his father comes from Sligo and that's quite close to where I come from and we both played flute and we play in a similar style . . . a brilliant player he is and all. Apart from his dancing career, he's a great traditional flute player.

"I mentioned him working with the Chieftains to Paddy Moloney and Michael was up for it. We were well aware of his brilliance as a dancer. Michael was invited along [to tour with the Chieftans] and, of course, he was a show stopper. Even at that stage there was no stopping him. He was given his head. Being the man he is he was inventive and was creating different things and suggesting things to Paddy and asking what we thought of this and that. Of course everything and anything he did was brilliant so you let him off. That was Mike. He's a gentleman to the last. Very generous fella. I always found Mike generous to a fault in fact. Even when he didn't have it.

"He is a different animal when he hits the stage! I suppose it might have upset some artists along the way but Mike always had a very clear focus when he hit a stage, and was a perfectionist. He stands by it. Then again, he was a long time waiting at the bus stop if you like. He came across the big time and there was no stopping him. You know, he's competitive and he's a fighter. That's the boxer in him!"

Chapter Twelve

Down and Out in Beverly Hills

Michael Flatley can tap dance at thirty-five beats per second.
Only his bank account ticks up faster.

The Sunday Telegraph,
London, October 11, 1998

Mr. and Mrs. Michael Flatley hit America with grand smiles, and life seemed great. Beata and I were welcomed home as husband and wife. After the craziness of Europe, being back in America felt good.

I was married and madly in love. My family adored Beata; everyone seemed to be happy around her. She certainly made me smile all the time. My construction business was booming, and I was still taking every opportunity to dance.

I created a business plan for my company so I could bring in managers to take care of the day-to-day work. I thought this would allow me time to build my own show, an Irish dancing troupe that I imagined would tour throughout the United States. Having traveled with the Chieftains, I'd learned that there was indeed an audience that was eager for my kind of dance, and I was further encouraged by the recognition I was winning. I was the youngest person ever to be awarded the National Heritage Fellowship by the National Endowment for the Arts–a great organization, by the way, that always gave me lots of encouragement. I considered the fellowship a huge honor, as it is awarded according to the vote of other artists, who usually give it only to more veteran performers.

As if this weren't enough, word had gotten around about the speed of my tap dancing. *The Guinness Book of World Records* got in touch, but they had to verify my abilities in order to grant me a world record. So in May 1989 they set up a test at a recording studio in Alsip, a Chicago suburb. Guinness Book representatives flew over from London, joined by Alsip's mayor, whom they brought along as an independent witness. We used sophisticated sound equipment and a tape that recorded very quickly, at thirty-five inches per second. They set a machine to beep every second, so that sound engineers could mark the tape with a wax pencil showing where each second began and ended. The whole process was incredibly difficult, but when it was over, they found that I'd been dancing at twenty-eight taps a second–a bona fide world record.

National Geographic also got into the act, naming me one of their "living treasures." They took a superb photograph that made me appear to be "flying" across the Chicago skyline.

Patrick Flatley: "With the construction business, Mike went to the north side of Chicago where the money is.

"Mike and I both got our licenses so we always had something we could fall back on. He kept his options open. . . . He had nineteen trucks on the road inside of a year and a half, which was unbelievable. It was one of the biggest businesses in Chicago.

"Whatever he puts his mind to is successful. He's driven. He has a real drive to him, a combination of Mum and Dad, who were both successful. Dad built all the houses since we were kids, kept moving up the ladder.

He always worked Sundays when he didn't have to, and me and Mike would have to go out with my dad.

"Dad always thought big, kind of like my brother. My mom did as well. My mom and dad worked as a team, determined to make it, having come all the way from Ireland. Dad and Mike are an awful lot alike.

". . . All the dancing came from my mom. I'm sure Mike got his drive from my mom and dad—except he took it a step further."

Abe Villagomez dug sewers with Michael Flatley. Interviewed at his home in Chicago on August 7, 2004, he recalled: "[Mike and I] stood together digging—and I think Mike worked like he always wanted to get to Australia first. He always had that look in his eye, and we'd be a little competitive in getting the job done. He was a good worker and would stay there until the job was done. He did any job and could do any job.

"I worked with him, and I worked for him—and it was no different. He worked as hard whether he was paying the wages or collecting them the same as me."

Life seemed to be dealing me nothing but face cards, winners all the way. But then, once again, trouble struck. The very success I had achieved gave rise to a new kind of failure.

Basically, in my efforts to liberate myself from the daily demands of my business, I had grown my construction company too fast. I'd wanted someone else to run my business so I'd be free to go on tour, so I hired a headhunter to find me a second-in-command. The headhunter presented me with a former executive of a major company. He seemed to be just what the doctor ordered, and with a light heart, I took off for yet another tour with the Chieftains.

A few months later, I was fast asleep at New York's Mayflower Hotel when the phone rang at 3 a.m. It was my second-in-command. He'd been up all night worrying.

"Boss, we hit the skids," he told me. "You better come home—fast."

I was facing bankruptcy. It all started when I'd franchised my company. For $100,000 to cover the costs of the paperwork, anyone could buy the rights to start his or her own branch. Buoyed by all the cash coming in, I moved up into a big office and had forty trucks on the road.

But when you franchise a business, you're only as strong as the guys who buy in, and I wasn't always getting the employees to match my ambition. To be brutally frank, I thought some of them were real bums.

I think this was when I adopted my basic motto: *Never count on anyone but yourself.* This was also when I discovered the most important principle in my life: *Never choose money—do what you love.*

The company's resources were gone, and now we had nothing left. I was furious at myself for being so trusting. I could have punched myself in the mouth. Hard.

To casual onlookers I still had it made, driving around in the brand-new Mercedes that I had bought for my wife. But now I was overextended like you wouldn't believe. My payroll alone was over $50,000 a week. Plus I had put a giant marketing strategy into place, so I had bills for advertising as well.

As always, I was willing to work hard. I'd leave home at 5 a.m. to drive north for an hour on Highway 355 to Addison, where our headquarters were. But the men who worked for me weren't always turning out as they were supposed to. And when they did show up, it wasn't uncommon for them to take all day to do one small job.

My expenses were sky-high, and my income was dropping fast. But out of sheer stubbornness, I refused to admit that my business was doomed.

One Thursday morning, twenty-four hours before payday, Beata and I were driving to the office together. I can still see the time on the dashboard clock–7:06–as Beata said in a forlorn voice, "Mikey, what are you going to do? You can't pay. The men will be waiting for their money. They'll want to kill you."

I pulled my expensive car into a roadside restaurant. "I don't know," I told her. "I've got to figure something out. I've got to think."

It was a beautiful sunny morning. We sat down in a booth and the waitress came over. Beata ordered pancakes, and coffee with a little cream. I ordered a double Jack Daniel's. (And in those days, I rarely drank!)

When I'd finished my drink, I looked at Beata. "It's time to let go, baby. We have to just let it go."

We did let go–and I did it right. I paid off everybody I humanly could–and I never filed for bankruptcy.

Beata was strong. But she was also clearly dismayed about what was happening. I had our house mortgaged to the teeth to help finance the business, so we'd had to sell it. We had nothing left but the car–which still had payments due. So we took to the highway, heading for California. We hoarded what little money we had, not stopping except to get coffee and to go to the bathroom.

We rented a tiny apartment in the middle of Los Angeles. I thought I'd hit bottom–but I was wrong. After I'd failed to make two payments, a repossession company took my car.

I fell to my knees as I watched them do it, kneeling on the ground with my head in my hands. I felt as though someone had kicked me in the stomach. I didn't give a fig about the car itself. But watching it go, I could hear a voice crying out, "You failed. *You failed.*" My humiliation was complete.

I tried to get some work but that's tough in L.A. if you don't have wheels. I tried laboring, showing up on street corners at 5 a.m. for the chance to earn a few dollars a day. But in California, it's mainly immigrants who do that sort of work, and they usually wouldn't let me wait with them. Then I started bartending school so I could pick up a bit of cash working the bars. But I was always looking for something better.

Next, I got the idea to teach a few dance classes. The dance studios were miles from where we lived, and I didn't have the price of a bus fare or a cup of coffee. But I had no intention of failing. I walked.

Our money went quickly for rent and food and all the other expenses of day-to-day life. But as hard as I was working, I was committed to keeping up my discipline. How could I remain a dancer if I didn't practice? I started working out in an old theater off Third Avenue and La Cienega, a local hangout where a bunch of black tap dancers used to work on their moves. I remember this one guy who liked to get my juices going. "Hey, man," he'd shout. "You're going fucking crazy with your feet. Why don't you slow down? Just walk around for a while. You've got it all wrong, man. Hey, man, the way you dancin', you're going to be dead in ten minutes."

We danced and danced. When that place closed down, I found another dance building over on Dupre and Third, not too far from Cedars-Sinai Medical Center in Hollywood. The structure was crumbling–and condemned. But it had a wooden floor to dance on.

For me, as for most dancers, it's very important to dance on a sprung floor–a wooden floor designed to absorb the shock of furious dancing; a floor that gives when you dance on it. Otherwise, you risk hurting your legs and ruining your knees. The floor can be any sort of wood you like, but it must give, at least a little.

The place on Third Avenue had a sprung floor–but it was also locked up, chained, and tough to get into. I used to climb to an upper window–a difficult climb. I couldn't bring any music in with me–it was already too tight a trick to get in the window. I made my own music using the rhythms in my head. Sure, it wasn't perfect–at that time, not much was.

Yet I did have one superlative moment in the City of Angels.

When the Chieftains were booked to appear at the famed Hollywood Bowl, they asked me to dance with them. I couldn't imagine a bigger thrill.

All the great names have appeared at the Hollywood Bowl, from Judy Garland to every big-city symphony orchestra; from Jimi Hendrix to Pavarotti; from the Beatles to the Dalai Lama. The open-air Bowl is located high in the Hollywood Hills, with Los Angeles laid out like a dazzling carpet beneath. It opened in 1922 as a canvas-topped wooden platform. Now it's one of the world's famed theaters.

When we appeared, we had a sell-out crowd–18,000 people standing up and screaming. From the stage I could see the cheering crowd, framed by hills that stretched all the way out to the Pacific Ocean. It was the biggest show of my life.

Despite this extraordinary high point, I was all coiled up. My low-paying jobs had me like a caged tiger. I'd get home to the little place Beata and I shared, and pace around the living room in frustration. I only knew how to measure my progress by how much I could earn–and I wasn't making very much money.

My poor wife, God love her, worked hard to support me through these difficult times but now she was very successful in her own right. She was head make up artist at Givenchy in Beverly Hills. She had a whole new circle of very rich friends and started spending more and more time socializing and I began to see less and less of her. I knew I had to do something quick, because I couldn't bear feeling so unsuccessful. Despite my dreams of being a dancer, I decided I had to advance in the business world.

Then one day I saw an ad in the paper advertising for brokers. I put on the only suit I had from my days as a bachelor and went off to my interview with high hopes.

When I arrived at the offices, I was told to meet with one of the company's executives.

"The boss?" I asked.

No, I was told. Another man.

"Well, then, no, thank you," I replied. "I'll meet the big guy. If not, I'm wasting my time, and I'll go to a better place.'

The secretary looked me up and down. "Wait right there," she said. I heard her making a call. "All right, *the boss* will see you now," she told me.

I walked into the office without missing a beat. I'd been a boss myself, so I knew just what to say: "You have never had a broker in this place like me. I'm the best salesman that ever lived." When I heard myself lie, I cringed.

"Have you ever done this work before?"

"No," I admitted. "But I'm a businessman and I know more about numbers than you ever will. Try me. Just prep me for your tests, and if I don't ace them, you can fire me."

I won't bore you with the details. Suffice it to say, he didn't fire me! In fact, I got the corner office with the window. Finally, I thought. Now, for sure, I was on my way.

Chapter Thirteen

My Big Chance

A man oughta do what he thinks is right.

John Wayne, *Hondo,* 1953

I'M NOT PERFECT. Far from it. Confident? Oh, yes! I wasn't born to finish second. I believe if I'm going to do something, I'll do it right, and I'm going to give it 150 percent while I can.

So there I was, sitting in my office in this firm. It was a beautiful office, for sure, and the money was okay. But when I realized what I had to do to earn my salary, it made me feel ill.

To put it bluntly, I wondered if the brokers at this company had any ethics at all. These guys in their sharp suits seemed like they were simply investing for the main chance. Blackjack players got better odds in Las Vegas.

The salesmen had list after list of old people who had money—probably the last money they had in the world. Everyone called the old ones "suckers" or "lambs." Our guys tried to sell the suckers oil fields—God knows where these bonanzas were even located—and as they were making their pitch, they'd cover the phone and have a good laugh. Anyone foolish enough to invest in one of these ventures was just shoveling money into a drain—and I think we all knew it. In fact, the whole time I worked there, I doubt anybody ever made any money from anything we sold.

So here I was, finally having managed several months at a stable job. I'd even gotten myself some nice suits! But even though my boss was breathing down my neck, I wasn't selling anything. I wasn't trying. I couldn't be one of the sharpers taking advantage of the old folks. I wasn't brought up that way. I'd just sit there behind my desk looking out at my view, and in my head I was dancing in Madison Square Garden or performing sold-out shows in football stadiums across Germany. I couldn't stop thinking about my art.

One day I was on the phone when another life-changing call came through on my second line. This time, it was a young lady from Tyrone Productions in Dublin, inviting me to come dance in a show called the Mayo 5000.

"Mayo 5000: The Celebration Concert" was set for June 1993, to commemorate the finding of the ruins of Ceide Fields, a five-thousand-year-old County Mayo settlement. It surely sounded like a great production—an eighty-five-piece orchestra, scores of drummers, a giant choir of some two hundred singers, and the singing group Anúna. Composer Bill Whelan's "The Spirit of Mayo" was to be the planned centerpiece of the event. The guest list included Mary Robinson, Ireland's first woman president, along with many other luminaries. The best of it was that I'd be allowed to create my own dance.

What an opportunity! But how could I take this chance and keep my job?

I tried to play it cool, saying I'd consider it and call her back. Then I switched back to my first call—a lovely old woman somewhere in the Midwest.

"How much is a share in that oil field?" she was asking me. As I started to give her the price, I looked up, and through my window I saw right through to my boss's office. He was staring at me through the glass window and I suddenly realized that he was listening in.

I told the lady that I could probably let her into the deal for a mere couple hundred thousand. But of course, I said as I'd been taught, the more shares you buy, the better your rewards will be and the quicker you'll see them.

"Well," replied the lady, "I really trust you, Michael–you seem like such a nice, honest young man. This is the last of my money. But if you say that this is the right thing to do, then I'll send you the money because I believe what you're saying to me."

From the corner of my eye I could see my boss reaching up with his hand as if he was grabbing a whole pile of gold and pulling it back. Then he reached for his throat and pointed at me as he mouthed a few angry words: *Take the fuckin' money.*

"Michael, what do you think I should do?" the lady asked. "Where should I send my money?"

My boss's face was literally turning purple. But I couldn't go through with this. I just couldn't.

"Oh, my God, ma'am," I found myself saying. "You're not going to believe this, but the last share has just been sold. I'm so sorry."

I could see my boss jumping over his desk, knocking over trash cans, knocking his secretary out of the way, heading for his glass door to run at me.

"Are you sure?" the lady was saying. "I really need to make some money."

My boss was now in full stride, knocking over everything in his path to get at me.

"I'm sorry, ma'am," I said. "I'll call you back if we have anything else."

I put the phone down just as my boss got there. He called me a bunch of names I'd never heard before and screamed for me to "get the fuck out of his office." He even started throwing things out of my desk.

My heart sank. This had been a good job, and now, once again, I was a failure. But I felt like I would have been stealing from that lady. I just couldn't do it.

When I got home, things got worse. Beata was very young, and I don't think she understood what I was going through. When I told her that I'd been fired and that I was going to Ireland to dance, I saw that I'd become a failure to her, too.

"You wanted to be a broker and now you want to go back to do dancing," she yelled at me in her Polish accent. "Why, Mikey, why?"

I didn't know how to explain it to her. Although we'd had a very loving partnership, my unhappiness at work had put a huge strain on our relationship, which no longer seemed perfect. This latest decision made the strain even worse. All Beata saw was me not being at home—going off to Ireland to dance and having no job. They'd offered me $4,000 to appear on the show.

What I didn't realize was that for Beata, who'd already been through a near-bankruptcy with me, a one-shot fee didn't offer nearly the security of a steady, full-time job. She was in a foreign country where she was totally dependent on me, and even with our jobs we were struggling to pay the bills. I was thirty-five years old and desperate for a chance. Pretty soon, I thought, I'd be too old to dance. What would happen then?

Somehow, I talked Beata round. At least, I convinced myself that I had. Beata stayed on in Los Angeles. And I went off to Ireland, my hopes higher than they'd ever been before.

But as I left on the plane, I could only think of Beata—how hard she had worked to help pay the rent and support me in every way possible. All she wanted was to have a husband who was successful. A broker is what she dreamed of. I'm sure to her, I was a failure.

Israel Gonzalez got to know Michael Flatley in 1992 when they were both attempting to get a start as actors. Gonzalez said in Los Angeles on September 17, 2005: "It was a tough time. We didn't have the price of a cup of coffee. But Mike would pace up and down the apartment saying he was going to be a winner. He always believed in himself. There was never any question that he would give up on his dreams. But he got kicked back time and time again–we all did; young guys trying to make it in Hollywood are two a penny. It's just that Mike had that solid gold backbone that kept him going. Yet, now he's made it as a star around the world, he has never forgotten the hard times or the people who were with him."

Chapter Fourteen

Mayo 5000

I saw Michael Flatley—and I hadn't seen him for yonks—coming out with his chest all polished up and bare, [wearing] a leather jacket and a minstrel hat, and I said: "Holy Jesus!"

Seamus O'Shea, Irish dance teacher, March 16, 2004, on Michael Flatley's entrance at the Mayo 5000 festival in Dublin, 1993

Dancing in the Mayo 5000 was wonderful. The week-long festival of Irish culture gave me the chance to bring my work home to my people, and I was thrilled to be there. On opening night, I put on a show in a Spanish outfit and was rewarded with huge applause.

Mary Robinson offered her congratulations along with many others, including Moya Doherty, a producer at RTE, Ireland's national TV station. As I soon learned, Moya was also the wife and former colleague at TV-AM in London of John McColgan.

Moya was straightforward and attractive, slightly older than me. Talkative and enthusiastic about my dancing, she kept asking me about my future plans.

How could I give her a straight answer? I'd come off the Mayo stage a hero. But when I went back to the States, I'd be just another unemployed, aging performer, with no idea where my next meal was coming from.

Moya wouldn't leave it, though. "What's next for you then?" she kept asking. I couldn't resist. I told her about the show I'd been dreaming of for so long: a line of dancers—thirty or forty or even fifty of them—a chorus line of performers moving as fast as they could across the front of the stage. Behind the dancers were the singers, plus a full, fantastic orchestra and a big band. That was my dream show—a show that I'd already danced, scene for scene, in my head. I shared this dream with Moya as though it was already a reality, and I could see it catch fire for her, too.

When Moya and John invited me to lunch at the Conrad Hotel, opposite Dublin's National Concert Hall, I laid it out for them again. I told them that there was a huge, hungry audience for such a show, especially in America, an audience I'd come to know during my ten years of touring. It might seem fantastic, I admitted, but I was sure it was true: a show based in Irish dancing could even play Radio City in New York.

Moya and John couldn't have been nicer. The three of us got on famously, and I couldn't help feeling wistful. Wouldn't it be wonderful if they *did* want to produce my work? I must say I really liked them.

But I must have been missing my crystal ball that day. For as we said our goodbyes outside the restaurant, I felt only a mild kind of disappointment. No, I thought, as I watched the two of them walk away. No point getting my hopes up. Chances were, I'd never hear from either of them again.

Seamus O'Shea, at the Clonsilla Hall, Dublin, March 16, 2004, recalled: "Moya Doherty saw Michael when he appeared at the Mayo 5000 in 1993. My wife Aine and I were celebrating our twenty-fifth wedding anniversary so I remember the day very well. . . .

"I always seem to have been around for Michael's big appearances in Ireland. I saw him when we had a huge ceremony for the European Special Olympics in 1985. Jean Kennedy Smith came over with Teddy Kennedy, and they opened the Games. We had a mass display of Irish dancing right along the field. . . . Then Michael came out . . . in an all-black suit, and he was excellent. . . . I look back at the video, and it has all the steps he created . . . his steps, the mannerisms that he has. He had already developed them all. . . .

"So the concept of all this kind of showman thing had already been developing in his mind . . . nine years before Riverdance*."*

In the official book of Riverdance *(Andre Deutsch, London, 1996) written by* Irish Independent *columnist Sam Smyth, Moya Doherty says of first seeing Michael Flatley dance: "When I saw Michael I thought: 'Wow!'"*

On February 9, 1995, Doherty told Eileen Battersby of the Irish Times*: "That night in the Concert Hall [when I saw Mayo 5000], I was so struck by Michael Flatley's innovative approach to Irish dancing.*

"He has introduced an entire series of new steps and rhythms."

Act Two

Riverdance

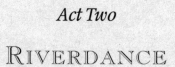

Everything that happens happens as it should,
and if you observe carefully,
you will find this to be so.

Marcus Aurelius, *Meditations*

Chapter Fifteen

The Birth of Riverdance

I think he has single-handedly changed the face of Irish dancing.

Moya Doherty, February 9, 1995.

Shortly after I met Moya Doherty, she was appointed executive producer of the 39th Eurovision Song Contest. The contest, founded in 1956 to promote European unity, was traditionally hosted by whatever country had won the contest the previous year. Ireland won in 1992 and 1993, so 1994 was definitely her year to host.

In fact, Ireland's national broadcast network, RTE, had produced the 1993 contest, and it looked with little enthusiasm on the prospect of repeating the experience. The show was generally thought of as a pretty long evening and so people like David Blake Knox, RTE's head of entertainment, were committed to livening up the production any way they could. But how could you spice up a three-hour broadcast that essentially consisted of song after song after song? The fact that they turned to Moya shows how much faith they had in her ability to create an entertaining evening.

Moya's been quoted as saying that her biggest concern was the five-minute act for the intermission–a time when millions of viewers usually head for the bathroom. If only she could create a compelling five minutes, she'd be well on her way to giving the viewers a brilliant evening–and she'd be showcasing Irish culture as well. She loved my idea of the dancing line. So she gave me a call from Dublin.

At last, a chance to make my dreams a reality. A chance to create a show that I could never have afforded to produce myself. A chance to show the world what Irish dancing could be. Before Moya could even explain her offer, I had said *yes* so fast it surprised even me. What else could I say?

Work began with remarkable speed. Moya sent me tapes from the show's composer, Bill Whelan, who'd also worked on the Mayo 5000 and who would be writing our lead-in and intermission music. Over in California, I started choreographing the show, working out solo routines for myself and group routines for the glorious line I'd been envisioning for so long.

In January 1994, the producers flew me over to Dublin to start work in earnest. They warned me to keep a low profile. Even then, I think they had some idea of how big this thing would turn out to be, and they wanted it to be a huge surprise.

In Dublin I met a choreographer who was a longtime friend of Moya's. She was to be working with me on the show. A Londoner, she had no Irish dance expertise but that was not a worry for me. Not yet.

She and I were set to begin rehearsals at Diggs Lane studio in the center of Dublin. Diggs Lane, to put it kindly, was well past its sell-by date. It was literally falling apart. In fact, the building was eventually condemned and a bar is now on the site. It was perfect for me. I've always been more comfortable in the shabby, down-to-earth spaces that have seen a bit of life, a bit of the past. They suit me better than the new, shiny buildings that don't seem to have any history at all.

The building was no problem–but what about the performers? I had assembled a crack team of Irish dancers, including fifteen world champions. Well, I'd been a champ, too, in my time, but now I was thirty-five and I hadn't competed for years.

Worse, I'd gone way out on a limb with my style—flamboyant, theatrical, and, let's face it, *sexy.* Not the way these Irish kids were used to viewing *their* national dance.

Worst of all, I wasn't Irish—not in their eyes. Their teachers had told them that some effin' Yank had blown into town to choreograph their celebration of Irish culture. How would they ever let me work with them?

All the way over to the theater, I tried to come up with a strategy. I looked down at myself and realized that I'd even dressed like a Yank—cowboy boots, torn blue jeans, and a big old leather coat. When I walked into the studio, my heart was in my mouth.

In the way of young dancers, they'd all been laughing and joking as they waited for the choreographer to arrive. But as soon as I walked through the door—silence.

Action, I decided, was better than words. I put on my tap shoes. You could have heard a pin drop. But everyone was watching me. So without even warming up, I let off some of the meanest dance moves I had—heel clicks in the air, lightning steps, the kind of speed that had put me in the *Guinness Book of World Records.* For ten furious seconds, I did work that no one in the room could do.

Then I stopped, breathing hard. Dead silence—but full attention.

Slowly, deliberately, dancer Colm O'Shea walked across the stage and stuck out his hand. "Nice to meet you," he said. The others rushed to join him.

That moment remains one of the high points of my dance career—and not only because these talented young champions had accepted me so warmly. Until then, I'd been focused only on my own work. Suddenly I had an entire troupe that was burning to learn my style. These were top-flight dancers–the best Irish dancers in the world–but they didn't know how to do it *my* way, and they were bursting to learn. They soon discovered that what I was asking them to do was harder, faster, and a lot further out than anything they'd ever done before.

At the end of the first day I asked, "Had enough?"

"No," said half the troupe.

"Yes!" exclaimed the other half. They were exhausted.

"Good!" I said. I sat down and took off my shoes. "Let's go down to the pub and get hammered."

They roared with appreciation. We all went down to the Hairy Lemon and ordered a round–and from that day on, that was our tradition. For all the many weeks of rehearsal, we drank pint after pint together, sharing stories, telling jokes. I loved them all like my brothers and sisters–and I loved some of the girls just a bit more than that.

But it was the art that really turned me on. Finally, I was creating for myself–and for a company. We were doing a number called "Riverdance," the kind of dance drama I'd been developing over the years, with a foundation of traditional Irish steps but with a lot more innovations that I'd also been working out, portraying the life of a river, and through that, the story of the Irish people. Together, we were about to change the face of Irish dance. This was the life I had dreamed of.

Dara O'Shea, daughter of Seamus O'Shea, was in the line of dancers that performed for the Eurovision contest and went on to be the first dance captain for Riverdance. *She was interviewed in March 2004, near her family's dancing school at the Clonsilla Hall on the outskirts of Dublin: "When we turned up at 9 a.m. one Sunday morning . . . to do our initial audition with Michael, we didn't know what we were auditioning for. We spent the whole day dancing with him and that was our audition. You were either chosen or you weren't. . . .*

"People always ask me what it was like to work with Michael, not even knowing that I worked as closely as I did. He worked as hard as he made us work. I will take my hat off to him any day of the week, because that man came into a studio and he made us work so hard. He was our captain. He was the mentor and he sweated every bit with us and took no second measures. That man just drilled.

"That's my memory and that's what I keep in my heart."

Dancer Niamh O'Connor spent five years with Riverdance. *She, too, got her start dancing for the Eurovision broadcast. She spoke in Las Vegas, in February 2004: "I did the very first audition. . . . I was in college at the time and used to take off early to go down to rehearsals.*

"We knew when we started to get Michael's routine together that this was definitely going to be something big. Michael was just excellent. He kept making us work really hard, but you actually wanted to work really hard. He's a perfectionist. We knew it was going to be a hit on the night. He choreographed all the numbers. He was there one hundred percent of the time. He came up with everything."

Areleen Ni Bhaoill was a dancer on Riverdance *and* Lord of the Dance, *and another who began with the Eurovision show. She talked at her home in Biloxi, Mississippi, in February 2004, and in Dublin, in March 2004: "There were so many of us from the O'Shea School, we all knew the same material. Michael got us up, all in a line, and we all did the same step. It was fantastic. And then he taught us the new steps and we knew that's what Riverdance should be–and that's how it ended up. . . .*

"Michael had the vision years before. I've seen him dancing on videotape as a youngster and the similarities to Riverdance *are unbelievable. He brought it forward, but you can still see the same steps were there."*

Dancer Cormac O'Shea from the O'Shea Dancing School was also part of that original line: "I was aware of Michael. I had met him as a child when he performed at the Special Olympics. He was renowned, and dance people around at the time were very aware of him. Immediately in class he was quite innovative and using unusual strategy and unusual techniques. It was immediately apparent how talented he was.

"All of our training, all of our rehearsal, all of our directing in anything, was all performed by Michael Flatley. All of our involvement on a dancing level was almost exclusively controlled by him."

Kelley Byrne first met Michael Flatley during the preparations for Eurovision; he was the one person she didn't know on the first day of rehearsals. She talked in Dublin in February 2004: "All the dancers knew each other through competitions at weekends and about sixty people were called to audition for Eurovision. Moya saw us, as did Michael and Jean [Butler, the main solo female dancer and Michael's dance partner].

"We were in Diggs Lane from ten in the morning until ten at night, seriously getting it done. . . .

"Everybody admired Michael and respected him. He was the best dancer. He was the best showman and he was the hardest worker. He would expect one hundred and ten percent from everybody, but he'd be giving one hundred and fifty percent himself.

"When it came to practicing for the shows, he worked us so hard. Some of the girls were leaving the room to go and throw up, we were working that hard. But nobody complained because he was working harder than the rest of us. He kept going. We'd all dropped and he was still going. We had to admire that. We all trusted him. We were confident he knew what he was doing."

Dancer Ronan McCormac, talking in Dublin in February 2004, said: "Michael was great to work with. His enthusiasm was amazing. I have to say that anything he expected us to do by way of dedication to work, he was one hundred times more. It was a pleasure to do it.

"He had this amazing knack, the psychological trick, of just making you want to do your best for yourself, to give your best performance. . . .

He wanted you to be able to say, 'Hey, I did my best today.' Not a lot of people can manage to bring that out. . . .

"Charisma is the word that sums up the first impressions of Michael. For me, with Michael, while he is an impressive dancer and technician, it is his charisma that makes him stand out. If you were to get ten guys dressed in black and they were told to walk across the stage and Michael was one of them, he's the one you would look at. He attracts your eye to him. . . .

"There was a lot of socializing that went on around that time, and it was just great, great fun. Anyone who worked with Michael at that time very much enjoyed his company outside of the whole workplace.

"Everybody got on with him. For somebody in the studio, he was someone you stood back and looked up to. When you were in the pub, everyone was equal. When it came to the socializing, he was very much one of the guys. One of the gang."

One conflict that arose during the Eurovision rehearsals concerned the role of Moya's choreographer friend from London. I've got a lot of respect for her as a choreographer of modern dance. But I felt her vision just didn't work for *Riverdance.* Instead of basing her work in Irish tradition, as I did, she was going in a whole other direction. It was hard for me—and I think even harder on the company. Eventually, we ended up with more Irish moves—but we had a few tough moments there for a while.

Dara O'Shea: "[The other choreographer] was around, but she was basically a director. A few nights before the dress rehearsal we had a meeting with Michael and he decided he would change her choreography.

"That's when that line came and it stayed in a line. We had the dress rehearsals which were for all the parents and invited guests, and it absolutely blew everybody's mind.

"We really realized that this was something! It just became something—the impact. People still talk about it."

Niamh O'Connor: "[Earlier in the rehearsals, the other choreographer] was there, and Michael, and we were doing different choreographies [for each of them]. Once we came in, and Michael had arrived early with one of the other dancers. He'd come up with this idea, and he taught us the steps in about ten minutes, put the thing together and that was it.

"She came in then and saw it and said 'yes.' That's how Riverdance *started."*

Areleen Ni Bhaoill: "[The other choreographer] tried to throw a little bit of modern dancing in there. We tried that for probably about a good week and a half, and it looked like Irish dancing trying to do modern dancing. It just looked out of place, and we all felt that.

"With the material Michael was showing us, we felt that we were going to do something special. We were all a little fed up with the situation.

"We went to the Hairy Lemon pub and we all said our piece to Michael. I guessed we all knew he wasn't happy with it, but he didn't know that we were as unhappy as we were.

"We told him we didn't like what we were doing, and he said that we should meet two hours earlier the next day and that's when the whole line-up thing came into it. . . .

"Moya and John had the last say. They would have been happy with whatever dancing came out of the rehearsal studios, but once they saw what Michael had changed and the way we looked, they knew that was the way to go."

Kelley Byrne: "Moya had hired a friend who had staged pantomimes and modern dance. I don't really know why she was brought in. We were doing this dancing that none of us were comfortable with.

"We went to the Point [Theatre] to rehearse and had to show Moya what we had. Moya and the others said it was good, but all the dancers weren't happy. Michael asked, 'How about we do something else?'

"We came in out of hours to work with Michael and worked on the line step, which is what it ended up as.

"Michael obviously went up and was talking to Moya and said, 'What do you think?'

"She said, 'Yeah, yeah. It's good.'

"He said, 'We've been working on something else. Will you have a look at that and see what you think of that?'

"We did our stuff, the line step. It was very simple, very effective, and everybody loved it. All the technicians were watching and they shouted, 'Yeeah.'

"They were really enthusiastic. We got a great reception from them and so Moya said, 'Oh, yeah.' Anyone who saw it would say definitely now it had to be that one. It was what we were all good at. The next week, that was all we did. As soon as Michael showed us what he had in mind, we were more comfortable. It was Irish dancing but with that special twist. It wasn't modern dance but Irish taken to outer limits.

"Michael kept it Irish, which is what we were and what we were good at. We did a couple of rehearsals with just crew around and they loved it."

When Moya saw how well our work was going, she increased the intermission act from five minutes to seven. Meanwhile, Bill Whelan was still working on the music. One day, he came in with a tape of something done in an off time, a strange time signature. I was used to dancing to a more regular beat, and I was intrigued by what Bill had brought me. I'd never actually danced in that time signature before. Trying to choreograph to it was confusing, but exciting. And the music was really catchy.

But I didn't want to be limited to that rhythm. So I asked Bill to create a piece of music for me in my favorite 2/4 or 4/4 time–a more steady, even beat–and it was great. Our big fight was over the ending, to get him to come back to 6/8 time–steady and rhythmic, not like the off-signature that he'd brought in at first. I thought the audience needed something to hang on to coming home. Bill fought me on that, but eventually he gave in. I'm glad he did, because I think that end piece of music was his best, the one that rocks out. The key to creating a successful evening of dance–or any kind of theater, really–is collaboration. In the end, Bill and I proved to be strong collaborators who brought out the best in each other. Bill is a musical genius. *Riverdance* could not have happened without him.

Another great addition was Jean Butler, who became my dance partner. She was a fellow Irish-American, and she did a marvelous job. People used to speculate about our relationship offstage. It seems everyone was looking for controversy. Whatever was or wasn't going on between us in our private lives–and it was strictly professional, I assure you–we definitely had a strong sexual dynamic onstage. It had to be there to make the dance work–the mare and the stallion. All I'm going to say is what I said back then: "I'm proud to have her as my dance partner. She's a lovely girl. And how could I not love Jean? Her grandmother's name is Flatley!"

Gerry Ryan, host of his own Dublin-based "TwoFM" nationwide radio show, was the cohost of the 1993 Eurovision Contest. He grew up with Moya Doherty and remains one of her best friends. His wife Moira went to school with her in Dublin, where he talked at his home on the outskirts of the city in February 2004: "I met Michael in rehearsals a couple of weeks before the show. The entire technical crew, cynical people who have seen everything, used to stand down when he would take to the stage. The sound staff, the orchestra, the lighting technicians, the floor manager–people who would normally scurry off to a bar if it was open, or go for a cigarette–would sit down and watch Michael and this extraordinary spectacle unfold.

"The technical staff would normally rather fart in your face than look at your best efforts. . . . But they stopped every time Michael was rehearsing Riverdance. *They stopped every time he was directing the steps. I think I saw* Riverdance *rehearse about forty times. I don't recall one*

single rehearsal when the entire technical staff didn't down tools and stop and watch.

"I remember looking at Michael and going, Wow, this guy was like Jimi Hendrix. It was so electric and he was incandescent. He was combusted in rehearsal, every single time. . . . He never dropped the gate. It never went down, it was never anything other than one hundred and ten percent performance. I remember looking at this and going, 'Christ, this is going to overtake the whole show.' . . . Irish dancing was finally being infiltrated by sexuality. It was so exciting to be there and watch Michael at the center of this."

Chapter Sixteen

"Riverdance": The First Performance

Nobody could have foreseen the scale of the success.
And nobody did. Except Michael.

David Blake Knox,
RTE head of entertainment during
the Eurovision production

On the evening of the Eurovision broadcast, I was doing what I always do before a performance—pacing up and down the corridors and psyching myself up. Suddenly, I bumped into this guy who asked me if I could help him with his bow tie.

He had no idea who I was. But I recognized him. He was Paul Harrington, who, with Charlie McGettigan, had composed the Irish entry in the Eurovision contest, "Rock 'n' Roll Kids." In other words, he was the star of the evening.

I was happy to tie his tie for him (we've since become great friends), and we talked for just a moment before we each had to get ready to go on stage. We knew there were to be three thousand people in the theater and more than three hundred million worldwide watching us live. But I didn't feel I had a nerve in my body. This was what I did, what I had trained for—and this was a great shot.

Right up to the last minute, there had been controversy about the arm movements. In traditional Irish dance, you don't move your arms—it's a sexual thing—and in my dance, you do—also a sexual thing! Even at this point in the game, RTE executives were nervous about breaking too much with tradition. "Please, please," Moya had begged me. "Don't do this." As late as the night before the Eurovision broadcast, word had come from above asking me to change the choreography, saying they didn't want to look foolish in front of the world.

But I was having none of it. Why was I there, if not to do my own thing? I told Moya, "You chose me for the way I dance. I won't change. I'll go home first."

She gave in. And from that moment on, she stood firmly with me, even in the face of the ongoing disapproval from the higher-ups. Fair play to her!

By the time I flew on stage, it was too late for any more second thoughts. The controversy had made an impact on me, though. As I danced, I felt I had eight hundred years of Irish repression on my back. And below me, buoying me up, my thirty-five years of hard work.

I was dancing for Ireland, for my parents, for my fellow dancers, and for myself. When I finished it felt like scoring the winning goal in the World Cup. The greatest feeling of triumph I'd ever had. Even before the audience broke into applause, I knew I'd done what I'd set out to do.

But the audience, in the words of Moya's husband John McColgan, broke into "[not a] cheer, but a primeval roar." Mary Robinson was leading the cheers. All over the auditorium, people were applauding while the tears streamed down their faces. With all the hankies out it looked like the audience was waving white flags. In fact, they were.

The surrender of Irish repression. The victory of a new, sexy, self-confident style of dance.

The opening night of "Riverdance" was one of those nights that come along once in a lifetime. There was just something in the air that night, something magical like a beautiful light that was glowing around all of us. The music was brilliant. The dancers were on fire. My partner, Jean, looked stunning. And the singers were in great form. I'd worked my whole life for this one moment in time. Dreams do come true.

As I'd flown across the stage that night, the whole world seemed to stand still. It was as if I was in exactly the right place at exactly the right time. Maybe for the very first time in my life. It was what the universe intended for me, and it was happening. Ireland was finally proud of its national dance.

Kelley Byrne: "Our parents and special guests came to the dress rehearsal and that was a full house. The reaction was amazing. I was, 'Oh God. We probably won't get that tonight!'

"We did. . . . None of us had ever experienced anything like it.

"I can only imagine it must be like taking drugs, the high. I never needed to take drugs because that was such a high."

David Blake-Knox: " 'Michael brought a sense of show which was very American. He was also open to different styles of tap and other forms of dancing. He was obviously an extremely dynamic individual.

"It became obvious from rehearsals that the talking point was going to be the [intermission] act because it was fairly sensational. Ireland won that Eurovision and people can hardly remember who it was.

"I had heard about it and I had been down there and had seen bits and pieces of rehearsal, but the first time I saw them performing it was just like a bullet between the eyes. It was a fantastic act.

"It had dimensions that were bigger than the act, that tapped into all sorts of things that were going on in Ireland at that time. It captured the

mood of a country that was freeing itself from its history. Often, because of our particular history, elements of Irish culture have been treated in a purist way. The point was simply to preserve them and not to offend. This, [by contrast,] was a radical engagement with a culture that had defined itself as immune to change.

"When I was growing up, Irish dancing was regarded as the most uncool thing that anybody could do. It was also a heavily desexualized form of dancing: hands were rigid, only the ankles moved, and the girls wore traditional Celtic costumes that obviously nobody ever wore . . . outside dancing.

"Michael's role in 'Riverdance,' specifically where he famously lifted his arms, said this was altogether something different. He had integrated into the traditional idea elements of American tap, and his final line move is clearly a chorus line. There was a revolutionary shift, and part of the reason it made such an impact on so many Irish people was seeing elements that you knew very well transformed in a way you never thought possible.

"It coincided with a period in Irish history when the tiger was taking off and young Irish people weren't having to emigrate, when there was a sense of relaxation, a reason to stay at home. That Irish identity, which for centuries had been plagued with problems, had changed; people felt at home in their own skin.

" 'Riverdance' showed affection and familiarity with the traditional side of dancing, but also the boldness, the vision, the sense of excitement that you could draw upon. It was a really, really important moment in modern Irish culture which extended far beyond Eurovision. It completely eclipsed the event that it was part of and became a phenomenon.

"It boosted that wave of international success that the country was enjoying. There was the cinema and the work of Jim Sheridan and Neil Jordan, the bestsellers of authors like Roddy Doyle. Even the Irish soccer team, which for many years had been a laughingstock, was, with the help of Jack Charlton, looking good. The economy was absolutely booming. There was a real sense that as a country we were on a roll. . . .

"Michael made a lot of Irish people believe that anything was possible. That was great."

Gerry Ryan: "[On the night of the broadcast,] Michael was dancing out of his skin. Michael was like a bull coming to stud and Jean was like a gentle flower being chased across this bed on her wedding night. . . .

"The Eurovision moment was the moment. That's when it happened. In cultural, artistic and stage production terms, it was Pink Floyd on tour–to capture it on television was a huge challenge.

"I remember standing at the side of the stage with a whiskey in my hand and watching Flatley flexing like a boxer before he went into the ring. And watching that moment when he would adopt that Grecian stance, that matador stance, and watching him dash onto the stage, I go back to Jimi Hendrix. There was nobody else in the world who could do this. Only Michael.

"People also tend to forget that Ireland also won the Eurovision that night. No one remembers. Pat Cowap became one of the best camera directors in Europe, Moya Doherty became the producer of one of the greatest televisual moments in European broadcasting history. Flatley became the man who changed Irish dancing forever."

John Suragan was chairman of the RTE Authority at the time of Eurovision. In Dublin in November 2004 he recalled the triumph: "Extraordinarily successful would be the overview. Seldom before has there been an act that has dominated a Song Contest–anywhere, I would expect. It was an enormously successful event, and then it was a huge subsequent success, obviously on the international as well as national stage. It has been one of the great success stories. . . .

"You can't really imagine the effect on tourism and the economy. We are a country of four million people, so there is no other way we'd get an international audience on such a grand scale and then make an excellent impression on them. You can't hope to do better than that, really, can you?

"It was stunning. Everybody in the theater was stunned. Obviously it had the same effect on the [television] audience but clearly, it had a stunning effect on the six thousand people that were present in the Point Theatre. . . .

"Two of the most successful shows in the world over the last ten years have sprung from Michael. The original idea came out of Michael Flatley. What he has done for Irish culture and Irish music–it's not measurable really. We're now known all over the waters, and for a small nation that's an extraordinary achievement."

President Bill Clinton, speaking on March 15, 2001, at the Irish-American Lifetime Achievement Awards, Plaza Hotel, New York: "Michael Flatley is one of the most gifted dancers ever."

CHAPTER SEVENTEEN

Riverdance: *The Stage Show*

It was Michael Flatley's obsessional drive for perfection in rehearsal, both for himself and the other dancers, that turned the unabashed enthusiasm and raw energy of last year's amateurs into this year's polished professionals.

—The official *Riverdance* book,
released for the debut of the full-length production

"RIVERDANCE" had begun as a seven-minute intermission act for the Eurovision broadcast of April 1994. With Moya as producer and me creating the dance, we went on to present a full-length show.

Riverdance, the show, opened at Dublin's Point Theatre on February 5, 1995, and went on to an extended five-week run there, playing to sold-out houses and wildly enthusiastic crowds. We were booked as well for four weeks through Barry Clayman into Labatt's Apollo Theatre in London in May. No one knew how an Irish show would play in England. But all the signs seemed good by the time I arrived. I was asked to pose for lots of publicity photographs, and I knew that both tickets and the video that had been made of the show were selling out.

The moment I really knew we'd knock 'em dead was the hour

before opening night, when I was warming up. Suddenly, I heard screams that grew louder and louder. Fans had circled the theater. They couldn't wait for us to begin.

They were even noisier at the end of the performance when we received five standing ovations!

What could go wrong with a success like that?

After our triumph in London, we returned to Dublin, intending to go on to a second London run. Yet even before we got back to Dublin, there were rumblings of discontent. You might have heard rumors about me–that I was unrealistic, demanding, difficult to deal with. All I can tell you is that the show meant everything to me. Because of my commitment to it, I was willing to work for weeks without a contract–and with no pay–while we tried to settle things.

As far as I'm concerned, the money and material considerations were settled relatively quickly. The issue that remained was artistic control.

Here's where things get complicated. Moya, I believe, felt entitled to control the show because she'd raised the money for it. In fairness, *Riverdance* could not have happened without her. As she put it to Dublin's *Evening Herald* in a public statement on May 24, 1995, "As producer, I can do as I choose. Michael Flatley is the star of the show."

But I was the one who'd created the dance, so in my mind, it was my baby. But I thought Moya, John, and I were all friends, and I was sure we could work it out. After all, we'd never had a confrontation. We were all too busy enjoying our success. We even appeared at a summer charity gala before the Queen and Princess Margaret. I regarded *Riverdance* as a family, and you'd expect a family to have a few arguments. I was sure they'd all be resolved and we could settle back to concentrating on the dance and the show.

Our second London run was scheduled to open at the Apollo Hammersmith Theatre on October 2, 1995. Already, we had millions of pounds of advance ticket sales, so the stakes were high. By now, it was my picture alone on all the London posters. I had become a very bankable star. I was going out frequently with John and Moya, whose motto was, "We'll knock 'em dead all over again." We were all very close but it was Moya I would talk to the most when problems over our business relationship started to pile up.

Chapter Eighteen

Collapse

If thou has eyes to see, then see!

Creto

As the increasingly bitter contract disputes were going on, I was continuing to do eight shows a week at the Point Theatre. One night, I simply collapsed, unable to move. Lord knows what might have happened were it not for the help of the *Riverdance* therapist, Derry Ann Morgan.

The collapse didn't come out of nowhere. I'd been going at an incredible rate for weeks, choreographing, rehearsing, and dancing on a grueling schedule, I loved what I was doing—but any dancer will tell you that it's exhausting beyond belief to ask that much of your body, day after day, night after night.

The show depended on me. I was in several numbers, and I'd won a great deal of acclaim.

Whenever I was feeling tired and worn, I was given a prescribed shot of something to pick me up. Soon I'd feel more energetic again, and I'd be able to dance my way through the show. Then, afterwards, I'd feel worse than I had before.

Each time, the cycle got worse. I thought maybe I just needed a rest. But there was no time. The prescribed magic painkillers and pick-me-ups helped me get through the shows.

One day was worse than all the rest. I collapsed, unable to move, and I felt that something was terribly wrong. I sent for Derry Ann, whom I would have trusted with my life, and she rushed me to the hospital.

Later, I learned her boss, producer John McColgan chastised her for taking me to the hospital without consulting him or the other producers. When I found that out, I was very upset. Why hadn't they trusted both of us to do what was necessary, after I'd collapsed in such a terrible way?

She told me she wouldn't be coming to London with *Riverdance,* which upset me greatly. Then she told me something that upset me even more. "Michael," she said. "I don't believe you're coming to London either."

Her words were like a prophecy. As everyone knows by now, the producers fired me on the opening night of the show.

Derry Ann Morgan, a former Riverdance *employee, spoke at the Westbury Hotel in Dublin in February 2004 about her memory of the afternoon she discovered Michael Flatley seemingly unconscious backstage at the Point Theatre: "I went straight away down to Michael and he was in quite a state. Someone had said to me that he wasn't feeling well, and I was rushed straight in to him.*

"I knew that previously he had been given stuff to kill his pain so he could dance. I knew then that he'd never dance in London. I just knew.

"He was frighteningly unwell. He was on the floor and there was just something wrong. Seriously wrong.

"He mumbled something about hospital but he could barely get the words out, he was so sick.

"He certainly was in a panicked state. I was scared. God forbid, I didn't want Michael dead.

"And I was on my own looking after him. I stayed calm and got on with that.

"I needed to get him checked out as fast as possible [so I] got him out to my car and took him to the Mater Hospital in Eccles Street. He was able to walk but I had to hold on to him, and he stumbled into the emergency room.

"He was going on about the next performance, which was only a couple of hours away. He was under pressure, but he wouldn't want to let somebody down. He was in such a state I didn't think he had a chance of being back to work that night.

"I managed to get the medics to see him as quick as they could. They ran all sorts of tests to make sure that he was okay. He was in such agony, he was so disoriented.

"We were on a fine line of time but we made it back in time for the next show. I brought him back into his room and then I was called into the production office. I was told I was in trouble because I took Michael and didn't tell anybody. What did they want me to do? Send a memo? And then try and discover what was wrong with him? I didn't have time for the niceties. Michael could have been dying for all I knew.

"John said I couldn't possibly have got all the tests done and I said that I had. . . . I apologized that he was annoyed but [said] that I wasn't sorry that I had taken Michael because that was something that I felt that I had desperately needed to do in that situation.

"All I knew was that he seriously needed to be seen to. I wouldn't have done it if I wasn't concerned.

"I walked away pretty upset about it but I didn't tell Michael. I didn't want him to get upset as he had to go back out on stage. He would have become concerned for me if I'd told him. That's his nature.

"John said, 'But you couldn't have gotten all those tests done in that period of time.' I explained that I [had] talked to people and said what it

was all about and that Michael needed to get back on stage—and I got the tests done.

"They had spent quite a lot of time trying to track us down when I brought him to the hospital.

"But Michael asked me to take him to hospital, so I knew it was something. I was willing to do it, because as far as I was concerned, he was number one and that was it. And also he was so unwell. I got a shock when I saw him.

"They were right—nobody would walk into A&E and get all those tests done.

"But because Michael was really determined with me—for whatever reason—I'd go in and break every rule in the book to get around everybody, and I did. . . . And they did do it! He was able to come back saying he was fit to go on stage.

"I couldn't figure out why the two weren't meeting.

"I knew nothing . . . about those other things that were going on in negotiations. Why would I know all about it? I certainly didn't. . . .

"I went in to Michael and pretended nothing had happened, but I was extremely upset. . . . I actually said to Michael, 'I'm going to say something to you—'

"I said, 'I'm definitely not going [with the show] to London.'

"He didn't say anything.

"And I said, 'But Michael, there's something else.'

"I said, 'I don't think you are, either.' . . ."

Steven Byrne was a dancer with Riverdance *at the time Michael Flatley was taken to the hospital. He now lives and works in Boston, and there he said in October 2004: "Derry Ann [Morgan] came to me after she had been to the hospital with Michael and she said she was very upset by what happened.*

"She felt first and foremost that her loyalty was to Michael and to his well-being, that was her job. She felt she was doing her best to . . . see that he was okay.

"I don't know how anyone could have a problem with Michael. I always thought he was great, had great charisma, and his leadership and motivational skills were just brilliant. Thousands and thousands of people wouldn't have had their lives improved in one way or another [without] Michael [and] what he did. I think he deserves everything that he got–in the positive way. He really did a great job in so many things."

Chapter Nineteen

Night Moves

He's one of the sexiest men I've ever seen.

Jennifer Lopez, February 2004

While all the contract negotiations were going on, I was continuing to enjoy my private life. I'm not ashamed to have an eye for the ladies, for I believe that sexual energy is a vital part of success. Most successful men have an incredible sex drive. I'm all for sexual energy–it's what you do with it that counts. If you can transmute the energy into something more productive, then you can create something really special. But we all need to have a bit of fun along the way!

True, I've been particularly weak in that regard. I adore beauty in everything. I particularly love to admire the beauty of women. And I've always enjoyed the good things in life. When I was only eighteen and my buddies were drinking five-cent beer over at Mother's Bar on Oak Street, I'd be saving up my nickels to buy martinis at the Pump Room at the Ambassador East. I'd get all dressed up, saunter in, and chat up the little blonde bartender that I was sweet on at the time. Eventually, we clicked.

Now, more than twenty years later, it wasn't much different. I was hanging out in Lillie's Bordello, a fashionable Dublin nightclub frequented by big-name entertainers, a very classy, private place. Owner Dave Egan became a good friend and he used to save a couch for me in the oak-paneled VIP room—my escape from the crowds and the madness.

By now, I hadn't seen Beata for several months, and our marriage was on the rocks. Meanwhile, I'd fallen head over heels for Kelley Byrne, a beautiful young dancer.

My involvement with Kelley was like a bolt from the blue. One cold and rainy Dublin night I was walking home with a little group of dancers from the show. As I headed toward my little apartment at the top of Leeson Street, the others dropped off one by one, until it was just Kelley and me.

We passed my favorite pub—O'Brien's at the top of Leeson Street—and headed up around the church. Kelley had this incredible auburn hair. Mountains of it. But more important, she had fire in her soul. I looked at her. It was windy and the rain was just pouring down. She was huddled up in a big, long coat with these Doc Martin–type army boots underneath. We were talking and all of a sudden, something happened. I don't know why. We just started kissing.

In one split second I was madly in love with Kelley Byrne. And my whole life changed.

Our love affair began with a grand ferocious passion that was almost too much to bear. We were crazy lovers, making love wherever and whenever. She had the most incredible body I've ever seen in my life—all hidden underneath big sweaters. And she was loyal, honest, and proud.

Offstage she was always wearing army boots. She dressed terribly, she had no manners, but Kelley Byrne was straight and would not let me buy her a drink unless she could buy the next round.

I'm afraid that was the absolute end for my marriage. I knew it was all my fault. I'd left Beata in Los Angeles, and I'd been running away ever since from the fact that our marriage had died. I still loved my wife in a deep, deep way but I could no longer live without Kelley and that passion. Beata was a lady. I had let her down. But my passion for Kelley was overwhelming, and all I could do was submit.

My passion for Kelley was the kind you rarely find in your life. We were all over each other at every possible opportunity. I just had to glance at her to want to love her. It's almost impossible to disguise such passion, though at first we managed to. But only just. Usually, we met in tiny little places, in the back bars of pubs or in groups. We had our secret signals for when we wanted to take off to make love. The secrecy, the sneaking off, gave our love extra excitement.

Then fate stepped in at Lillie's Bordello. Kelley and I were alone on the couch in the upstairs lounge.

It was a quiet night. We had broken our taboo to sit separately in public. We'd probably had a little too much to drink and our guard was down. Kelley started going for me. She was kissing me, having the time of her life, when the door of the lounge opened. And there stood the world's biggest motor-mouth reporter.

"Flatley's Undercover Lover"–it was all over the press. Everyone wanted to know who Kelley was because no one could identify her. We agreed to be more discreet.

I was able to take Kelley off to St. Tropez, where we had a great time. But Kelley has a fiery temper, and she's insanely jealous. So we knew our share of stormy weather as well.

One night I was in Lillie's with Kelley and my brother Pat for a party, and it was all wild. One of the girls came over and kissed me on the mouth. Another kissed me and made of show of putting her tongue in my ear. A third dancer kissed me and put a condom in my hand.

Then Kelly came over and all hell broke loose as she pulled the long, stage wig from the third dancer's head. Can you blame her?! My bodyguard had to pick Kelley up and carry her out.

PRIVATE COLLECTION

My grandmother Hannah Ryan was a champion dancer in Ireland. Here she is dancing as my mother plays the accordion. I save an empty seat for her at every one of my performances.

PRIVATE COLLECTION

That's my grandmother with the flute and my mother with the accordion. Music is in my blood.

My grandmother Hannah Ryan was born in Brownsford Castle in Kilkenny. She taught me you could get anything you wanted in life if you worked hard.

PRIVATE COLLECTION

My parents were married by an Irish priest on August 25, 1956, a day after my mother's birthday.

PRIVATE COLLECTION

PRIVATE COLLECTION

My father wanted to get ahead and was willing to work all hours to do so. That's him with the shovel, working a construction job.

PRIVATE COLLECTION

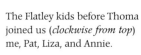

My first passport photo, with sister Annie.

PRIVATE COLLECTION

The Flatley kids before Thoma joined us (*clockwise from top*) me, Pat, Liza, and Annie.

PRIVATE COLLECTION

We always dressed for dinner. Thanksgiving Day in the 1960s.

PRIVATE COLLECTION

Jack Love was the high school athletic hero who I fought in a boxing match in front of the whole school. Against all bets, I won the fight. In 2003, at my twentieth high-school reunion, he was one of the first people to say hello. A great guy.

PRIVATE COLLECTION

Here I am dancing with the Chieftains at L'Hermitage in Beverly Hills, California, sometime in the early 1980s.

PRIVATE COLLECTION

In 1985, while on tour with Chieftains in London, I met the woman who was to become my wife, Beata Dziaba.

Beata and I are best friends and she's still one of the most beautiful women in the world. She visited me at Villa La Masquerade in 2003.

PRIVATE COLLECTION

PRIVATE COLLECTION

The announcement of the launch of *Lord of the Dance* caught the whole world by surprise. Seated at the press conference from left to right are Jim Aiken, John Reid, me, and Harvey Goldsmith.

The two sexiest leading ladies of all, Gillian Norris and Bernadette Flynn.

COURTESY OF BRIAN MCEVOY

Celebrating *Lord of the Dance*'s $500,000,000 in sales with Sir Cliff Richard and Lisa.

COPYRIGHT © UNICORN ENTERTAINMENT

The lads from *Lord of the Dance*. Some of the greatest dancers in the world are in this line up. Do you think we took it seriously?

PRIVATE COLLECTION

My relationship with dancer Kelley Byrne was as wild as a bog fire–full of passion and jealousy. Here we celebrate New Year's Eve 1997.

PRIVATE COLLECTION

Kelley and I are still great friends. We had dinner together at Joseph's Restaurant in St. Tropez in 2002.

PRIVATE COLLECTION

Trying out the stage at Neiderlander Theater on Broadway.

BRIAN MCEVOY

My shoes are the tools of my trade. The metal heels are made of the same metal NASA uses to make the nose cone of the shuttle.

Being interviewed backstage at SFX in Dublin in 2004.

BRIAN MCEVOY

PRIVATE COLLECTION

With Mom on a private jet in 2003.

PRIVATE COLLECTION

A recent gathering of the whole Flatley family in Chicago: (*From left to right*) Lisa, me, Mom, Dad, Thoma, Pat, and Annie. I love them all so much.

PRIVATE COLLECTION

Patrick and I love to go to the fights together. We saw Lennox Lewis win the Heavyweight title over Vitale Klitschko in Los Angeles in 2003.

PRIVATE COLLECTION

I got to spar with Irish boxing champion Wayne McCullough in 2004 in Las Vegas.

PRIVATE COLLECTION

Backstage with sister Annie.

My mother and my grandmother.

PRIVATE COLLECTION

PRIVATE COLLECTION

Marie Duffy became my dance master and right-hand person in 1996. When she married her wonderful husband, Mike, I gave her a car for a wedding present.

PRIVATE COLLECTION

Being handed the Irish American of the Year Award by Bill Clinton.

PRIVATE COLLECTION

I love my parents so much. They're the greatest parents in the world.

PRIVATE COLLECTION

With my best buddy, Dave Egan.

My brother said, "Mike, she only does that because she's crazy about you. That's true love."

It was. It was incredible. But it was hard for both of us, being so intense. I loved her, but there were the other girls trying to get my attention. On tour, it's easy to forget about right and wrong. The girls didn't care, and I didn't, either. It's wild and crazy on the road, like being licensed to have fun.

I'm not saying I'd do it again! It took a long time to grow up, but I'm glad I had those wild days—they were great experiences. I now have a much clearer picture of what I want. And, more important, what I don't.

Kelley Byrne: "Michael and I got on from the very first. He told me about his wife. She was in America. He was in Dublin, kind of on his own. He didn't have a lot of friends. Every night there'd be a whole gang of dancers and we'd all go out.

"When we were putting together Riverdance, *they rented an apartment for Michael. He had no money. I was working part-time in a shop. He wasn't working, he didn't have any other work other than the dancing. But he was very generous; he'd always buy everybody a drink. Once he told me, 'I'm really stuck. I haven't got a penny.' I got fifty quid out on my credit cards, it was all I had, and a friend had to take it to him because I couldn't even get into town.*

"He would say to me, 'I'll never forget that fifty pounds you gave me.' A few years later, he was a millionaire. It was really great. I wasn't in it for his money. He would say to me: 'At least I know I can trust you.' Michael has since bought me two cars—a BMW and a Mercedes. A good return on fifty quid!

". . . He got on well with the dancers like we all did and we'd go out in a gang and just have a good time. He'd no other friends here. He was in more need of company, really.

"He was a funny guy with a good sense of humor. I was still like a teenager in that way. We had a great friendship and we got on very well.

He needed someone to talk to and help him with what was going on. It took off from there.

"We kept it a secret; we didn't broadcast it at all but, of course, some of the dancers knew. And the producers.

"I did Riverdance, *the show. My contract wasn't renewed after the first five weeks in Dublin. I was quite upset about it, but then I was off working and finishing college.*

"I still had five years of Michael. I still got to travel the world. I don't feel like I missed out on Riverdance, *the show."*

Areleen Ni Bhaoill: "I loved Michael to death and we had a lot of fun together. . . . Many of the girls in the shows wanted to have sex with Michael. What was he to do?

"I probably would have stayed with him forever. I loved him very much, and I would have stayed with him. I loved being with him–I loved the sex with him. We'd have fun–and games.

"When we were on a break from the show he'd take Kelley away. I lived in hope that one day it would just be me but that didn't happen."

Chapter Twenty

Showdown

Michael was *Riverdance.*

Gerry Ryan

This guy was an absolute pro.

Dave Kavenagh

. . . His child in a sense was taken away from him
and he had to develop a new child.

David Blake Knox,
former RTE head of entertainment, February 2004

At 11 p.m. on October 2, 1995, the night before we were to open in London, the telephone rang. Contract negotiations over *Riverdance* had grown increasingly difficult. And there was my attorney, Robert Lee, saying that for me, it was all over.

"You're out, Michael," he informed me. I felt that they'd pulled the plug on my world. "They do not want a star. They want a show where anyone can be replaced."

I didn't even answer him. I couldn't. I just put down the phone and stared out the window at the rain. A fire crackled in the fireplace behind me, and Kelley stood by, keeping the vigil with me. We didn't speak for a long time as I just stood there, watching the rain come down.

Later that night, I talked to my father. We're both busy men and we never have enough time to talk, but that night we took all the time we needed. I wondered if he'd understand. He'd seen me broke and struggling my entire adult life. All I'd had to do was sign a damn contract, and I'd've been able to continue with the artistic success I'd earned, not to mention a fortune of money.

Tonight, I was close to tears, and he could hear that. There are times when he talks to me, and I'm still that little lad fooling around in his truck playing the penny whistle. Dad spoke to me in his soft voice that comes straight from the heart, and it was like sweet music to me. He used his sayings and his cliches, all the warm Old World stuff I'd grown up with.

"What goes around comes around. The darkest hour is before the dawn. You've got to believe in yourself. Let them say what they want– you get back to business right away. Walk tall."

Then he clinched it with the words I'd cling to for the coming year. "Look, Mike," he told me. "You built *Riverdance*–you can create another one."

Kelley Byrne: "It's strange, but I don't remember so clearly Michael's break-up with Riverdance. *I think I may have blocked a lot of it out, as it was so very upsetting. He was devastated. I think he can get depressed quite easily, quite moody sometimes, but my feeling at the time was he wasn't going to give up, he was going to go and do the show. I was totally with him, even though I wasn't living with him.*

"On his own he was thinking, but when I saw him he would be a bit more talkative because he hadn't seen anybody, and he'd talk about it; it wasn't so bad for me. It was a bad time for him, but I had so much confidence in him. I never imagined for a second that that was the end of it. I knew he was going to do his own thing."

* * *

When *Riverdance* opened in London for the second time, the gorgeous Areleen Ni Bhaoill appeared in Jean Butler's place. It was announced to the audience that due to an injury, Jean would not be dancing but no mention was made of my nonappearance.

Areleen told me later that most of the cast were in shock that I was not performing. They'd read the papers like everybody else, of course, but they'd had no idea things had gone that far.

I was convinced I'd done the right thing in not signing the contract. I still believe it was the right thing to do. But I'll confess that it still upsets me to have people think that I was greedy, for that's not what it was about. I believed–naively, I suppose–that Moya, John, and I were partners. Moya had been like a big sister to me. And I'd helped create this huge money-making machine that she was now claiming belonged to her. I'd helped build something big, something that goes on to this day. It was a dream we'd all shared. It couldn't have happened without Bill Whelan doing the music. It couldn't have happened without Moya raising the money. But it came from *my* dream, the one I'd been creating for thirty-five years.

I'd have danced for free if need be. In fact, I'd been dancing for free for three months. But I wanted what was mine: artistic integrity. I would never have the chance to appear in *Riverdance* ever again. I have to admit it broke my heart!

It's difficult to convey the depths of pain that I felt. *Riverdance* wasn't just a piece of work–it was my life. It was thirty-five years of dancing, sweating, working, dreaming, thirty-five years of forging an entirely new kind of Irish dance. It was built out of my family's history, my years of struggle, my experiences of yearning, succeeding, and failing. In *Riverdance,* I put everything I knew about falling in love, about the women I'd desired, about my own sexuality. No one in Irish dance had ever held up his arms when he danced, or bared his chest, or invested such sexual feeling into the moves. No Irish dancer had ever run across the stage like a bull, chasing the girls as they scattered before him. The deepest wound I ever felt was in learning that the producers of

Riverdance appeared to have gotten their replacement dancers to imitate me–my persona, my moves. At the time, it seemed to me that they hadn't just taken a source of income, or even a work of art. At the time, I felt, they'd taken a part of my soul.

Now that I've got a bit of distance, I understand that there are many different ways to look at what happened. None of us expected *Riverdance* to take off so quickly, to bring in so much money, to become such a huge hit overnight. We were all a bit thrown by the instant success–at least, I know I was. Which made it all the harder for me to understand at the time how the people with whom I'd made this incredible journey could now be saying that they–and they alone–had the rights to decide when I was allowed to dance the steps I'd created, and how. Which made it all the more painful to learn that I had been replaced with dancers who appeared to be imitating me.

I just wish money hadn't got in the way. But I've got nothing bad to say about that show or the people connected with it. I hold no grudges. We were all great friends at the time, and I'd like to think we still could be if we ever met again. In April 2004 I hosted a party for the tenth anniversary of the original seven-minute *Riverdance* performance at Eurovision. It was a party for the original dancers, most of whom turned up. It started at the Hairy Lemon pub in Dublin, and continued into the small hours at Lillie's Bordello. So many great memories. Let me be the first one to put my hand out. And let's give Ireland back that great night without any scars!

The official Riverdance *book quotes Moya Doherty: "We have to draw a line in the sand; we can't go on like this, we must protect ourselves and the show. . . . No one dissented when the decision was made to replace Michael Flatley."*

In London's Sunday Telegraph, *on July 28, 1996, a* Riverdance *official described as a "member of the management" was quoted as saying*

Michael Flatley wanted to take over the show: "Finally, Moya gave up and said: 'Flatley, my dear, I don't give a damn.' And he was out."

On October 1, 1996, in The Times *of London, Moya Doherty said, "I have the highest admiration for Michael as a dancer and choreographer but he was and is a solo player. Getting rid of Michael was a traumatic decision. I didn't want to lose him and would have liked him to dance in America."*

Seamus O'Shea: "It was blown up it was about money, but it really wasn't. The newspapers printed all that.

"It was definitely artistic freedom and creativity. He just wanted that."

Jean Butler told the London Sunday Mirror *on August 25, 1996, "Michael leaving the show affected me enormously. I felt I was losing my right hand."*

On October 31, 1999, she told London's Mail on Sunday, *"I knew he wasn't happy. He probably felt he was being undermined artistically. But because I never got to speak to him properly about it, even afterwards, I felt stranded. I'd been so used to performing with him–indeed I'd never performed with anyone else–that it was a bit scary when he left."*

On October 26, 1999, Jean, who had quit the show in 1997, told Kevin O'Sullivan of London's Daily Mirror: *"I earned loads of money and traveled the world, but 'Riverdance' became a monster.*

"In 'Riverdance' it got to the point where the lawyers were more important than the performers.

"I'll never be in anything that gets nasty, ugly, or legal again."

Dancer Niamh O'Brien said at the Venetian Hotel in Las Vegas in February 2004: "When Michael left we were in rehearsals and everybody was distraught and devastated. We didn't know what was going to happen. He'd been the driving force for all of us to keep up. He'd kept us motivated so it was a really horrible time for everybody.

"I think there was something lost for all of us. He was there from the start. He was the one that had pressed us to keep going and told us we could be the best show in the world.

"They needed to find a replacement for Michael but nobody had the same style as Michael. Nobody was as vibrant or had as much stage presence as he did."

Dancer Eileen Martin said in Dublin in March 2004: "Without Michael it was never going to be the same show. Everyone knew that.

"And it wasn't."

Cormac O'Shea: "It all broke down in a calamity . . . which was extremely upsetting. . . . It felt like it was the end. It was the first time that we had had a substantial amount of rehearsal not involving Michael, and it had a very different feel. From that moment, the whole structure of the show changed in many ways; it was a very different vibe.

"It was a very confusing period, I think, the first six to eight weeks. Many people were involved and performing lead roles and there wasn't a ready-made character that could fall into that position.

"Although people repeated the footwork and repeated the expressed moves and everything, it was very different. It took dancers a long time to come close to realizing the same kind of stage personality that Michael brought to the show. . . . His contribution was very unique."

Penny Wark reviewed the first night of the second London run of Riverdance *in the* Today *newspaper on October* 5, 1995:

"The new 'Riverdance' is different in tone to the version in which Flatley starred.

"Dunne, a man with the build of a leprechaun and hair that badly needs barbering, does not have Flatley's presence or the sex appeal that lifted 'Riverdance' into entertainment's super-league."

Dara O'Shea was with Riverdance *when it debuted without Michael Flatley at Radio City Music Hall in New York in March 1996: "It was really exciting to do it in America, and the show did stand on its own without Michael. But no one could deny that his creation started it all off.*

"Although he wasn't in it it was still his legacy. We all felt that.

"Michael displayed real class and sent flowers and a good luck telegram to all of us including Jean Butler wishing 'every success' at Radio City.

"We had all known what was going on between him and John and Moya and it affected us on a personal level. . . . We used to go and see Michael [during the contract disputes] and he was still training right up to the end. . . . There would be tears. It was like the family was broken. He would say he was still training and he would say he was still hopeful they could work it out. He didn't want to leave Riverdance. *He practiced right up to the end."*

David Blake Knox said in February 2004 at the Westbury Hotel, Dublin: "In a curious way, I think [the fact] that Michael could be replaced . . . is testimony to his contribution to the show, his choreography. When I see another dancer doing his roles I can see Michael's signature all over it.

"[Being sacked] was an extraordinary test of character for Michael because a dancer's life is quite limited in terms of, in most cases, just the physical. Michael had only achieved the success of Riverdance *at a relatively late stage of his dancing career. It would have been extraordinary for any dancer to have achieved what he achieved. It's doubly extraordinary for a dancer to achieve that at his age.*

"It seemed at the time doubly cruel . . . having achieved this. . . . Most people would have cracked under the weight of that disappointment. . . . He was able to meet that crisis and he announced immediately he was going to do his own show.

"Celtic Tiger *turned out to be the biggest hit in all time, actually. All his plans came to fruition, and I think that that story is one of the most remarkable in show business. . . .*

"He has to be considered as an artist and recorded with that kind of status. Things like the fancy costumes that alienate some people are

superficial. Underneath that there is a very, very serious, dedicated artist that has been working for decades at his art. The fact that he is so successful sometimes makes people not realize that his soul is still that of an artist.

"All his career shows that. He is not some person who just got lucky. He clearly enjoys doing deals but it's a fundamental misconception to think that Michael is driven by material success. Because if he were, he would have stayed in Riverdance."

Gerry Ryan: "Michael Flatley is a megastar. In stratospherical terms. This is a superstar. . . . Michael brought to the show Jimi Hendrix and a blazing guitar. I don't think money was ever a problem. Money was an issue because Riverdance *became a hugely lucrative business. Michael wanted to own the artistic creation he was responsible for. All Michael wanted was to be recognized as the creator.*

"I spoke with Moya and John by telephone after Michael and they separated. They were at the Apollo Theatre in London and I think Moya was absolutely, utterly freaked out at the notion of Michael leaving the show.

"Moya rang me up and she was beside herself. She was pretty close to tears–and I know that the cynics may be reporting that she was close to tears because part of her box office percentage was disappearing. I think she was emotionally traumatized, like John, by the idea that Michael was leaving.

"Michael was waking up to the fact that he was a very fundamental and pivotal part of the production, and he also believed very strongly that he was also a part of the creative process that made the production so successful. It seemed to me to be where the argument lay.

"Michael was a franchised artist, they were business people, and they had to keep the show going.

"She rang me up and said, 'Look, I'm terribly worried about the way this announcement is going to be perceived at home in Dublin, the home of Riverdance.'

"She made suggestions as to how the announcement should be made

in Dublin. I pointed out to her that we had a long history together, and that it was very unlikely that I was going to say anything that would be either damaging to her or unfair to Michael.

"Moya, very graciously as I recall, sent me a fax—it was in the day of the fax—[that] said, 'I trust your judgment and I know that you will say the right thing.'

"There have been times when it has been suggested Moya, John, and I had a falling-out. We never had a row, ever. We never had a cross word. On my honor, we've discussed the situation many times over a drink and in our cups and we're the best of friends, and we see each other much more now than we ever did before.

"These guys became billionaires. I was still Gerry Ryan trying to scratch a living in broadcasting in Ireland. That's really why we didn't see one another. There was a never a moment of animosity. . . .

"It was very evident in these communications, whether they were on the phone or on fax, that Moya and John were going through a lot of pain over this.

"Don't forget—this is a multimillion-dollar decision. Plus, don't forget, they believed in Michael. He was the very essence of the 'Riverdance' piece in the Eurovision [broadcast]. For them to have to arrive at the moment where commercial necessity forced them to move on from Michael's argument with them must have been a very difficult moment. . . .

"Michael was Riverdance.

"You know something honestly? I never said [to John and Moya about firing Michael], 'Do you think it was a good idea?' But I might occasionally say after a malt whiskey, 'Well, was it as good without him?'

"I don't think they ever thought it was good without him.

"I felt very strongly that Riverdance *was the poorer for the loss of Michael. That was a personal opinion. I still hold that opinion. . . . I felt they should be moving heaven and earth to keep him in it. . . . Michael was right to demand his just reward and credit for the input that he had made artistically and creatively. There was no way that the guy under the*

circumstances could continue to dance in the show, which I think was a great tragedy of modern contemporary theater.

"I was being sentimental.

"John and Moya weren't."

Record producer Dave Kavanagh spoke in Dublin in May 2004, about his own version of events. Kavanagh was good friends with John and Moya, who brought him in to try to negotiate an agreement with Michael. Kavanagh was also involved in the controversy through his co-ownership of the Celtic Heartbeat label, a joint venture with Atlantic that had signed Riverdance *composer Bill Whelan: "You could see very early in the set-up that there were going to be divisions because it was, for everybody, a unique opportunity.*

"I think everybody had rolled their dice. On the surface it looked fine. There was a lot of smiling.

"The reality behind that is people were looking at a picture which obviously meant a lot of money. There was a lot of money about to arrive on the table in some form or other. It was a question of whose was it? Whose Riverdance *is this? Is it John and Moya's because they put the dough up and they are the producers? Is it Michael's because he's the creative force and he's choreographed it? Is it Bill Whelan's because he's written the music? Everybody had a bit of muscle.*

"What was clear was that for the public, the person who interested them most was Michael. He was going to put bums on seats. He was going to sell records, even though Bill wrote the music. It was the image of Flatley that was going to sell everything. He was going to sell the merchandising, the DVDs, the seats, everything. Without him this was not a winner. . . .

"Moya and John were trying to do a balancing act and maybe on a Tuesday they were boxing in Michael's corner and on the Wednesday they were in Bill's. Eventually there was a bit of a breakdown. I remember having to attend meetings, representing the [record] label but trying to

ease the tension that was starting between Bill and Michael and Moya and John. . . .

"What John and Moya wanted to try and do was try and cap whatever Michael could take out of the show. Michael's concerns are what really always stuck with me. Obviously, some were financial, but that wasn't a big issue. The hardest part of it for Michael was I don't think he felt that people had given him enough recognition for his contribution to what was now happening.

"This guy was an absolute pro. He worked very, very hard. He worked through pain I'd say, the legs suffering. I think that he choreographed everybody. His detail was immense.

"I remember going down to a couple of rehearsals and he really, really flogged everyone around him. He expected the same standard from them but he was a perfectionist. That's what separated that show and that's the reality. You were spellbound by the attention to detail, of the movement, of the choreographed movements. I think that what Michael really wanted was for people to say, 'Look, this is what he's doing.'

"He wasn't getting that. The billing was the same for him and Jean. The poster was him and Jean. It was Bill Whelan, Riverdance, *and 'Abhann Productions Presents' . . . and everything appeared above Michael, and he hadn't even got the star billing as the dancer.*

"That was a commercial decision they made, which was that people were interested in Jean and Michael under the sexual tension type of thing. Whether that's true or not, that was the way it was presented. The reality for Michael was, 'Look, I did this. Where is my recognition?'

"I think that hurt him and it alienated him. What it did, unfairly, was it made Michael look like a moody star. But he was very calm.

"I was there mediating. I was saying to them: 'Look, this should be a very enjoyable experience, this is the greatest thing that's ever happened to you.' Instead, they were very defensive relationships, that's the best way I can put it. . . .

"It got to a point where Moya and John said to me, 'Look, you get on

well with Michael, would you have a conversation with him? Find out exactly what the problem is, and why he won't sign the contract.'

"I went in and said to Michael, 'The problem here is there is an absolute time frame about when this contract needs to be signed. They are very nervous about opening in London without that contract being signed.'

"It was a certain ultimatum from Michael's perspective there. He was basically being told, 'Sign or we're not opening.'

"To Michael in his mind he thought, 'The show can't open without me.'

"The financial arrangements as far as I understood were fine. I went through that with him. There was a lot of money involved, in excess of fifty grand a week or something. He had a royalty even on the record. He had a royalty on everything. I didn't get the impression from him that was the problem.

"All the deals I had done in my life, and I had twenty major deals, were really all about money, that's all anyone would ever talk to you about. In Michael's case there was another issue . . . about him as a human being, his treatment, about the recognition that he desperately wanted. He wanted people to say, 'This guy made this thing happen.'

The show at that stage was getting too big and too valuable for anyone to admit that. There was no way that Moya and John were going to turn around and say, 'Look. We can't go on without you.' . . .

"I went back to Moya and John at some stage and said: 'Ultimately it could come down to billing. This could come down to you accepting that Michael essentially is really Riverdance.*' . . .*

"They said they couldn't do that.

"I went back to him and said, 'Michael. There is a time frame that we're nearly running out of. . . . These conversations will just end. What happens after that, I'm not in control of. People will make decisions.'

"I was unaware at that stage that John and Moya had already brought over a world champion dancer to replace Michael. They didn't inform me about it. I continued to talk to Michael for another couple of days. We talked on the phone a couple of times. We got to some stage

where we seemed to be close, and I called him the next morning and I said that I thought we could make this thing work. . . .

"I think Michael was isolated. I think that the longer this went on, the more isolated he became. . . . I remember going in and you could see him sitting in the dressing room on his own. I would go in and sit in front of him and we'd talk. You could go out and meet John and Moya, there would be a bunch of promoters around them. . . .

"All I know is that I got a call saying, 'Dave, there's no point, don't be contacting Michael. The conversation's over. He's out.'

"I said, 'What? You do know you're opening tomorrow night?'

"They said, 'Yes. We've a new guy in. He's been rehearsing. We didn't tell you because we wanted you to keep going with the best intention.' They were right. If I had known that I would have felt substantially undermined and I would have felt that I would have had to communicate that to Michael. . . .

"There was certainly a thought process which was the minute they said this is 'Michael Flatley's Riverdance*' they couldn't move without Michael. By not having Michael you could have multiple shows. . . . That is the art form of the likes of Andrew Lloyd Webber and Cameron Mackintosh and people like that. Where they cast people that are essentially replaceable. . . .*

"Moya and John at that moment had to make a business decision with the investors in the show which was very simple, 'If we go on with Michael without the contract signed, we're not going to be in charge of the show anymore.' They took the decision that that wasn't something that they were willing to work with, and therefore they were willing to roll the whole dice and have one go.

"Michael was shattered. I felt that I had failed because when I saw the way the package unfolded and as quickly as it did, there was mayhem. This was major news on television and radio and in newspapers; Michael was on television saying, 'I can't believe it. This is the show that I created and now I'm out.'

"The reality was the back-up band were playing the music. What

Moya and John and the promoters had to do on the night was to offer a refund to anyone who didn't want to see the show without Michael.

"It was a very, very lonely night. . . . The guy who wrote the music, the guy who choreographed it, and the leading female star were out of action. Gone, on an opening night in London. It didn't look particularly great from that perspective.

"This new dancer guy had only had two days of rehearsals I think, maximum three days, which I don't even think he could do with the troupe because they were unaware that Michael was in the situation he was. . . . Moya threw up on the night. Physically.

"I looked at the show with her for the whole night, and it was a terrifying experience from her point of view—and it worked. What transpired that night essentially was that the show was now what was selling tickets.

"What was also clear was that Michael probably was bigger than the show. Now, he still had to pick himself up. To me, when he launched himself with Lord of the Dance *after that, the point was he was bigger than any show he was in, no matter what he did. That's exactly what would have happened in* Riverdance. *The reality is that it would have been Michael Flatley's show. . . .*

"I don't mean this in a cynical way, but they all got their toys. They just ended up playing with them in different rooms. . . .

"Think about it in real terms.

"Here's a small country with little Irish dancing which is more popular in America than it is in Ireland. It was a failing piece of Irish culture which no one was really that interested in. You wouldn't see an Irish dancer on television unless it was a 1948 movie with Barry Fitzgerald in it.

"It was turned into probably the biggest-grossing thing in entertainment. This did numbers at the box office that were phenomenal. The merchandising was phenomenal. It sold a phenomenal number of records. Every part of our industry was impacted on. A massive amount of jobs were created. They ran out of Irish dancers. They couldn't make shoes quick enough. Here was a bunch of Irish kids touring around the

world, staying in good hotels, earning a couple of grand a week which was being sent home to their accounts. They were coming back here and buying their houses.

"This was an industry that started with a small dream. It is sad in that Michael started that journey and I don't think he even got down the first lane.

"Most people would just crawl away hurt and try to get away with a load of money. Hire a lawyer and say, just go in there and molest those people. Do whatever you have to do but hurt them and get me loads of money.

"Instead Michael went off and he went through a process, 'How do I come back? How do I show these people that I really am as talented as I know I am and what I have done for them?'

"That was a very tough thing to do. Without that support system. With having to pick yourself up like that.

"That to me is the confirmation of what Michael's abilities are. How he behaved in adversity, [which] is the measure of everybody. It's very easy to be magnanimous when you're winning. His ability to behave well in adversity showed the strength and character in great style. You get that [prize] taken away from you once, there's very few people who come back. I'd say that's the moment that made him.

"It confirms the greatness."

Act Three

Lord of the Dance

I go to encounter for the millionth time the reality of experience, and to forge in the smithy of my soul the uncreated conscience of my race. Old father, old artificer, stand me now and ever in good stead.

James Joyce, *Ulysses*

Chapter Twenty-one

Sexy Dancing

You notice his thighs quiver and shudder in a way that I've never seen in a man who wasn't horizontal.

Chrissy Iley, *The Sunday Times Magazine,* London, June 9, 1996, on Michael Flatley rehearsing *Lord of the Dance*

Dancing is sexual energy. The greatest feeling in the world. I think I gave Irish dancing some feeling, something above the knees, and that's exactly how it should be.

On stage I can always feel the audience reacting. They get the emotions we're creating for them and they feel the passions within themselves—sex, romance, anger, joy, and Lord knows what secret desires. We're all blessed with those.

So whenever anyone wonders why *Lord of the Dance* became such a sexual show, there's your answer. It's the nature of dance itself.

Lord of the Dance began in the dark. Eleven days after my departure from *Riverdance* I awoke abruptly and sat straight up, knowing I had a number I'd call "Planet Ireland." That was the foundation of what would arguably become the most successful touring dance concert of all time.

To the world, *Lord of the Dance* was a revelation. But I'd had the rhythms and movements in my head since I was a youngster. And even while I was on stage with *Riverdance,* I had imagined *Riverdance Two* and *Riverdance Three.*

I believe in the elemental struggles of good versus bad and love versus lust, with the good guy winning in a super feel-good ending. I wanted audiences to leave the show feeling like winners. So *Lord of the Dance* is the story of a Celtic spirit and her dream. It has some good guys, some bad guys, and a couple of beautiful girls–one an angel, the other a temptation. And in the end we see these forces come together to determine who's going to be Lord of the Dance–and who'll get the girl.

The cynics among you may see more than a hint of my own personal drama in this story. After all, at the time I was splitting up with my wife, whom I really, dearly loved. Nevertheless, I was trapped in lust with Kelley, who drove me crazy and whose charms I could not escape.

Or perhaps you'll see my professional history.

Or maybe my inspiration came from somewhere deeper, more primal–a profound connection to my Irish culture. Where did I come up with "Cry of the Celts"–the opening number of the show? Why "Cry of the Celts" and not "Dance of the Celts"?

Where I got the inspiration for *Lord of the Dance* may be an enigma, but there's no mystery at all about why I moved so quickly to launch the project. Not only did I need a place to put my sorrow and anger over the loss of *Riverdance,* but for purely professional reasons, I had to act while people still knew who I was.

Kelley Byrne: "When we were on holiday, in the K Club in Barbuda and in the Maldives, when Michael was still very much part of Riverdance, *he was talking about putting together another show. He'd be up all night writing out ideas. He never stopped, twenty-four hours thinking, thinking, thinking, and all I heard was about the new shows.*

"He never really sleeps. He has to take a sleeping tablet or he would be up all night with ideas. His brain never stops working. He just has to write it all down. That's why he is where he is, and he deserves everything he gets. He works so hard. You have to give it to him. It's not money or anything. He can't exist without doing stuff. He can't sit back."

Luckily, not long after my departure from *Riverdance*, I was invited onto a TV show hosted by the veteran British singer and popular talk show host Des O'Connor. My dancers and I worked around the clock at the St. Xavier Hall in a grimy alleyway in Dublin to create "Warlords," the number that was later performed toward the end of the first half of *Lord of the Dance*.

This time, I vowed, I'd be in control of the finances. I'd learned from *Riverdance* to keep my gloves up and protect myself at all times.

Still, launching a new show, difficult at the best of times, was especially hard for me, and especially hard in Ireland. Finally, with *Riverdance,* Ireland had had a true international success, one that used the talents of many Irish artists. I was still a Yank, and the press didn't look kindly on me for what they saw as trying to piggyback on *Riverdance*'s success—even though I was a creator of *Riverdance.*

Luckily, I've learned to use negativity as rocket fuel. I've programmed my subconscious mind to become even more determined with every critical word. People who tell me "I can't" only make me work twice as hard and twice as fast.

My vision for *Lord of the Dance* required a few dozen dancers—and no way could I afford to hire them when I started creating the show. Given how expensive it is to mount a show, and how little money I had at the time, I knew the show had to be all worked out in my head before I could start working with the full team. My preparation was all the more important because of how great the demands on the dance team would be. They were going to be doing twelve to fifteen taps a second simultaneously, hitting the floor at exactly the same time. Before I could even begin to teach them the steps, I had to have my rhythm patterns perfectly set up.

After all, I was to be the director, the choreographer, and the star. No way could I afford to have my dancers looking at me nervously, watching me stutter and stumble as I tried to figure out a combination. I was asking these kids to take time out from college or full-time jobs and gamble with their futures. I had to be worthy of their trust.

I put all my energy, all my skill–all my love–into my dances and my dancers because I believed in them. In return, I received at least as much as I gave, for nothing is more exciting than helping young people follow their dreams. I had been where they were–in many ways, I was still there–and now I could do something to help them achieve the greatness that I had been seeking all my life. I'll never get tired of that–seeing the young people in my shows, creating new solos for them, pushing them, getting them to aspire, to push themselves. It's a beautiful thing, and I love it.

I love people–especially dancers–but I can be extremely tough on my cast when I'm working. Great dancers want that and love that. They appreciate the leadership. They don't want a softie in charge. They want someone who's a hard leader, because they know that this is the guy who's going to break through new barriers, the guy who can defeat everyone. They want to learn that way of life. There's a gentleness and kindness underneath it.

There are a lot of people in the world who get a kick out of being mean and using their power. That's a horrible way to be. I don't believe you need to be a bully to be admired. But sometimes you have to shout.

I've always had to deal with one big public knock: that I had a big ego. I have always had a laugh at that, for that's not me, that's the product, an essential of stagecraft.

* * *

Dancer John Carey remembers Lord of the Dance *rehearsals quite fondly: "It was the best experience, definitely the most fun time I've ever had."*

Michael Flatley was appearing in Riverdance *when promoter Peter Aiken first met him. They met again when Aiken Promotions was consulted about* Lord of the Dance. *Aiken recalls: "We just couldn't see how he was going to come up with a show. To us, it was like a rock band trying to be another U2.*

"Eventually, though, we could see that the guy was going to pull it off. He's very driven, he works so hard at it, from 8 a.m. to midnight.

"Ego? I've never seen it offstage. Onstage, he has to have it.

"He looks after his dancers. Of all the rock bands I've worked with, he has the best catering.

"Most of the groups I work with demand more than Flatley. And he's the only artist I know who willingly meets fans after the show.

"He's nice to people. He might walk with a bit of a swagger but that's just the way he is. He's Rocky in dancing shoes."

Kelley Byrne: "If you ask any dancer who ever worked with him, I don't think you'd find anyone who said they didn't like him—even if they didn't get on with him, which is unlikely, because he's very friendly. He's got time for everybody. Everyone respects him.

"If he gave off the wrong impression sometimes, it was because things were twisted. In Chicago, an Irish journalist asked, 'Do you think you're the best dancer in the world?'

"Michael said, 'Yes, I do.'

"The headline was 'Flatley Ego Monster—I'm the best dancer in the world.' He couldn't really win. You shouldn't knock a hard-working and decent guy. He's never ripped anyone off. I don't think he ever intentionally did bad things. I think at times whole situations would overwhelm him and he would go along with it."

* * *

When I started developing *Lord of the Dance*, I couldn't afford all forty dancers. I was paying for everything out of my own pocket–salaries, rehearsal space, and all the rest–and I could only bring in a few dancers. We were back working in the old broken-down dance building in Diggs Lane as I tried to hang on to what was left of my dream.

I remember one afternoon, the dancers had gone for lunch, and I was at my wit's end. I was running out of money fast and still no hope of launching a new production. I was exhausted beyond belief. I hadn't eaten yet that day. My personal life was in tatters. And the bad press about my fight with *Riverdance* was relentless.

I sat down in the hallway, completely on my own, as I had been so many times in my life. I opened a newspaper to take my mind off my problems, only to find another big spread about my giant ego and all the negative things about me you could imagine. As I read it, my anger at the injustice of it all turned to an emotional dam that was about to burst. Just when I could feel the tears coming, a woman walked round the corner and said, "Jesus Christ, Mick, how are you doin', boy?"

It was a well known theatrical star, Twink, a lovely woman with a wonderful personality. By chance, she was in Diggs Lane to take a dance class and she'd run into me.

I'm sure she could see how low I felt, and she immediately set about trying to cheer me up, asking me how things were going.

"Never better!" I lied. "I've got 'em all just where I want 'em."

We hugged and laughed, and she walked away smiling, giving me one of her inimitable winks. I let the paper in my hand fall to the ground and walked back into the tattered dance studio with the broken mirrors. Unable to hold back any longer, I fell against the wall and sobbed like a little child. I was almost out of money, and I knew the end was near.

But I couldn't let my dream die–not after I'd been through so much. So I came up with a very unusual way of raising money. I contacted VVL Video, a division of Universal, to see if they'd be interested in buying the advance video rights to my new show.

Lots of movies are financed these days by advance sales of the video rights, but–then and now–it's unusual to finance a stage show this way. Both sides were taking a gamble. If my show was a hit, the video rights would undoubtedly be worth much more than I could sell them for at this point. But if VVL bought the rights and the show flopped, they'd have lost money.

Reluctantly, VVL agreed to send their representatives out to see a piece of the show in rehearsals, but they stressed how skeptical they were. Lightning doesn't strike twice, they told me. People won't accept *Riverdance Two.*

Where there's Coke, there's Pepsi, said I. Where there's McDonald's, there's Burger King.

The big day came, and our team was ready. I must confess, we were all fairly nervous. Bad press tends to do that to you. So we'd all gone out to the Hairy Lemon the night before and had more than one too many. By the time the Universal people arrived, I was nursing a beauty!

When they walked in, the room went silent. We all felt a bit overwhelmed for they were clearly not in good humor. You could feel how uninterested they were–this was just one more call they had to make, one they clearly wished was already over.

I shook hands with the first two youngsters who walked in the door. Then in came the big honcho, a man named Bill Tennant. When I put out my hand to greet him, he ignored it. He simply strode past me, saying, "Let's see what you got."

The first number we performed was "The Cry of the Celts." The two young people did a complete one-eighty–they loved it. But from Tennant–nothing. In a cold, businesslike voice, he said, "Let's see another one."

I winked at the lads. "Warlords," said I. That was the name of a very dramatic number–sixteen men and I, dancing a capella, accompanied only by the sound of lightning-fast taps all clicking in unison.

We lit the place up. We gave it everything we had. People even gathered from the neighboring studios to watch—we could see them looking through the studio windows.

We finished, breathing heavily, and the two youngsters were now ecstatic. But from Tennant—still nothing.

The dancers were only looking for a pat on the back. I must confess, I was expecting one myself. Tennant's next words would live with me for a lifetime: "Come on, come on, let's see another one."

I'd had just about enough. "I'm sorry, time's up," I said. "That's all you get."

Tennant got up with a disdainful look on his face and headed for the door. Before he reached it, my Irish pride couldn't resist. "I want your answer today."

He looked at me with the look only Tennant can deliver. It was the first smile of the afternoon. Needless to say, I got my money. And he eventually became my manager.

The £800,000 I got from Universal, coupled with the half a million I had of my own from *Riverdance*, was just enough to launch *Lord of the Dance*—and it kept my dream alive.

No one will ever know except the dancers and me the pain, the emotion, the agony, and the ecstasy that we experienced during those long, hard weeks in that broken-down studio. We deserved the success we all got, because we never backed down. We fought to the end—and we won.

Just in case that half-million pounds from *Riverdance* sounds like a lot of money, let me say again that I put it *all* into *Lord of the Dance*. It went for costumes, musicians, theater rental, advertising, and all the other costs of putting on a huge show. I was so broke, I had to borrow fifty quid from Kelley one night, just so I could have a pint with the lads.

In fact, the hardest part of creating *Lord of the Dance* was the commercial side. In order to produce the show myself, I had to detach completely from myself as an artist and look at myself as a product. How many seats could my name sell? What did people expect when they bought a ticket to see "Michael Flatley"? What kind of show was I known for? What did I *want* to be known for? These were questions I wasn't used to asking–but I had to ask them now.

Meanwhile, we recorded "Warlords" for *The Des O'Connor Show* in November 1995. It wasn't screened until January 1996, but on December 28, 1995, we presented "Warlords"–the seed of *Lord of the Dance*–at the National Concert Hall in Dublin. At the same time, *Riverdance* was honored as "Performance of the Year." Even though *Riverdance* had dropped me, I considered it a double triumph.

CHAPTER TWENTY-TWO

Putting It Together

Cometh the moment, cometh the man.

Folk saying

I WAS REACHING FOR THE SKIES. But I couldn't do it alone. Especially after the *Riverdance* experience, I knew I needed some back-up. So I set about putting together the best team I could imagine.

I'd met John Reid a few years previously on a trip to St. Tropez with Beata. Reid was a manager of high-profile music clients. He seemed very clued-in and had represented the likes of Elton John, Billy Connolly, Andrew Lloyd Webber, and Queen. He told me he could resolve my *Riverdance* legal and financial problems with "one meeting on advantageous terms," which sounded grand to me. In October 1995 we made a handshake agreement that he would represent me for three years.

I was off to a great start, for sure—but how was I going to pay for the show? One of the most helpful things John ever did was introduce me to promoter-producer Harvey Goldsmith CBE, a grizzly, fifty-something, throaty-voiced character who is one of the great names of music. Harvey gathered the big-money names in the entertainment business into his upstairs London office, and I just sat there, listening to the moguls talk.

The world's experts were all there, all the top money guys, as well as directors, stage designers, lighting designers, sound engineers, managers, submanagers, assistant managers, and choreographers. They talked for hours about what a Michael Flatley show should look like without ever thinking to stop and ask me. And they say I have a big ego!

Luckily, I already had my vision. I wanted to marry an ancient art form with an ultra-modern stage design, costumes, lighting, and sound. Although my medium was the centuries-old form of traditional Irish dance, I wanted to create a show that could give today's rock and pop bands a run for their money. And I was willing to gamble everything I had that such a spectacle could play in the world's biggest arenas, just like a top rock 'n' roll band. I wanted a big, bright show with all the showmanship and zest of a Broadway extravaganza, complete with pyrotechnic effects, dramatic dance numbers, and huge sounds.

Of course, the experts waxed eloquent on all the things I *couldn't* do. But finally, someone thought to let me speak. I'd had the show worked out in my head for so long, I was able to talk for thirty minutes nonstop, from the first entrance–me dancing onto the stage in a cloud of smoke–to the splashy, soaring leaps, the elaborate mid-air heel clicks, and the sexy dance numbers, all the way to the final encore. I explained the entire look and feel of the show, from the big picture to the subtle, almost subliminal, messages it would communicate.

Finally, I fell silent. No one said a word. I surely wasn't about to speak. I bit my lip. Waiting, waiting. . . .

Finally, one of the potential producers said he would invest.

Then another, and another.

That was all the confirmation I needed. "Thank you, gentlemen," I said calmly, "but in the event, I'll be bankrolling the show myself. I don't need your money."

Wow! They sat there with their mouths open. But I'd gotten what I wanted: to find out whether the most shrewd and skeptical bankers in the U.K. would be willing to cough up the cash. I'd wondered if I'd be able to hook these fish—and now that I had, I knew I had a bankable idea. But I didn't want their money. Instead, I was ready to bet my entire savings on it.

John Reid couldn't believe I was trying such an audacious move. He kept sending his subagent Derek McKillop to try convincing me to let others invest in the show. "You can't do this alone," Derek would say on John's behalf. "No one can. It's financial suicide. We can save you."

I just sat and listened.

Derek also told me that he thought *Lord of the Dance* was the stupidest title he'd ever heard of. "It'll never work," he kept insisting. "You'll lose your shirt." Lucky for us all, I didn't take him seriously.

Of course, most shows *are* produced by a group of investors, for very few people have the ability—or the wish—to take the entire financial risk upon themselves. I, however, believed in myself and I was ready to invest in *Lord of the Dance* to my last penny. If the show failed, well, then, I'd lose everything I had—and more. I'd walked into Ireland with nothing but my talent and my pride, and I was perfectly willing to walk out of it the same way. On the other hand, if the show succeeded, I wouldn't have to share the money—or the creative control—with anyone, not ever again.

For sure, I'm a proud man. Maybe too proud. But I'd just been burned and I wasn't ever going to trust anyone again with control over my life's work. Yes, I was on a tightrope but I liked it up there!

Harvey Goldsmith spoke at his central London offices on April 28, 2004: "I first met Michael Flatley when he was performing in Riverdance, *and I went backstage to meet him. I thought he was incredible. . . .*

Eighteen months later I got a call from John Reid [. . .] to say that he was managing Michael and wanted to put a show together. I met with Michael, who explained he wanted to do his own show.

"We were meeting two or three times a week and working on different designs, and then he came up with the title of it, which we all accepted, and the show started to evolve."

Now it was time to put the artistic team together. My first thought was to call Bill Whelan, the composer on *Riverdance.* I really like Bill—he's a great man, incredibly talented, and our creative process was marvelous. Sure, there were times we fought like cats and dogs, but underneath it, there was a deep respect and admiration.

In the end, I couldn't get past his ties to *Riverdance.* I wanted a clean start. So I called Ronan Hardiman, a composer whom I'd worked with on a 1996 piece for the Prince's Trust. We'd gotten on well, and I thought he'd be terrific for *Lord of the Dance.* I went to his home, where I found he composed in front of a huge television monitor, making the sound echo here, there, and everywhere with just the flick of his finger.

Ronan and I were in tune. And we were both happy to get to work immediately and to stay at it. I put a lot of pressure on Ronan, firing off ideas at him every second, but he responded to it. He's a genius.

I would pace up and down—he said I had my feet in my head—as Ronan tried to keep up with my thoughts. At first, he wasn't that keen on the *Lord of the Dance* theme—the hymn, based on a traditional Shaker melody, that is known as "Lord of the Dance." But instinctively, I knew that tune belonged in the show, along with some traditional Irish songs, and in the end, it all worked wonderfully well.

The rest of the music was a collaboration. I gave his imagination free rein and like a great race horse, he hit his stride. We were working at a terrific rate so that the music would be ready as the dances were being created. In the words of the old saying, I wanted it fast *and* I wanted it good. I wanted scintillating, splintering precision. And Ronan delivered.

At Ronan's, I would dance throughout his house and act out scenes. Often I had the dance details all worked out before he had time to take notes. I left my imprint on Ronan–and I left black shoe-marks and dents on his newly sanded sitting room floor. I only discovered my misdeed when he presented me with an aging wooden board on which to improvise my steps. Greater love hath no man than to let his choreographer tear up his floor. For sure, Ronan's a great friend, and I love him dearly.

Ronan Hardiman spoke at his home in Dublin in May 2004, describing the killing pace at which he and Michael worked: "I watched Michael producing, directing, choreographing, and overseeing the set, lighting, costumes, sound, and music, and was amazed how relaxed he appeared. I had ten weeks to do my job and he had the same deadline for the whole show. . . .

"The way [Michael] is generally depicted–arrogant, egocentric–is at total odds with what I know of him as a person–and I have worked with him under pressurized circumstances. . . . He's very driven and focused. He drives the people around him very hard. Some people don't react well to that, and they tend to be negative and a bit bitter, and the relationship doesn't continue. But the people who are committed to being perfectionists in their work can see where he is coming from.

". . . The only problem I had was getting the ideas consistently down on paper. . . . Michael has an idea per second. He's one of the global superstars and by the very nature of that, there's going to be certain personality traits that go with that.

"One of the things that I find most stimulating, and it works both ways, is when he starts throwing out ideas, pacing up and down the room. I can hear the music as he's talking; it sort of paints a picture.

He's got loads of ideas going through his head all the time, and I can interpret them. That's an important chemistry. It doesn't happen with every creative relationship. . . .

"He definitely gets the best out of you. I have to say that he's just a nice guy. He's Irish. He's got a good sense of humor, and he's got a sense of the ridiculous, and I identify with that. But the magic is in being able to read his ideas.

"I go through his thoughts in detail and ask a thousand questions. I see it as part of my job with anybody that I'm working with, including Michael, to extract their vision. My job is to bring something creative to that. The first starting point is to get on paper what Michael sees. I have yellow legal pads filled with notes, with phrases like 'incredibly violent,' 'dripping with sex,' key emotional words. . . . He'd be walking around doing mini-versions of the big production numbers, a miniature version of what is going to be in front of the public. . . . The charisma and the energy that flows from him in that small space is exactly the same as in Central Park or Hyde Park. It just oozes out of him. . . .

"I saw this as potentially a great break for me. I don't think anybody would have foreseen the phenomenon that the whole thing was. I think it was a fair return on the kind of energy and the gut-instinct commitment that Michael put into it. If you put in more than you're asked to do, you'll always get it back tenfold."

Ronan was someone who could keep up with my energy. I wanted the rest of my team to feel the same way. At that point, I rarely slept at night. I was so driven that people must have found me hard to be around. I'd stare out the window of my hotel room at 2 a.m. or 4 a.m. or 5 a.m, listening to the rhythm patterns in my head, pacing about, waiting for the day to begin, waiting for everyone else to join my day. Everything was riding on this for me—everything.

I found Jonathan Park to design the set. He'd done the Rolling Stones' "Voodoo Lounge Tour," so I knew he'd understand the big rock-star feeling we were going for. Patrick Woodroffe, who'd worked with Michael Jackson and Tina Turner, signed on to create the lighting. He, too, understood that I wanted my show to be sexy–not titillating, but healthy, athletic. I didn't want the girls *trying* to be sexy. I wanted them to feel comfortable with their own sexuality. If they could enjoy that part of themselves, the audience would be comfortable with it, too.

I also had to recruit and teach a dance troupe, so I brought in the best-qualified person in the world. Marie Duffy became my dance master and righthand person, and I will love her forever. In 1996, when we started working together, Marie had more than forty years of experience and was one of the most well-respected and successful Irish dance teachers and choreographers in the world. For *Riverdance,* I'd trained all the dancers and gotten them in perfect shape, shown them how to use their arms and every other part of their bodies, how to smile and create a stage persona. I'd ushered them into my own style of dance and performance, drilling them for the whole rehearsal time, choreographing all the steps and then rehearsing those steps in the new style. Only then could I start to direct them–to work with the whole group of them on stage, figure out where they needed to be, find out what little changes might make the whole stage picture come alive.

With *Lord of the Dance,* I had the same type of overall responsibility, but I put Marie in charge of the day-to-day drilling: "Okay. Third from the back at the end, you're out of line, do this again. . . . Make the line tighter–you, on the end, move out to here." This time, that was Marie's job, and she did it brilliantly. She also auditioned every dancer herself and proved to be a wonderful choreographer.

Marie Duffy said in London in September 2004: "Michael contacted me in the very early days and told me about his idea and his dream and all he wanted to do, and asked me if I would be interested in working with him, as he liked and appreciated the kind of work I did. He thought we could get on well together, which we have done.

"It has been phenomenal, because we seem to think quite alike. He would just talk about something, and I would know exactly what he meant.

"I of course was over the moon at being invited to work with Michael. It was a great honor for me. It was the icing on the cake as far as I was concerned in my career. . . .

"We auditioned and then about a month later he spoke to me about Ronan Hardiman being involved and listening to his music and putting ideas together. And from there we picked a working group of about sixteen or eighteen. We did numbers to promote the show. . . . At that stage we had no costumes, no nothing. The first item we did was for the Prince's Trust in London, and from there we never looked back.

"Again, the show was only in its infancy, three-quarters of it hadn't been put together, but always he had a vision in his mind. He knew exactly what he was doing from day one. He had the whole vision from the start to the finish in his head. I think in March/April then we brought in the rest of the dancers and from mid-April we worked through to the opening in Dublin.

"It has just been phenomenal. There were very nervous times and long hours put in of hard work, and Michael worked tirelessly. . . . He was very inspiring and very motivational. As soon as Michael talks to you, you get the bug.

"We just built on it. Day by day. The same with costumes and everything. . . . I will never forget my first impressions when I walked into the theater a few days before opening and saw the set for the first time. I just stood. I couldn't breathe, with the excitement."

I wanted my dancers to be the highest-paid in the industry. I was happy to reward them for dedication and loyalty. Eventually I'd put together a team of top-notch dancers, an even split of boys and girls. They were all champions several times over.

From then on it was hard work, ten- and twelve- and sometimes fourteen-hour days. I hired Anne Buckley as my soprano soloist. For musicians, I brought on the All-Ireland fiddle champions Cora Smyth and Mairead Nesbitt.

I had to be certain of my choices for the leads. I had a studio full of world champions, but I could tell the very special dancers, the ones who should be featured.

I made Daire Nolan the bad guy, Don Dorcha. Bernadette Flynn became Saoirse the Irish Colleen, the good girl. Gillian Norris was Morrighan the Temptress, the bad girl. Bernadette and Gillian are both stars, brilliant dancers in their different ways. I loved them both.

Bernadette held six world titles and seven All-Irelands. As soon as we met, she understood without me having to say too much. At sixteen, she was the baby of the bunch. We were able to dance together for ages without me having to talk or to explain anything about the movements. She knew what to do–and what to do next. She has the heart and soul of an angel. It was magical.

In June 2004, Bernadette Flynn recalled: "It was our dream. [However,] grasping the steps, especially those in the Encore, was extremely difficult. Michael had most of the world champions, from my age group up, and I could see that they couldn't do the steps either–it wasn't just me. Gillian and I stepped into our roles and started to arrive early to rehearse and leave late."

Gillian was also an extra-special addition to the cast. She was so hot. She had the best body in the troupe, and she had a passion in her heart that burned like a gypsy. Gillian was the type of performer you couldn't take your eyes off. You knew something was going to happen at any minute–you just didn't know what it would be.

Gillian Norris: "It was like running away to the circus. . . . Michael was my idol. Still is.

"I always seemed to work very well with Michael. If he wanted me to do something in a certain way, I'd do it, or if I ever wanted to do something, I could always suggest it to him. I never felt intimidated by him.

"I couldn't believe it when I got a lead role. One day Michael and Marie Duffy called me out and said I was to be given an understudy. Then I didn't hear much about it until Michael put on the 'Gypsy' music and called me out and asked me to do the lead part in it, to do whatever I felt myself, what came to me at the time.

"He obviously liked it, as I got the lead. It was a big shock because I was so young, only seventeen. I thought it would be someone who had been dancing longer than me but he had a different opinion.

"He wanted who he wanted, and luckily I was who he wanted.

"I wanted him, too–but that's a different story!"

It had been the start of a new life, walking into my rehearsal studio, facing all the hope and all the worries, the young people with their ambition and their talent. They looked at me eagerly with big, bright eyes, like little birds waiting on the worms.

This time, I wasn't the unknown. The unknown was whether the public would respond to *another* Irish-themed dance show. Preview performances began at The Point on June 28, 1996, and my whole future was riding on what happened there. I had staked everything I had on this show, and now I was broke. I *knew* my gamble would pay off–but would it?

Chapter Twenty-three

Braveheart

He deserves credit for sheer balls.

—*The Times,* London, October 25, 1997

I WANTED TO BE in the best physical shape possible for *Lord of the Dance.* That meant extreme focus, so I'd gone into strict training. Every day I would walk from Dublin's Westbury Hotel across Grafton Street and over to the south side of St. Stephen's Green where Pat Henry has his gym.

Pat's an expert on fitness. He trained with some of the best people in Hollywood before returning to work in Dublin. He's helped get many actors and athletes into great shape. And he's so aware that the only way to achieve results is through discipline and hard work. He's appeared in several movies, most memorably as the executioner who chops Mel Gibson into pieces in *Braveheart.* I thought he probably had what it took to get *me* into shape!

Pat Henry usually begins training his clients in the early hours of the morning at his basement gym in Upper Pembroke Street in Dublin, where a giant poster of Michael Flatley in his Lord of the Dance *pose has pride of place. He spoke there in February 2004: "I've trained a lot of famous names, and they all know that they get the best training they're ever going to get anywhere, including America. . . .*

"I have never trained anybody as determined and focused as Michael Flatley. Ever. He had unbelievable focus. Once you told him to do something, he would do it. We set out a plan, and he trained every single day and never missed a day. Even when he was very sore, he'd never miss a day. He came back and worked extremely hard. . . .

"He was never in bad shape. He had great symmetry of the body. His legs were in good shape but the upper body needed tone and muscles. The plan was to increase the muscles on the shoulders and tighten the waist up and get the abdominals going, get the arms looking good.

"When he stripped off on stage on the first night, people just went 'Wow!' because he looked fantastic.

"He was like a stallion. He used to dance on the stage and his muscles would ripple with the light shining on. That was an amazing moment.

"All through rehearsals, even when he was really tired, when he was exhausted rehearsing the girls, he absolutely never missed workouts. I think that's probably one of the reasons why he's so successful, because he has a target and nothing is going to get in his way. Even if he was sick, he wouldn't let it get in his way.

"When you meet someone that can train that hard, it inspires you to train them even harder, because you know that they are not going to mess around. Michael wanted to know how he was doing and if he could push himself harder. There are very few people that I've come across that can do that.

"If they can do it in that area, then they can do it in life in other things.

"He would listen to you and have respect for what you do. The respect part was important, because when you get to that career stage other stars wouldn't have respect for people, but he did. He was able to respect that you knew what you were talking about. . . .

"Michael Flatley is able to be where he is at the moment because of his mind. He is total concentration. He could focus on any body part and get results quicker than anybody else. When he visited the gym, he never

allowed music. He said he would only concentrate on one thing at one time. That was muscle. Michael Flatley wanted to do nothing but train. He wasn't interested in talking to the people. When the training was finished, he would speak to them. . . . When Michael was training, don't disturb him, let him concentrate on his work. When he was dancing, don't disturb him. . . .

"Michael didn't have a problem with privacy. He'd be waving at the girls as they went by. The girls waved back. The secretaries used to whistle at him as he went along. He'd come out [of the gym] and he'd be covered in sweat and we'd go running. It was like 'Rocky.' Everywhere people would be shouting, 'Keep going, Michael!' They love him here. This is before he became Lord of the Dance. They see him as Irish. . . .

"When he was in the gym and working on his chest, you could see it almost growing in front of you, because when someone is that focused with that much meditation it happens. People were crying when he was dancing, bursting into tears with the feeling that they get from him dancing, because he's become meditation in action. That can help so many people's lives, because it triggers something all through them.

"When you train somebody, and they can meditate to that level, it can be scary. I've seen him in the gym on the punch bag, and he'd be on that punch bag maybe doing six rounds, three-minute rounds, and the sweat would be pouring off him, and his knuckles would be bleeding, but he wouldn't stop until he had finished. I think that's what makes him so great. . . .

"People who meditate don't have any fear. There's no such thing as 'not going to be able to do this.' If you're in the presence of these guys before they go on stage they become tigers. They're no longer there at all. They are in their own 'other' space. They are in this meditation, and they move into that, and nobody and nothing can stop them. They're superhuman because they live in a different world.

"When you move with Michael, you can sense this energy level. It's an energy field he's in. He wants to whip people up to give them this energy as well. Most people like this don't sleep very much, two or three hours a

night maximum, because their mind works so fast. They don't need rest. They convey the energy and eat it very quickly, like a vampire. Their subconscious sees this energy and it just sucks the energy from them. . . .

"When he first danced in his own show he became who he was meant to be, and I think that's the secret—become who you are meant to be.

"It all sounds really strange but it's like a presence of God in a moving form. That's what it was. He wasn't there. It wasn't Michael Flatley, it was this movement that was flying through the air."

When a production like *Lord of the Dance* is riding on you, you discover lots of odd responsibilities. World-class training was the least of it. I also had to have my legs insured. They were—for £25 million. As I recall, Harvey Goldsmith paid the premium, which was £168,000.

The shoes I wore to create the show were also very special. One pair had aluminum taps made from the metal from the nose cone of the NASA Shuttle. Scientists in Houston sent the aerospace-grade metal to me saying it would help my performances. I intend to keep those shoes as long as I can.

I also still have the dancing shoes I wore on Eurovision night, although I've had to have them rebuilt many times. I tend to save my shoes from my most important shows so I can auction them off later for charity. But I use the Eurovision shoes all the time. They have their own special sound. The taps are from Chicago, the heels from New York, and the Spanish soles from Seville. They're three or four times heavier than most other shoes. I wear them to create steps and routines, and until about five minutes before I go on stage. Then, when I put on lighter shoes, it's easier to fly across the stage.

Kelley Byrne: "Everything Michael does, he does to perfection. He's a proper perfectionist. I'd be reading a novel and he'd be reading volumes all about improving your knowledge and how to do this, and how to do that, and he'd never take a minute off. Never.

"All he does is walk, walk, walk and think, think, think. Most of us would be happy sitting there watching TV. He never watches TV, always thinking, thinking, thinking. He loves movies but wouldn't know what was on TV. He knows what music he likes but doesn't listen to the radio. He's one of these creative people who have so much going on in their own minds that other stuff is an intrusion."

Chapter Twenty-four

Goodbye, My Love

WE HAD THE FINAL DRESS REHEARSAL of *Lord of the Dance* at 6 p.m. on June 27, 1996. My show was about to take off, but my marriage was collapsing.

Everyone who meets Beata tells me I'm a fool—that I should have stayed married to her. I agree. How could I walk away from one of the most beautiful women in the world? One of my best buddies said he felt like punching me after meeting Beata. He said he wanted to knock some sense in me.

My family loved Beata, and so did I. I still do.

I know it was all my fault. I'm a driven sort of guy, and I can't do anything to change that. I'd achieved great success later in life—after Beata and I had married—and I was intoxicated by that. So maybe I wasn't thinking straight. For years I'd been the only professional Irish dancer in the world. I'd lived out of suitcases, but we'd kept the marriage going. Now that I'd made it, our relationship had become far more distant and difficult. And there were other temptations for both of us.

I couldn't expect Beata to wait until things got back to "normal." And, hand on heart, I wanted to be free, to be able to concentrate on my work—and my new life—without any lies or guilt.

Was I too selfish? Maybe! Did I want to look back and say with regret, "I had a nice marriage. I ran home after *Riverdance* with my tail between my legs"? Or did I want to say, with pride, "I created new shows that will live on. I stayed and fought. I created years of work for many, many talented people"?

My private life was frantic, but it could not take my focus off the challenge, the fight that lay before me. My shows would go on to employ hundreds of people. My marriage involved just the two of us. I had to stay on in Dublin and fight for my dream.

Patrick Flatley: "Beata was awful close to us. She had a great sense of humor hanging around with us.

"She knew all the jokes, and Mike never stopped laughing. They get along great. He sends her flowers on her birthday. Just totally one of the family."

Michael Flatley, Senior: "Beata's a big, tall beautiful girl. It's a shame. They didn't get a divorce because they didn't get along . . . it's just that his world was so different to hers. They just grew apart."

"Don't you want a nineteen-year-old to make love to you?"

I was having a face-off with Kelley Byrne. And I'll admit that wasn't exactly what she said. In reality, she was much more passionate. But I'll just leave the rest to your imagination.

I'd moved to a terrific little house in a square just off Marlborough Road in Dublin. Kelley was not living there but was staying with me most of the time. I was still married and still hoping to work things out with Beata.

Beata and I talked constantly on the phone, and I thought if she flew over from California we might be able to resolve our relationship.

Meanwhile, the situation was tearing my heart out. I was being eaten alive between my passion for Kelley and my deep love and respect for Beata. It was too much–especially on top of the show and all the financial pressures.

So one night I decided that in all fairness, I must go back to Beata. It was the true-hearted thing to do. Even when Kelley came over to the house–and she looked stunning–I turned down the chance to have sex with her, for maybe the first time in our relationship. I heard myself saying, "No. No means no. I'm going back to my wife. I can't do this anymore. She's coming over in a few days to see me. So that's it, Kelley. I can't. This is just wrong."

Kelley had an inimitable style, like no one else in the world ever had or will have. She tossed her beautiful hair back from her face, threw off her sweater, and revealed herself. "Don't you want me?" she said.

I looked at her and felt her eyes burn through me. We were madly in love whether I liked it or not. I realized I had no choice anymore. I was her slave.

My wife arrived three days later, and I sat her down and told her the truth. Kelley drove me crazy. I couldn't escape from her charms. She was a perfect match for that time in my life. Kelley was Irish through and through. She was also a dancer who understood all the goings-on with *Riverdance.* We would talk for hours at high speed.

Kelley was as wild as a bog fire but she truly loved me. Meanwhile, Beata and I hadn't truly talked for many months. Fate had driven us apart.

But when I told Beata the whole truth, it broke her. She banged her fists on the kitchen wall and dissolved into tears. Never will I forget those beautiful bright blue Polish eyes filled with pain as she listened to my words.

I hated myself. But I couldn't keep on betraying her. It was killing me. It was killing everybody.

Beata is a brave woman. She knew I had to stay and contend with *Riverdance*. In a way she was so much more mature than me, and she respected my will to fight.

We suffered through our days together in Dublin and we both knew that our parting was for the best. We didn't make a final decision then–that didn't happen until Beata was back in Los Angeles–but we'd started the process that would end in our divorce.

I knew I'd failed her as a husband. I'd failed to be her white knight. I must have been a terrible disappointment to her. She is such a classy woman.

I'll always love her.

Chapter Twenty-Five

Victory!

I described the Michael Flatley phenomenon
as Irish dancing meets Michael Jackson.

Liam Miller,
former Director of Programmes for RTE, 1997

On July 2, 1996, *Lord of the Dance* opened at The Point Theatre in Dublin. I couldn't have asked for a warmer reception. I knew the true believers were out there in the theater. They all showed up that night, and I got exactly what I wanted. But it wasn't until the fifth encore that I began to cry.

People have a great way of reading between the lines. There had been so many stories in the press labelling me greedy and egotistical after the *Riverdance* split. In buying tickets the Irish people were supporting me, showing that they believed the rift was about artistic control for me.

There was magic in the air, and the dancers were all fired up. The audience gave us so much. The show soared.

Lord of the Dance was a hit. We could have sold out for a year! I thanked God for what had been achieved. I was raised a Roman Catholic and as a youngster I went to mass every Sunday. I still attend when I can. I try to pray to God, especially when I want to thank Him.

I'm spiritual in that I believe the universe has a method to everything, and everything that happens is for a reason. I may not be as religious as I once was, but after the opening night of *Lord of the Dance*, I felt truly blessed.

I was also exhausted. For weeks of rehearsals–not to mention publicity, production duties, and a million and one other responsibilities–I'd been going way over the human speed limit. Each performance, with eight solos and nine costume changes, was always a test. Afterwards, I had to spend nearly half an hour resting on a bed of ice to bring down my body temperature. And if I didn't eat soon after a show, I'd soon lose several pounds. I took to eating steak for breakfast and a second high-protein meal around 5 p.m. A nutritionist worked with me to make sure I got essential fats and lots of green food like spirulina to boost my energy and alkalize my system. Wheat-grass juice was also a big help. Soon, careful eating had become part of my routine, along with the weight training, shadow-boxing, skipping, stretching, and of course, the all-important warm-ups before the show. Missing even a part of this routine might mean I wouldn't have the energy to make it through the show–and there were eight shows a week! And not just in Dublin. We were also booked to travel around the U.K. Then on to the Coliseum Theatre in London.

Big plans, to be sure. But it looked as though we were going to make it.

Against all the odds.

London's Daily Mail, *July 5, 1996, set off its review beneath the headline "Fantastic Lord of Irish dance," with a rave notice from the critic Michael Coveney: "Michael Flatley, begetter, inspiration and erstwhile star of Ireland's most successful export since whiskey, butter or blarney, sensationally proves that there is indeed life after* Riverdance.

"Glorious life, too.

"If his latest creation, Lord of the Dance, *is intended as a two-fingered gesture to the global company he launched so memorably for Ireland's Eurovision Song Contest, and which subsequently dispensed with his services, then it is the Irish equivalent of a Churchillian salute.*

"At once heroic, commanding and awesome.

"Certainly his refusal to even mention the name of his former triumph in his programme biography speaks volumes for his feelings on the matter.

"In Lord of the Dance, *Flatley moves traditional Irish dancing even further across the boundaries of dance expression than its predecessor.*

"The unthinkable has been achieved.

"For Flatley has married an erotic liberation of flamenco to his more circumspect but closely-related, Irish counterpart. . . .

"Flatley himself is ideally cast.

"His is the avenging force which overcomes the menacing powers of evil which threaten the ancient spirits of the clans. And to it he brings those qualities which mark out the truly great dancer, no matter what discipline he or she embraces.

"It is the charismatic presence matched to a superb technical mastery which has the power to transport the audience into the realms of fantasy.

"He also excudes a muscular gravitas which is the stuff that stars are made of.

"All this adds up to fully justify the triumphalism of his euphoric curtain calls as he leads his company over and over again through the rhythmic stomping of their exultant finale.

"It most certainly looks as if the indomitable Mr Flatley is poised on the edge of another worldwide conquest."

The film director Michael Winner said: "I was brought up on Fred Astaire and Gene Kelly. I never thought I'd see another dancer to compare.

"But Michael Flatley in his own show Lord of the Dance *is their equal."*

* * *

Riverdance *and* Lord of the Dance *veteran Niamh O'Brien: "He made Irish dancing cool. And that was just the beginning. So much has happened in so little time. A revolution."*

O'Brien's sisters, Aoibheann and Derval, have also danced in Riverdance *and* Lord of the Dance. *Aoibheann was a long-term member of Flatley's Las Vegas-based troupe, where she said: "We've met stars who have come to the show like Madonna, Tom Jones, Jack Nicholson, Diana Ross, and Celine Dion.*

"I know it's a cliché, but the whole thing really is a dream come true. We once danced for one hundred and ten thousand people in an open-air concert in Budapest. It was like a football crowd–it's impossible to describe. And I can't remember one night Lord of the Dance *hasn't had a standing ovation."*

Marie Duffy: "We've had so many opening nights, and each one has a special memory. . . . I suppose the opening in Dublin was just unforgettable. It surpassed all our wildest dreams."

Cora Smyth is one of the original Lord of the Dance *fiddle players. She said in Dublin in October 2004: "Michael wanted us to be part of a spectacular show–almost like a rock 'n' roll event.*

"Growing up being part of the Irish music scene, Michael was very familiar with the backgrounds that we came from. So he understood that we weren't particularly show girls or used to a big show like that, so we had our own kind of take on it. It worked out great, and he was happy, and he was very encouraging and inspiring all the time.

"I was involved in theater, so it wasn't totally new to me at all that I would have to move around the stage. . . . Obviously Michael was hugely encouraging and totally supportive. . . .

"I think everybody learned an awful lot from him, because none of us would really have been alongside someone who would have that sort of stage presence and star quality. . . .

"You need to create an atmosphere on stage, which was what Michael wanted us to do—to involve the audience with that so they were part of it and would clap.

"Well, I like to enjoy what I'm doing. I've never really seen the show as a job or anything. Every night you want to get that adrenaline rush from an audience. I love being on the stage and I love playing music. . . . We have had a fantastic time and we've been incredibly successful with the show."

Chapter Twenty-six

Agony and Miracles

If you are distressed by anything external,
the pain is not due to the thing itself but your own estimate of it,
and this you have the power to revoke at any moment.

Marcus Aurelius

After the success of our Dublin opening, I knew we could go to the top. I also knew we had no financial security. *Lord of the Dance* was a money-hungry production—the rent, the publicity, the stagehands, the musicians and dancers. It cost a small fortune to keep the show up and running, and if tickets weren't selling briskly—and constantly—the previous nights' standing ovations wouldn't help us a bit.

I was also concerned about the technical aspects of the show. I didn't want my dancers working in cramped conditions, without decent dressing rooms to prepare in and no room to warm up in. I didn't consider space a luxury, but a necessity, and according to my standards, not all English theaters could accommodate us.

As I tried to ensure that my dancers and I would have the conditions we needed, I was looking toward our prime target—the Royal Command Performance for Prince Charles at the London Coliseum on July 23. As it happened, that was also the birthday of my late grandmother Hannah, so it felt as though there were a special blessing on that day.

Before it was time to dance for His Highness, we had a booking in Liverpool, where we got a sensational reception. Then we went on to the Manchester Apollo Theatre, where we were scheduled to play four nights before the huge event in London. And then disaster struck.

Pain is a part of every dancer's life, but I've never allowed it to worry me. If you let it, pain—and the fear of pain—can take over your life. The key is to make friends with pain: accept it, release it, and then get on with your life. So I'd noticed the sore Achilles tendon that had been troubling me for the past few days, but I hadn't paid it much attention.

Some might say I was being reckless. I'd been working extremely hard, and I was already thirty-seven years old—a fairly advanced age for a dancer. The average age of my troupe was only nineteen. And I, as the soloist, was working much harder than anyone else in the company.

To make matters worse, the Manchester Apollo was not a huge theater, leaving me little room to undertake my usual warm-up. Warm-ups are crucial for a dancer, allowing you to stretch out tight muscles, to literally warm them up by getting the blood flowing. Feats of agility and grace that would be impossible "cold" become, if not easy, at least doable when you've warmed up.

But that night, we were running late, so my warm-up—usually an hour—had to be cut to only five minutes, and in a cramped space, at that. Then the music started, the audience was waiting, and I heard my cue. What could I do? I flew on stage for my usual dramatic entrance.

Seven seconds later, I tore my calf muscle. The pain was sudden, sharp, and overwhelming, as though a bullet had ripped into my flesh. I'd never felt pain like that in my life.

Almost worse than the pain was the sensation of literally hearing the muscle tear—a terrifying sound to a dancer who depends upon his legs. I tried to catch my breath.

The audience heard the rip as well, and they were gasping, too, averting their eyes and then looking back at me in horror. I felt as though the room had suddenly shifted into slow motion as I mechanically continued dancing away. Should I stop? Was I going to fall? I bit my lip so hard it bled.

The agony rippled through me, stronger than before. *I must get through this,* I thought. It seemed unthinkable not to finish the dance. Then my front foot slipped to my side instead of kicking up over my head. Somehow I managed to hobble through the rest of the steps, but the audience could see that I was in serious trouble, and the cast was mortified. They had to carry me off at the end of it.

In the dressing room I slammed down two double shots of John Jameson Irish whiskey while I waited for medical help to arrive. The pain bit at me like a rabid dog. *It's all over,* I thought. *What if I never dance again?* It was a thought I could not allow to remain within my consciousness for more than a split second. Ruthlessly I suppressed it. But I knew I was facing my worst nightmare.

If I'd been more in control of myself, I might have wondered why my manager John Reid hadn't come over to see if I was okay. But the rest of the cast was stepping through the show with the understudy, and nobody was there to hold my hand. I thought about what might happen to the show if I couldn't return to my solo role. No one would be saying, "Never you mind, Michael, you just rest up and feel better." What they'd be saying was, "We want our money back!"

The anger I felt energized me. *No,* I thought. *I've come too far to stop now. It'll take more than this to keep me off the stage!* I was determined that this injury would *not* be the literal Achilles heel that finally brought me down.

I got the emergency help I needed. Then it was time to call in the best physiotherapists in the business. How could these experts help me dance again?

The first physiotherapist announced, "If you stay off your leg and you really go through the therapy that we prescribe, in six months you'll be walking normally. But you're not going to be dancing for at least twelve months."

No, I thought. Unacceptable. Who else could help me?

The second guy had worse news. "This is a very serious injury, Mr. Flatley. I'm afraid your dancing days are over for the foreseeable future."

No way. Next!

The third physio, an Australian, examined me thoroughly and then gave me a long, hard look. I don't know what he saw in me, but he said simply, "Why don't we just see how we go, mate? I'll strap it up and let's hope for the best!"

I looked at him and saw nothing but hope. "You're hired!" I said.

The Coliseum was sold out. I had to be back on stage in London in four days. Of course, some of my concern came from pride, and some from my wish to dance for Prince Charles, and some from my sense of loyalty to my troupe, whose jobs depended on the show continuing to run. But to be honest, I was also in an extremely precarious position financially. The show was doing great—but we still hadn't broken even. If I let an understudy finish out the run for me, God knew what effect it might have on ticket sales. I ran the risk of losing absolutely everything.

So I turned to Derry Ann Morgan, the dance therapist I'd come to know and trust on *Riverdance.* Besides her expertise in massage and dance therapy, Derry Ann was a skilled healer in Reiki, a Japanese approach to channeling universal energy to help the body heal itself. So basically, I asked Derry Ann to help me create a miracle.

If she had any doubts, she never let me know. All I heard from her was faith. We sat together in a darkened room, and Derry Ann helped me focus my mind on healing the injury. With any type of treatment, it helps to have an open mind. Any doctor will tell you that the patient with a negative attitude is less likely to get better than the patient who's full of optimism and determination. With esoteric healing, which depends so heavily on mobilizing your mind and spirit, positive thinking is essential.

For four days, all my energy was channeled into healing my leg. I visualized light pouring into the muscles–healing light. I spent every minute helping my body to heal.

After the first few days I could feel the difference. But there was still no way I could dance. I couldn't even walk.

I didn't care. Somehow, I knew, I would dance in the London premiere. I didn't know how it would happen, but I was sure that it would.

On the fateful morning, I still couldn't walk. I was warned again and again not to dance that night–not even to try. I wouldn't go along with the doctor's advice. But I did agree to have a doctor and two physiotherapists off stage as a precaution.

A few hours before the show, my leg was tightly bandaged from my thigh down to my ankle. When the clock showed an hour till curtain time, they shot me up with hydrocortisone and painkillers and I convinced myself I could dance.

Slowly, I began to limp in circles around the stage. I felt twinges, but the pain was bearable, if only just. Gradually, building up momentum, I began to walk faster and faster. Then I started jogging and running. I had the strangest sensation that I was not alone–that someone who loved me very much was shadowing me at every step. It was Hannah, I realized. My grandmother. Even though she'd passed on a few years earlier, I'd never lost the sense of her. Now, suddenly, she seemed closer than ever.

And then I began to dance.

It was exhilarating! Only a few hours before, I'd been unable to move more than a few steps. And now I was leaping, flying, kicking up my heels.

I didn't want to overdo it before the show. When I determined I could dance, I slowed my movements, gently, gradually, until finally I had cooled off. "Leave an empty seat in the audience tonight," I told the house manager. Ever since then, every single time I dance, I make sure there's a seat for Hannah.

The show was a roaring success, even though my leg was still black and blue from top to toe. What's even more amazing is that my leg healed itself show by show from that night on, and I've never missed a show. Let me tell you, whatever happens to your body, it's all in your mind. I'd always believed it, but now I knew for sure: We can create miracles for ourselves if only we believe. But you can't just wish for a miracle. You have to work for it. And then you've got to *know*, with every fiber of your being, that it can happen. It isn't hope. It's faith.

I'm convinced I gave the best performance of my life that night. The pain was brutal when I stopped dancing, but I'd given my all with every step. I saw the audience rise to their feet, and I knew I'd made Hannah proud.

Although I'd never before been injured to that extent, I'd always known that Irish dancing is one of the most difficult and punishing forms of dance. Although my torn muscle was the first time I'd ever had to miss a performance, it was hardly the first time I'd been injured. During that first Dublin run of *Lord of the Dance*, the muscles in my hands seized up—I trapped some nerves in my neck and suddenly, I couldn't open my hands. They healed only after lots of massage and physical therapy.

I'd had other torn leg muscles over the years, and by now, my big-toe joints hardly move at all. To make matters worse, one of my small toes has a small fracture that can't heal, since I'm constantly on my feet. Another bone at the top of my foot bothers me when I do certain toe stands. I know when it's going to hurt, though, so I'm prepared for it. My back aches sometimes, my knees get very stiff, and my legs shake all night in my sleep. But I'm not complaining. These pains are how I know that I'm a dancer. I've made friends with my pain–I've earned it.

Martin Flitton: "I got a phone call on June 24, 1996, while I was working on another show for Harvey Goldsmith, that a production manager who was working on the Lord of the Dance *was leaving to go and do some shows for Michael Jackson.*

"Harvey asked me to take over all the technical and equipment side of the show for a couple of weeks.

"That was my first meeting with Michael. I explained the situation. He was fine. We went down and we looked at the stage.

"He reworked out how the dance and dancers could be used in the best way. He called all the dancers in and restaged the performance to suit the size of the venue.

"In Manchester we extended the stage out–and that's where Michael incurred a leg injury. Michael's understudy had to come on, and we had to arrange doctors, and he was in a lot of pain.

"After Manchester we had a big opening, so we did the rest of the shows with the understudy, which presented its own problems because obviously people pay to see Michael Flatley.

"Some people were refunded, some were very aggressive. It was a nightmare. We had people so frustrated that they could not see Michael dance that they were spitting at us. We were on tenterhooks whether Michael would do the opening night in London.

"I went to his dressing room that night and the doctors were strapping his leg, his thigh, and giving him pain-killing injections. He was in a lot of pain but nevertheless he did the opening night.

"That was unbelievable. Each night it was a case of doctors examining the swelling and strapping him up into shape.

"After the Coliseum we had a two-week break and we redesigned the whole set."

Kelley Byrne: "Michael pushed himself to the limit all the time. There were times [during the tours] he was on oxygen. He got very ill in Australia, and some shows had to be canceled. He was in hospital in Brisbane on nebulizers to help him breathe. In England he ripped his leg but was right back up for a London Coliseum show with a muscle that was only Sellotaped together.

"He gets paid a lot of money, but nobody has ever worked so hard for their money. He earned every penny.

"In London, doctors were injecting cortisone into his knees. He desperately wanted to do the show. I think the producers were very much, 'If you don't go on, the show won't go on.' It was in the first two weeks of the show and it was all dependent upon him. There was no question of him not going on. I don't think they forced him, I think he wanted to be there. . . .

"Michael told me that to achieve what you want you picture it, you put it up on your personal screen and then just before the time, let go. And it will happen. He's just so focused. There's very few people like that. Whoever they are, they're very successful types, because they just go for it no matter what it costs."

Pat Henry: "I was in London for the opening at the Coliseum and with my wife, I went backstage to Michael. . . . He opened the bandage on his leg and the blood just gushed out.

"He'd had an injection before he went on stage because Prince Charles and Diana were in the theater that night, and there was no way was he going to miss that show. It wouldn't have mattered if he had no leg, he was doing the show, and that's what he did. In his dressing room afterwards, his leg was in an awful state. . . .

"Michael never missed a step. It was amazing control; there are very few people that have that much determination that it overrides

everything. I think it goes into . . . his business attitude and it goes into his shows and it goes into his life."

Derry Ann Morgan: "In Manchester, when Michael came off stage he had a severe injury–the pain was like he had a bullet in the back of his leg.

"Michael was really upset that he couldn't go back on stage. There was an awful lot of confusion because it hadn't happened before–but they had understudies. I told them to get the understudy because Michael couldn't get back out.

"People were in denial. Michael was upset and I remember saying to him, 'Which pain is worse? The pain that you can't dance or the pain that shows as you walk?'

"He looked at me. And I said to him, 'You know you can't dance. You can't dance for a very, very long time.'

"I could see that light in his eyes and he said, 'Yes, I can.'

"We went on down to London. I got him to picture himself out on the stage dancing as if he had no injuries, with the energy going into the body. He was good at that.

"The day of opening night he was hopping around. We walked out on to the stage to the arena–[the same general area] where the injury had happened [in Manchester], and we had our little talk and just walked to the back of the stage. He said he was okay and he was ready to go.

"He literally . . . danced his way off that stage and never looked back. He never missed a performance. I don't think he has since. Did he dance with Hannah? Of course, he did."

Chapter Twenty-seven

Bigger Is Better

Nobody realized at the time how successful [Irish dancing in] arenas would be if you ever pulled it off. But Michael did.

HARVEY GOLDSMITH

I'D BUILT *Lord of the Dance* as a spectacular. I'd created a big, big show. I dreamed of bringing it to arenas and football stadiums—to playing in rock-star-sized venues. But John Reid and Harvey Goldsmith wanted to contain the show in theaters.

I knew the show would work in the larger venues. With the big screens that had been developed for rock concerts, the dance steps would be on full view for all the audience. As far as I was concerned, we were going to compete with Michael Jackson and we were going to beat him.

I saw myself as a man standing naked on the nose of the Concorde with my arms out, my eyes wide open, the supersonic jet flying as fast as it could possibly go. It seemed to me that John and Harvey saw me in the backseat of a Rolls-Royce saying meekly, "Thank you very much for that theater." And then they saw me driving home to my hotel suite with their voices echoing in my ear as they said, "Be happy with your lot, son."

I'll never deny that John and Harvey both had brilliant careers. They were two of entertainment's big boys and were used to calling the shots. With all their experience they could see many reasons why my plan would fail. What I wanted had never been done before and I was the new kid on the block. So why should they listen to me?

No reason—except the fact that I was proved right.

Finally, John lost patience with me and we had a long fight. "You can't do arenas," he insisted. "You're a fucking dancer, you'll never be the main act. You've got to do theaters."

I kept saying to him, "John, you're wrong. I know you've a great reputation, but you're totally wrong."

He shouted back, "Arenas? Big screens? Over my dead body! This show will never have big screens as long as I'm alive!"

When that fight was over, I came to a painful realization: for John and me, this was the beginning of the end. I didn't want any more negativity to plague my career. I wanted to be surrounded by people who shared my vision—and that wasn't John Reid, in my opinion.

Harvey was there while John and I were sparring. I turned around and said, "Harvey, I'm going to do this show in a football stadium some day."

Harvey replied, "You can't do the show in a stadium—you're a dancer." When I still wouldn't back down, he conceded, "Maybe we can do one arena."

They couldn't see what seemed obvious to me. They just didn't get it. John Reid repeated to me, "Over my dead body will you ever do arenas."

Who was the artist? Who was the creator? Who was the man in charge? And, more important, who was the man paying for it all? John Reid was about to learn just how determined I was.

Harvey Goldsmith: "When we set out to open the show in London, Michael started to show his prowess off as a showman, and we had a pretty wild party. The first run of U.K. shows was a huge success. Then Michael started to take the whole project over.

"Michael wanted to be in arenas, not theaters. There . . . were complaints that playing in an arena not all the people could see the feet, but Michael had an answer and had this thing that he wanted to go big and be big.

"He was driven. . . . He just had this whole idea in his head that he wanted to be bigger and better than anybody."

Chapter Twenty-eight

Going Global

Flatley is unique. He has spent the bulk of his life
doing something *nobody else can do.*

The Independent,
London, January 11, 1997

DESPITE JOHN AND HARVEY'S SKEPTICISM, *Lord of the Dance* turned into a worldwide entertainment hurricane, a high-energy mixture of theater, dance, and the magnificent spectacle that people had come to expect from a top-flight rock show. Our ancient dance, combined with futuristic effects, gave people the impression of going back in time—and being catapulted into the future.

I'd been told so often it could not be done. All you can do is climb to the top of the mountain, they told me. Then, you have to come down.

No, I said. Then you fly!

Harvey had done a brilliant job with the Down Under dates. The folks at *Riverdance* were trying to get an Irish dance exclusive run in

Australia—a move that only made it clear how afraid they were of us. But Harvey made sure we were booked across the continent, and we hit Australia like a tornado, selling a quarter of a million tickets in ten days.

The Aussies were a wonderful audience—they screamed and howled and generally weren't shy about showing their enthusiasm. They came to the shows ready for a good time and we gave it to them. This, I thought, was the real beginning of the show's international success. Who cared what happened with *Riverdance*? We were no longer the underdogs. We were kings. Money was rolling in from our tour and the video sales, and finally, around Christmas 1996, it looked as though I'd cleared my own investment and that we were about to break even.

Yet despite our runaway success, John and I were still having huge arguments, usually about using video screens for arena shows—if they would work, how they would work. But I'd believed in myself for too long to give up on my dreams now! Even though John was dead set against doing arenas, I went ahead and played one anyway, at Wembley.

Suddenly, there was John, forcing his way into my Wembley dressing room. I certainly didn't want to see him, not before an opening night. I'd already started getting ready for the show and I was keyed up, tense, focused on the extraordinary demands of the next two hours. But John stood before me, swearing, shouting, kicking a wastepaper basket, throwing faxes in the air.

My nerves were raging, and they went straight to my stomach. I gave as good as I got, but later, after he left, I vomited. How could he behave this way, especially before a show?

Our arena shows were huge hits. Wembley gave us a record-breaking sold-out run of twenty-one shows, proving once and for all that *Lord of the Dance* could play in rock-star venues. And yes, we used big screens, much to the delight of the audiences.

John was great when it came to dealing with questions and problems but it frustrated me when he didn't like my answers. He made me feel felt cornered, unable to run with my ideas. I was like a caged tiger.

Even though John was around to fight with me about arena shows, I didn't feel that he gave me enough attention at any other time. I was delegated to his sidekick and subagent, Derek. Derek was a nice guy but from my point of view I was paying for full-time management from John and not getting it, and at an especially pivotal time in my career.

John, on the other hand, seemed to be intimidated by me. Plus, he was a volatile man, which is not at all my style. I try to be strong, I'll surely fight to get what I want, but I'd rather not make a noise about it or go out of my way to upset people. My personal assistant during the early *Lord of the Dance* run was Sharon Ashley, a dedicated and hard-working woman, whose dealings with John were unpleasant, to say the least.

In September 2004, Sharon Ashley said: "I've tried to blank John Reid from my memory. I really don't want to remember what went on. There were some horrible moments.

"Once, backstage, he lost it with me and called me a 'fucking fat-arsed cow.' He ranted at me, saying I was fired. He couldn't even do that–I was employed by Michael as his personal assistant."

When I returned to London, I discovered that our *Lord of the Dance* video had made number one on the U.K. charts. No one had even bothered to tell me. That totaled up all the sums against John–I simply couldn't go on with him. I quietly began talks with lawyers in America and at the same time started meeting with Bill Tennant, the legendary and extremely well-connected Hollywood agent and manager who eventually did take over as my manager. He came on board while *Lord of the Dance* was playing to eight-thousand-seat houses in Newcastle, England.

I knew the breakup with John Reid Management would set off fireworks, but I was honestly astonished by the fuss that ensued. My lawyers had sent an official letter of dismissal to John Reid Management. Instead of handling the matter quietly, as I expected, they came back with a public statement:

> We have been informed Michael Flatley no longer wishes us to act as his manager. We regret, we have no alternative but to recognize the relationship cannot continue in these circumstances. We will nonetheless be enforcing our contractual rights against Mr Flatley.

Apparently, "enforcing our contractual rights" translated into a huge lawsuit for breach of contract against me, leaving me little alternative but to bring a countersuit, claiming deceit.

I'd originally hired Reid to take on *Riverdance*. Now, I was hiring Bill Tennant to handle Reid. Both times, I'd end up doing it all myself—alone.

Martin Flitton: "My mother died while I was in Australia and I flew back to England so I didn't see the last few dates—and again, the stature of the man. He booked me first class. I arrived back for the funeral. Michael had sent a wreath.

"The whole world was alive with him and he still took time to do that. I think that cemented the friendship with Michael. He actually did care. A lot of people said: 'Sorry to hear . . . ' He genuinely was.

"Later, the troupe came back and we were starting Wembley in January 1997, and doing all arenas. In Australia Michael had said we needed screens—and we did, to allow the vast crowds to see. We were playing to

audiences of twelve thousand a night in Sydney and I knew we could get screens in.

"[John Reid objected, and it] came to a head in Wembley. I was in the production office and Michael was in his dressing room. Derek arrived first and then John Reid. The first I knew about it was John Reid came out past my office door screaming and shouting. My immediate reaction was to go and see how Michael was. Michael was fairly calm–seething but calm.

"What you don't do is have these confrontations before and after he goes on stage. You don't suffer, but the audience will suffer.

"As it turned out Michael put on probably the best show I've ever seen up until that point. He was on fire. He's never had a bad show, but some nights he was on fire. . . . I think every new challenge brought a little bit more out of him. He shows it. I remember that night because I went out to watch thinking that he wouldn't be in good form. He was on fire."

Harvey Goldsmith: "Michael created a show that was too big to go into theaters, and he didn't want to play theaters anyway. He wanted to play Wembley Arena as opposed to a theater–and that's what he did.

"We did a huge marketing exercise and it really started to take off; there was tons of publicity and he was out and about at parties and being seen by girls like [the famous model] Caprice. . . .

"John Reid was scared [of the consequences of Michael's American tour]. He didn't think he could deliver [a successful tour]. Michael kept pushing him.

"There were arguments breaking out, and then Michael somehow got to the Oscar people and persuaded them that he and the company should appear, which was quite extraordinary.

"At that point Michael became unstoppable. I was kind of rode out of America. We did well out of it financially with what we did.

"The next thing is my father had just died, and I got a phone call out

of the blue from Michael. He was in Barbados and he phoned me up and said, 'I'm really sorry. I heard your father's just died.'. . .

"I really tried hard to get the pair of them [John and Michael] back together again. It was one of those things.

"At that time Michael was out and about everywhere. He was going through women at a rate of knots. His profile was everywhere and he was as famous as David Beckham. Michael was a bit of an enigma but to his absolute credit, he pulled it off financially and materially in what he wanted as a show. . . .

"He's a driven person. He knows what he wants. He has tunnel vision. I live with that. A lot of artists are like that. . . . I think he's been so successful on what he's done that there isn't a downside. I think he's done absolutely brilliantly."

What got me through this difficult time was my faith in *Lord of the Dance*–and the way people around the world seemed to love the show. I'd never had an audience response like this one. The audience would stand up three or four times during the performances and throw things at the stage with joy. Every night after the show, I'd find a crowd waiting for me, from age five to eighty-five–different races, nationalities, religions, attitudes–different people, all united in the pleasure they found in *Lord of the Dance.*

My fans took to the Internet, starting more than four hundred Web sites featuring news and gossip about *Lord of the Dance*, my career, and me. Some of my fans even started calling themselves "Flatheads."

There was one more almighty challenge ahead of us: the United States. I got a great response from my appearances on *Larry King Live* and Jay Leno's *Tonight* show, which helped to reassure me. But there was so much riding on the American tour. By 1997, when we were booked for America, we were certainly doing well–*Lord of the Dance* was bringing in more than one million pounds each week.

But we weren't out of the woods yet. America was still our biggest challenge–and perhaps our biggest prize. If we did well there, we would truly be on top of the world. But a poor box office in the States could bring everything crashing down.

David Wigg reported in the Daily Express, *London, on December 3, 1996: " 'Lord of the Dance' has become one of the hottest tickets in arenas around the world.*

"Original talent Michael Flatley's UK tour sold more than 210,000 tickets and grossed more than £5,300,000.

"More than one quarter of a million tickets for his Australian shows were snapped up at a cost of £13 million in ten days."

Martin Flitton: "I had lots and lots of discussions with Michael [about stadium shows]. Michael had a vision, and unfortunately other people pooh-poohed the idea. A dance show in an arena?

" 'What do you mean ten thousand seats? You're not going to get ten thousand people to come and see this.'

"Michael did.

"You learn that Irish dance is all over the world, everywhere somebody has emigrated [to], but the phenomenal success that Michael had experienced in Ireland and Britain and Australia created the Michaelmania Down Under.

"I mean, you hear about Michael Jackson and Madonna and the rock bands of yesterday, the Beatles and the Stones, and all the other hype, but believe me you've never seen so many people at an airport in Perth where Michael flew in.

"If I hadn't seen it, I could never have been convinced about such a pandemonium. It was that unbelievable. . . .

"Michael was bombarded by the audiences–all over the world he's been showered with bouquets of flowers, single roses, greeting cards, love letters, condoms wrapped in envelopes with telephone numbers and

email addresses. He's been presented with everything from teddy bears and sweaters to home-customized Agent Provocateur knickers.

"Before I really got to know Michael Flatley, I used to have this strange experience. I always used to go out and watch the opening part of the show and I always thought Michael was looking at me.

"It didn't matter where I'd place myself in that arena, he was watching me. I used to think, 'Oh, bloody hell, what've I done wrong? Am I in for a bollocking at the interval?'

"After a few months, I realized that that was his quality. It wasn't just me. Everybody thinks they're the person he's looking at. That is the gift.

"Nobody I've worked with–and I've worked with Sting, Billy Joel, Eric Clapton, and lots of others–have had that ability, and it haunted me for weeks. He has that quality. Michael is the ultimate showman.

"Not only can he dance, he is a showman. That's the blend of success."

Marie Duffy: "I go out to visit the troupes [performing around the world], and the hairs still come up on the back of my neck when I see people shouting and cheering and the standing ovations–and this is all these years later.

"You go to a different country, a different troupe, and you get that little tingle and pounding in your heart . . . to see the reaction of the audience.

"I feel that Lord of the Dance *is a classic. It stands there with the greats of musicals for all time.*

"You see dancers that come in very young at about sixteen years of age and you see the potential. And gradually, a year, eighteen months, two years down the line, you start to train them as lead dancers. It's inspiring to see them out there commanding a whole audience–so satisfying. Seeing how they develop–you never tire of it.

"Success hasn't changed Michael. . . . He has always kept his feet on the ground. . . . He always speaks well to people and of people and always has the time of day for everyone. When he would walk into an

arena, he would have the time of day to spend a few words with everybody, whether it is the stage manager or the cleaners–whoever, whatever, he has a special word. He's always very encouraging to everybody. . . . I think success has even made him a better person if that's possible, because I've never heard him do or say a mean thing about anybody.

"He loves the dancers, and he wouldn't allow anybody to do or say anything or hurt them in any shape or form. He's the first in to defend them no matter what, even if I'm scolding them for something!"

Kelley Byrne: "He looks after everybody. Michael's a decent human being. He's had his tough times and he understands life on the road. He was never in the business of making the dancers miserable. He's a dancer and always wants his troupes to be happy and content. . . .

"One time in Australia, one of the dancers rang up and said, 'Look, Michael, we're in a really dodgy area. The hotel's okay, but not a good area.' It was 1 a.m., but he got up, got in the car, and went to look at the hotel. Almost immediately he said, 'Right, get the coach and get everybody out of here. Put them in my hotel.' "

Marie Duffy: "The main thing is that it is such an energetic, powerful show and the energy . . . of the cast never fails to infect the audience . . . I think because it is such a live and visual thing, the dancing is so powerful. I find that when I leave the shows across Europe and America or whatever part of the world it is, audiences have the same reaction. They come out singing and clapping their hands and stamping their feet. . . . I think it's really the energy of the cast that plays a powerful part with the interaction with the audience. It is infectious. . . .

"The energy that exudes from it. . . . It breaks all barriers, be it age or sex. Whether it's young children or adults or men or women. There's no barriers. . . .

"I can tell you from the Irish dance side that it has taken Europe by storm because . . . it was very rare [before] if there were any Irish dance classes across Europe. Now they are registered with the Irish Dancing

Commission, and there's dancing classes all over Europe, and they are not only having the dance classes, but competitions which we call feisanna, are now held practically every weekend somewhere in Europe. That was unheard of before the show.

"It's unbelievable. And it's all because of Michael."

Chapter Twenty-nine

Heartbreak

Beata and I truly loved each other. But our marriage had to end. When that end finally came, I was appearing in Tasmania, disoriented from the time change and from the grueling demands of the Australian tour. I was also having trouble sleeping, so I was taking temazepam, a tranquilizer and sleep aid that helped me get some rest. Plus, I was "self-medicating" with alcohol–and drinking way too much. I knew the divorce was the right decision for both Beata and me. But it hurt like hell all the same.

I got the news of the divorce on my mobile phone–such an abrupt way to end a decade of marriage. That night I got on stage as the show was ending and roared my usual goodbye greeting. Only instead of saying, "We love you, Tasmania!" I shouted, "We love you, Temazepam!"

After the show I nearly collapsed with sadness. I went out with a couple of the musicians and drank to the last call. I had lost my wife–my little Beata. It was a brutal night.

Martin Flitton, speaking at the Langham Hotel, London, in December 2003: "After I met Beata, I told Michael I should knock some sense into him. Beata was very well looked after in the divorce. Michael didn't make any fuss but just paid her what was proper and agreed.

"He did it with some style, in his way. He said to me, 'I want you on a plane to Chicago.'

" 'What for?'

" 'My divorce papers. I want you to buy a Mercedes, fill it with flowers, and deliver it to Beata. Together with a big check.'

"Beata is a lovely lady. Again, a total believer in Michael. The ins and outs of why they split up is none of my business, but when the two of them are together, it's always special. The last time I spoke to her—which was probably two years ago—Michael went to spend a few days in France with her. You couldn't see why it didn't work. They were both totally in love with each other.

"It's funny, because she always used to check behind his back to see how he was, and he would make me check, behind her back, how she was. He always wanted to know how she felt and she wanted to know how he felt. I think there's always going to be a special friendship there."

Yet Kelley haunted me day and night. Kelley represented the sweetest wine—the sweetest, rarest vintage in the world. Her body was snow-white and pure. Her hair was everything that ever was in Irish history. The memories of being with her are with me for life.

I took her to Galway, where the wind was blowing us off the street. She's only five-feet-and-a-little-bit tall; watching her pound the pavements in her big long coat and her hair blowing was like seeing a Yeats poem brought to life.

Kelley and I traveled to many places together, and I never got tired of her romantic Irish looks—but I also discovered that we were totally different people. Our main love affair was in the bedroom.

Once, we were staying about twenty miles outside of Dublin at Harry Crosbie's new house in Wicklow. Harry Crosbie was the owner of the Point Theatre, and he'd invited us for the weekend. Kelley and I went out for a drive to a beautiful steakhouse which only has fourteen tables and is famous for Wicklow lamb. The chef said he would make us anything we wanted. This was the Ireland of my dreams.

I looked over at Kelley, and she was like a vision from God. We had just come from the house where we had made love and, after dinner, we were going to go back and start all over. It was all perfect, this happiness in the midst of my life's craziness. This irresistible passion was the only thing that could take away the pain of my divorce.

But then we had an argument. Then she cursed me and walked out. Everyone in the tiny restaurant was looking at me as I sat there. I gave a rather painful smile and wondered, "Well, Flatley, how do you get out of this one?"

I was starving, but I couldn't eat. I couldn't move. I couldn't meet the eyes of anyone in the restaurant. Finally, after the longest half-hour of my life, I said to the waiter, "Could you bring me the bill, please?"

Suddenly, out of nowhere, Kelley appeared. I quickly got up, paid the bill, and left. She came after me. "Come on, why are you acting like this? Can't we just make up?"

She could forget that quickly. I, however, could not. I realized that day that there was always going to be a problem.

Once, I remember, Kelley and I went to Palm Desert, California, where we met an old Native American woman, a healer. I was exhausted, all my muscles worn from months of dancing. My mental state was none too good, either. The old woman took one look at me and said, "I know why you've come." She brought me to a quiet room and began placing hot stones upon my chest. With the heat, an incredible sense of peace began to spread throughout my entire being.

"When you're sick in body, you go to the water," the old woman said. "When you're sick in mind, you go to the mountains. When you're sick in spirit, you come to the desert. Welcome to the desert."

* * *

Maybe there was too much passion, jealousy, or fire. When other girls were around, there was always trouble.

Yet, wild as Kelley was, I was besotted by her. I must have broken up with Kelley ten times. But I always went back for more. I could never get enough of her—my bittersweet love.

Chapter Thirty

Radio City: A Dream Come True

Of course, he's an ego. One thinks of Nureyev, Baryshnikov, Elvis Presley and Michael Jackson. Next to these, it can certainly be said he's no egomaniac–he's far too affable for that.

The Times, London, October 25, 1997.

I KNEW THAT THE KEY to success in the United States was getting to play the Oscars. John thought I wasn't ready for it but I believed I could do it. I asked my assistant to put a call in to Gil Cates, producer of the 1997 Academy Awards. We were successful, and I was overjoyed when we got the confirmation that we'd be at the Oscars, playing to an audience of more than a billion people.

I couldn't wait to return in triumph to Los Angeles, the site of so much misery and despair just a few short years earlier. But before we got to Hollywood, we were booked for Chicago, Minneapolis, Boston, Philadelphia–and then, for me, the ultimate venue–Radio City Music Hall in New York City.

* * *

The very first performance of *Riverdance* was at Ireland's Eurovision Song Fest in 1994. This photo is from that performance.

Who is this guy and where the hell did he get that shirt? Dancing on Eurovision.

Lord of the Dance opened at The Point Theatre in Dublin on July 2, 1996. I couldn't have asked for a warmer reception, but it wasn't until the fifth encore that I began to cry.

Rehearsing for *Riverdance* with Jean Butler at the old Diggs Lane studios in 1993.

I wanted to be in the best physical shape possible for *Lord of the Dance.* I went into strict training with Pat Henry at his gym in Dublin, and he helped me achieve the strength and stamina to give my all in every performance.

PRIVATE COLLECTION

For *Lord of the Dance* I was blessed with two amazing leading ladies, Kelly Hendry (*left*) and Bernadette Flynn (*right*).

COURTESY OF BRIAN MCEVOY

I take great pride in caring for my dancers, helping every one of them reach the peak of their potential. The male dancers in *Lord of the Dance* surpassed my dreams for them.

Niamh O'Brien has danced with me in every show, including the original *Riverdance.*

Here's Niamh (right) with the other ladies in our Las Vegas company of *Lord of the Dance.*

PRIVATE COLLECTION

I met Prince Charles after the Royal Command Performance of *Lord of the Dance* at the London Coliseum. He exuded class and dignity. He was very interested in the taps on my shoes and wanted to know how I tap so fast.

PRIVATE COLLECTION

We had our share of fun on tour. Here I am with Emma Pitcher (my PA) and Priscilla, my female bodyguard (she's the one doing the Mike Tyson impression).

PRIVATE COLLECTION

With long-time best friend Martin Flitton.

Lord of the Dance broke every box office record in South Africa. We celebrated in my suite at the Palace in Sun City. It went on for three days, and we went through 130 cases of champagne, some of which went into the hot tub.

PRIVATE COLLECTION

PRIVATE COLLECTION

I knew I wanted to buy my London home before I even got out of the car. Later, I found out it once belonged to Lillie Langtry, the beautiful actress who was mistress to King Edward VII.

Castlehyde in Ireland's north Cork was a wreck when I bought it. When I asked a builder about renovation work, he suggested we tear it down.

COURTESY OF BRIAN MCEVOY

My solo performance in *Feet of Flames* featured no special effects, no music—just me purely as a dancer. It gave me the most wonderful feeling, as if the dance were dancing me.

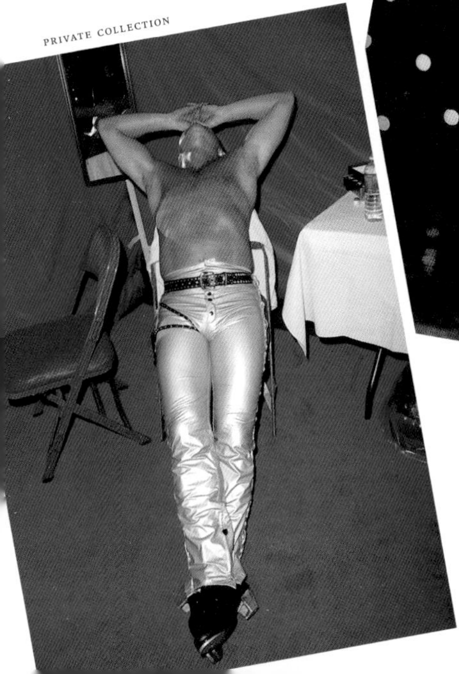

The show is exhausting. Backstage in 2000, Madison Square Garden.

COURTESY OF BRIAN MCEVOY

Lisa Murphy is a sweet, genuine, loving woman
who helped me find the peace in true love.

PRIVATE COLLECTION

COPYRIGHT © UNICORN ENTERTAINMENT

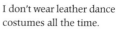

I don't wear leather dance
costumes all the time.

In Barbados, 2004.

While vacationing in Africa I literally got to swim with the sharks, which didn't scare me after *Riverdance*.

PRIVATE COLLECTION

PRIVATE COLLECTION

On safari in 2005.

While on vacation on the Maldive Islands, in the Indian Ocean, I fought this beautiful sailfish and won.

PRIVATE COLLECTION

PRIVATE COLLECTION

Warming up for the opening ceremonies of the G8 Summit, held in St. Petersburg during its 300th anniversary in May 2003.

I was honored to meet Vladimir Putin at the G8 Summit.

PRIVATE COLLECTION

COURTESY OF BRIAN MCEVOY

I was invited by Prince Albert of Monaco to present *Lord of the Dance* at the Red Cross Ball in Monte Carlo in August 2003, where I was awarded the Grimaldi Medal of Friendship. Lisa and I were honored to meet Prince Albert, Princess Caroline, and Prince Rainier.

PRIVATE COLLECTION

In September 2003, Lisa and I travelled to South Africa to meet Nelson Mandela.

Visiting with orphan children in Soweto who suffer from AIDS.

PRIVATE COLLECTION

PRIVATE COLLECTION

In New York City in May 2004, I received the Ellis Island Medal of Honor, which is given for professional and patriotic contributions to America. It was all the more meaningful because I knew my Irish grandmother would be so proud of me.

Dancing on the Great Wall of China in 2004.

PRIVATE COLLECTION

COURTESY OF BRIAN MCEVOY

I was proud and honored to receive a doctorate degree from University College Dublin in 2004.

PRIVATE COLLECTION

I've never stopped playing the flute, for personal pleasure and professionally. Here, I'm recording an album released in 2005.

PRIVATE COLLECTION

My forty-seventh birthday, July 16, 2005, London.

The best view in the South of France – from the balcony at Villa Masquerade.

COPYRIGHT © UNICORN ENTERTAINMENT

Celtic Tiger previewed in Budapest, where we sold out more than 100,000 tickets.

Brenda from Celtic Tiger: "Sex on Legs".

COPYRIGHT © UNICORN ENTERTAINMENT

COPYRIGHT © NIALL CARSON / EMPICS

With Niamh, the perfect bride, on our wedding day in 2006.

Our opening night at Radio City was March 4, 1997–exactly one year after *Riverdance* had played there. Since childhood, it had been my dream to play this historic theater, but I never had my chance to go with *Riverdance*, even though playing there had been my idea in the first place. Now I was looking forward to thirteen sell-out nights for *Lord of the Dance*–a sweet booking in itself, and all the sweeter for being better than *Riverdance*. On some level, every solo I'd ever created was created for that stage. It would be marvelous to actually see my work in its dream setting.

Harvey Goldsmith: "Michael was pushing and pushing that he wanted to break in America. I tried to get a lot of people to come over and see the show, but Riverdance *was taking off in America, and everybody was nervous about whether a second show would work.*

"For Radio City we'd only sold about sixty percent of the tickets, and the master stroke was that the night before we opened Michael did a show on America's PBS as part of their subscription drive. . . . He went on the program for two hours, and the reaction at the box office was unbelievable. The next day we'd pretty much sold every ticket there was to sell."

As I stepped out of the limo on opening night, I looked around in wonder at the hundreds of fans crowding around me. One guy came over to me and said, "Can I have an autograph?"

"Yeah, sure," I said as I happily signed my name.

The guy gave me an evil grin. "It's a writ, you fucking asshole. It's from John Reid. He said to say hello and good luck for tonight." He roared in my face with laughter and ran off down the street. Some people are all class! Even the fans were embarrassed.

John Reid was quoted in London's Daily Express, *on April 20, 1997: "Flatley wants everything–and he wants it yesterday. It's disgusting the way he treated me."*

* * *

The disturbing incidents weren't over. I walked into the theater and discovered that someone had left a book on the bureau in my dressing room—*Helter Skelter*, the story of the 1969 Charles Manson murders. The person who left the book had marked some pages that mentioned Bill Tennant, who was then Roman Polanski's business manager. Bill had been called in to identify the bodies of Polanski's wife, Sharon Tate, and the other victims of the Manson murders. Those cold-blooded killings had shocked the world with a new vision of evil, and by highlighting the passage in this book someone seemed to be trying to unsettle me.

> Just before noon William Tennant arrived, still dressed in tennis clothes, and was escorted through the gate by the police.
>
> It was like being led through a nightmare, as he was taken first to one body, then another.
>
> He didn't recognize the young man in the automobile. But he identified the man on the lawn as Voytek Frykowski, the woman as Abigail Folger, and the two bodies in the living room as Sharon Tate Polanski and, tentatively, Jay Sebring.
>
> When the police lifted the bloody towel, the man's face was so badly contused Tennant couldn't be sure.
>
> Then he went outside and was sick.
>
> from *Helter Skelter, The True Story of the Manson Murders,*
> Vincent Bugliosi with Curt Gentry,
> W. W. Norton, New York, 1974

Just as I was finishing the passage, Bill Tennant came into the dressing room, and I didn't know how to feel. Why had the book been left in my dressing room? What did Bill's connection to this awful tragedy have to do with me?

Then I decided that none of this was important. What mattered was that I was on the verge of achieving a lifelong dream. Whoever had left this book for me had stooped pretty low–the sure sign of a person who felt intimidated, by me, my success, my new relationship with Bill.

I'm proud of how I performed that night–of how all of us performed. I'll confess, though, that after the show, that freaked-out feeling returned. Who would do such a creepy thing? I found it very disturbing that someone had actually snuck into my dressing room. Once again, I had to shake all my anxiety out of my mind so I could make my appearance at the after-show party. There seemed to be an endless stream of famous faces to meet and greet. Among the many strangers' faces were my mum and dad, my brother Pat, and my sisters. It was great to see them after all the evening's shocks. Knowing they had been there to share my triumph made everything seem worthwhile.

Clive Barnes, the theater critic of the New York Post, *wrote in March 1997: " 'Lord of the Dance' is fascinating, rewarding, and above all entertaining.*

"Flatley has given it a sheer pop force that few would have guessed or dreamed of. Flatley's enthusiasm, gusto and guts–not to mention his showbiz flair and expertise–are, in any case, irresistible."

Radio City proved to be another turning point for our show. Success in Australia was all very nice, but New York City was one of the two entertainment capitals of the world. And suddenly, we were the hot new ticket.

I could see the change in the dancers–the beginning of a completely different outlook. When people like Phil Collins and Michael Jackson started flying in to see for themselves what all the fuss was about, the dancers took on a new sense of pride and confidence. To be sure, most of my dancers had achieved no little success in the world of Irish dance competitions. But now we were playing in a whole other league, the toast of the rich and famous. It was an achievement that all of us enjoyed.

Chapter Thirty-one

Hollywood, Here We Come!

> Any excuse will do to watch Flatley perform because the man is quite possibly the world's greatest living dancer. It's not just the speed of his feet, the height of his kicks or the clicking of his heels that makes him so fascinating to watch. There is an aura about Flatley, an unmistakable star quality that focuses all eyes on him.
>
> Eileen Murphy, *The Irish Echo,* March 12, 1997

And then it was time to get ready for the Oscars. Academy Award producer Gil Cates had given me the centerpiece slot between Celine Dion and Madonna. We were honored! The week before the show, I took over a studio in Los Angeles and we all rehearsed like demons.

As we stood together before the broadcast, I told the dancers, "This is like our Olympic Games. You're dancing tonight for Ireland." Our backstage area was crowded with movie stars getting ready to present awards or participate in onstage numbers, but I barely noticed them.

Suddenly, the drum started, the gates at the back of our set opened, and it was my turn to go onstage. I could feel my dancers behind me, tense with energy, just waiting to fly. As I sprang into action, I lost my sense of anything but the moment itself, just my body in the space and the dance that surged through me.

Lucky for me I had this depth of focus to sustain me, because so many things could have gone wrong. First, the stage was like ice. Then, the camera operator who'd been rehearsing with us had gotten sick, so we were working with a replacement, who had no idea of the kind of speed I brought to the stage. When I flew into my first steps, I knocked the new guy over, right in front of the celebrity audience and a billion television viewers.

After that, I nearly slipped–my back foot went up–though luckily, I managed to save myself. And when I did my stamp on the floor, I ended up putting my foot right through the little hole that had been set for Madonna to place her microphone. Thank God, I didn't break my leg.

This was a rocky beginning, but I don't think either the live or the TV audience paid much attention to anything except the sexy, high-energy dance that was unfolding before them. We went on to a brief interlude in which I had only a few seconds to change outfits. My dresser, Ashley Thurwell, and I had rehearsed the change at the hotel, though there wasn't any need–this was something we'd been doing for weeks, every single night of the show. I was supposed to fire off my shirt, put on my cummerbund and coat, and get right back out there. But Ashley freaked. She couldn't get the cummerbund done. I had to put my own coat on.

I put my hands on her face and said, "We're here, baby. Don't worry. This is the real thing."

She started crying.

It was okay. I was flying despite all bad luck. I was on top of the world!

Then I came out for the next number with the zipper on my pants slightly open and no cummerbund. Lord save us!

Despite it all, *Lord of the Dance* got a standing ovation. In the end, none of the mishaps mattered. I still feel great about that night and that solo.

I hugged and kissed Ashley, which is no duty–she's a stunningly attractive woman. It was her big night and she just got scared. Bill Tennant was angry with her, and I didn't like that–everyone makes mistakes. It was my first indication of the problems I'd later have with Bill. Although he did indeed help me deal with John Reid, he wasn't the right man for our team, either.

But I wasn't looking nearly that far ahead. All I could think was that finally, the whole world knew how good we were–the TV viewers around the globe, as well as our live Hollywood audience. In fact, Hollywood gave us a great hurrah, and I was invited to the night's most prestigious party, the one at Morton's restaurant. Ireland could be proud.

Ashley Thurwell said in London in October 2004: "I never ever saw Michael lose his cool–even when his costume for the Oscars went missing. I'd have freaked but he didn't.

"I did all his costumes. I would buy all his clothes. Did everything–on and off stage. We used to do a lot together. We used to go all over. I had great fun. We were best friends, it was great, we were really close. . . . We used to just laugh all the time. I'm sure Michael would say that as well. . . .

"About a week before the Oscars, we went to Palm Springs. At the hotel in New York all the luggage got sent downstairs and the concierge was going to put it in a separate car to go to the airport.

"I had all of Michael's costumes for the Oscars downstairs. But they didn't get to the airport with us. The Oscar outfits!! I only noticed by chance. A few days earlier my dog had died at home in Newcastle, and Michael had gone out and bought me a huge Dalmatian Disney stuffed dog. I was saying to Michael, 'Where's that dog? Oh, no, I must have left it in the hotel.'

"Then I realized the case with the costumes was missing, too. We rang the hotel, but they couldn't get the costumes on our flight because we were flying straight away.

"Then the cases got lost, and the costumes arrived about three days before the Oscars. I was just dying. . . . That was a bit of a close shave with those costumes, I tell you.

"Michael being Michael was 'It'll be fine,' and he didn't seem bothered at all; that's the way he is. He never, ever really lost it with us. . . . He was: 'Look. Don't worry about it.' That's Michael. He takes everything in his stride. He never really lost it. I don't think I've ever seen Michael really lose his temper. He was so easygoing, and he was funny as well.

"He's got a lovely, warm personality. He's great. He's very generous. Very genuine. He was loved in America. . . ."

Derry Ann Morgan: "At the Oscars, Michael and the show were the interval entertainment–a bit like Eurovison really.

"We were rehearsing in the afternoon, and I'd gone down to the stage with him and was walking back up when here was this lady standing at the top of the stage. She said, 'Michael, you probably don't know who I am, but I really would love to meet you. I just think you're so great and so terribly talented. I'm a great fan. My name is Celine Dion.'

"I was thrilled. She was with her husband, and Madonna was down the other side of the stage.

"Madonna was paying a lot of attention to Michael. She was intrigued by him.

"Celine had waited for Michael to come back so she could meet him. All the stars and performers were fascinated by him."

Dancer Catriona Hale recalled in October 2004: "Celine was really cool about letting us watch her in rehearsals for the Oscars, but she wasn't cool over Michael. She was really star-struck. After one of the dress rehearsals I walked past Michael's dressing room, and she was outside waiting. She had been waiting there half an hour to meet him.

"Michael was off doing business and didn't know she was there, but she was happy to wait for him to come back. She said to us: 'Oh, you're the dancers–how great to be with Michael all the time. I'm just waiting to meet him. I'm so nervous, but I have to meet him.'

"She and Madonna were fascinated by Michael. They were watching him all the time. They watched our rehearsals, got a sneak preview.

"When we were dancing at the Oscars I've never heard applause like it–and I started with Michael in Riverdance. *It was totally amazing. All these actors and actresses–you don't expect them to be standing up screaming. . . ."*

Lewis Segal, dance critic of the Los Angeles Times, *wrote in April 1997: "The Academy Awards made the milestones of film history into a mere backdrop for Flatley–and you ain't seen nothing yet.*

"Where 'Riverdance' faked its way through Irish folklore, 'Lord of the Dance' is a showpiece extravaganza.

"And best of all, it's got Michael Flatley, an epoch defining artist."

The late, legendary dancer Gregory Hines told a television interviewer before the 1997 Oscars ceremony: "I'm here this evening to see Michael Flatley dance."

The day after the 1997 Oscars, the gossip columnist Liz Smith reported in her Los Angeles Times *column: "At the big Oscar night parties the girls spent the evening admiring Michael Flatley's finest asset–those buns of steel which are hard to ignore, considering the cut of his trousers."*

On May 5, 1997, Michael Flatley was named by People *magazine as one of the fifty "Most Beautiful People in the World."*

Cora Smyth: "We've been in Radio City and . . . every massive place you could be in. You can only imagine being in these places, where rock bands go and you can't imagine yourself playing the fiddle coming from the country! And having other big stars in the audience looking up at you.

"We did this gig in Los Angeles and Jack Nicholson was clearly looking up at us. He came a good few times. We met him a few times and he was really, really into the whole thing, and there were a good few like that as well. It was just amazing."

After the Oscar performance, we sold out across America, playing to more than fifteen thousand people a night. We were taking in millions of dollars from ticket sales and merchandising.

When I officially became a millionaire early in 1997, it was a terrific feeling, for it meant that all the hard work and all my gambles had paid off. After that, the money situation seemed to change every other minute but I didn't complain about having to keep doing my arithmetic! In twelve months I'd gone from facing bankruptcy, ruin, and oblivion to being the highest-paid dancer on the planet.

Martin Flitton: "Michael loved the freedom money gave him. He looked after some of his family's outstanding commitments, he bought his mum and dad a nice Mercedes and beautiful watches and made sure they had no financial worries. He's always been generous in that way.

"He bought houses for everyone in his family. He bought businesses and buildings for them. He has bought new cars, mainly Mercedes-Benz, for scores of people including me and Marie. This year alone he's given away six cars."

Ashley Thurwell: "I remember when we were in Chicago and it was his sister Annie's birthday. His family all came to see the show and there was a Mercedes outside. Michael had bought her a Mercedes and it had a huge ribbon on it, a big red ribbon. It was such a nice moment, because everybody was crying and Annie was crying–and that was just Michael. He loves surprising people. . . .

"It's like everybody was a family when we were touring. I used to sit in

the dressing room, and after a show, we would talk for hours and hours, and he would tell me about the ideas he had. We would be the last people to come out of the venue . . . in the early hours of the morning. When he came off stage, he would always have the bucket, a kind of little bath full of ice and water, and Michael would put his head in there, and that would really cool him down. But obviously his adrenaline and everything was so high that he couldn't calm down.

"It would take him a long time. He was so hyped up. It was impossible for him to just relax after the show. He would spend a lot of time in the venue some nights, and we would just sit and talk for hours.

"We got on really well. He used to get the receptionist in the hotel to write little notes like 'Happy Ash Wednesday.' . . . He was just so funny. He would ring my mother at about two o'clock in the morning. We'd be sitting in the dressing room, and he would ring my mother and she really was fast asleep when she answered the phone. He would talk for hours with my mother. He is just such a really warm person. He got on very well with my mother as well.

". . . It was Derry Ann's birthday one night, and Michael had bought her some lovely presents. He bought clothes and a Rolex watch. She was really crying, and Michael had just come off stage, and I think he was just in his underwear actually, and he was just sitting there giving her the presents. It was just a moment but it shows what a happy family we all were."

Chapter Thirty-two

The Downside of Success

I LOVED THE SUCCESS I'd worked so hard for. But I knew I could not just sit back and count the cash. I had to retain my focus. We were flying fast and getting faster. The suites got bigger, the girls prettier, the cars faster–but the dance was still the main thing. There was still a long way to go, still lots of places and people to conquer.

Kelley Byrne: "He likes to spread around what he's achieved. . . . I remember the first Christmas Eve he had money, he spent the night driving around London, stopping and and giving every homeless person he could find money–twenty-pound notes. He knows what it's like to be poor. He's very decent. He's a good guy. He used to be Santa Claus every year.

"It's sad because so many people have not returned that goodwill. It's horrible to see how these people could be best friends . . . but they were all in it for themselves. Everybody starts to get that little bit more greedy. He could see that and he wasn't putting up with it. He went through a lot of people, but it wasn't because of some mean streak, some power trip. He

was extremely upset; he thought these people were good friends. It probably took about five people to do that to him to make him realize they were putting on an act; it took him a while to learn that and to understand it, for he could never be like that.

"He would be depressed and he'd just sit there and he'd be quiet. He was devastated. Someone had really let him down. It was a 'no–not again' kind of thing. All I could do was try and help him through it. He was hurt. He didn't take it out on me, he didn't make my life a misery. He wasn't difficult. He'd go through his depression but he'd always be focused on where he was going, and what he was doing.

"We'd always talk it through and he'd have quiet times to himself. If he'd been on his own it could have been really bad, but he knew he'd talk to me. He knew he could trust me. He was never suicidal or anything. Underneath it all, he had that self-belief, he knew he would get through it.

"He trusted so much because fame was new to him. Maybe now such betrayals wouldn't bother him so much. He wouldn't get so attached. He didn't really have a big circle of friends and it was all so new. He was on the road. He'd left everyone in America behind. He had his brother Pat and of course he'd talk to his dad. Matt Malloy from the Chieftains was a good friend, but I don't know if he'd tell Matt everything. He took it all on himself.

"So when people let him down, it really hurt; he realized that they were only after his money. He took it very hard but you learn things every day. I didn't think people could be like that. I think show business is horrible.

"Once we . . . were in Spago in Beverly Hills, and Wolfgang Puck and his wife Barbara came over and she said, 'Oh, Mr. Flatley, please let me choose your food for tonight.' We had three starters, two main courses, and probably three desserts, and with every course there was a different bottle of wine, and at the end of the night it was, 'It's all on me.' Not that many months before, he used to walk to that dance studio when he had nothing and he couldn't afford to buy a Coke or a cup of coffee in the

morning. Finally when he has money and he can afford it, he can have everything on the menu and it's all for free.

"I don't know—did he know that was waiting for him?"

Meanwhile, I had one more hurdle to overcome before I could fully enjoy the success that I'd worked so hard for. I had to deal with Bill Tennant—the manager I thought would save me. Martin Flitton had warned me about him, but in my eagerness to get away from John Reid, I hadn't wanted to listen.

The sad thing is, I always liked Bill Tennant. I know a lot of people didn't get on with him, that at times he could be brash and abrupt, but he got things done, and I always admired that. John could be cautious. "Some dreams can't come true," he once told me. Bill wasn't like that a bit. He had that wonderful American open-minded approach, that can-do spirit I appreciated so much. In no time at all, after he came on board, I was signed up with the legendary publicist Pat Kingsley, who had said she'd be honored to work with me. CAA, the biggest agency in America, called *me,* and I began working with two great agents, Richard Lovett and Rob Wright. Ten years later, I'm still with them.

But somehow things slowed down dramatically once we hit the road. Bill was there night after night, to be sure—but nothing was in the pipeline, no new projects were turning up. Looking back I can see that no manager could have matched up to my expectations but at the time I thought that Bill was underestimating me, and I soon grew tired of it. One day, after we finished up our show and I was on the way to the jet to head for Dallas, I called Bill from the limo in which Derry Ann Morgan and I were riding. Rightly or wrongly, I started a row with Bill, really laying into him.

I went on and on for what seemed like an eternity. I let him have it from both barrels, listing every shortcoming I could think of.

As he'd done the day we'd first met in Diggs Lane, Bill listened without saying a word. I'm sure I was the first—and maybe the last—

person who ever spoke to him that way. When I was done, he said just one word: "Okay." Then he put the phone down.

I waited, with my finger against my lips, wondering if I would get the response that I was hoping for. Meanwhile, Derry Ann and I arrived at my favorite Dallas hotel, the Mansion on Turtle Creek. I had a couple of glasses of wine, still wondering, and went to bed.

At ten the next morning, a young hotel employee knocked at my door and handed me an overnight delivery letter. I ripped open the plastic envelope and pulled out the contents. There was a letter from Bill Tennant offering his resignation.

"Yes!" I said joyfully to myself. "It worked!" Bill Tennant, like Jack Love before him, had walked into a straight right hand that he never saw coming. I was out of the contract in the blink of an eye, free to go on with no encumbrances.

Martin Flitton had opinions about Bill Tennant: "America [was] for me the start of a nightmare dealing with Bill Tennant because he wasn't from our end of the business. He was from the movie side and he could be aggressive. He and Michael had a relationship, but from my point of view he was rude [and] demanding on issues that weren't relevant to Michael.

"I used to dread the phone ringing. My stomach churned if it was Bill Tennant, and I've worked with some hard people.

"There was no way anything was going to happen to Michael while I was around. I was there to make sure the show made profits. Michael needed to make money. That was what it was about. Every night the accounts were done. I used to present Michael with his figures on a show-by-show basis, which is not usually done for an act, but Michael took that amount of interest. He's very smart. I used to stay late to prepare the figures so he knew where he was. . . .

"We never had a bad night; we grossed three hundred to three hundred and fifty thousand a night which was incredible. But Bill Tennant was giving me a real, real hard time.

"He had this philosophy that he was right on everything. You couldn't

have a discussion. You got lectured. I had, at that time, had twenty-five years in the business and everything we were trying to do was for Michael's benefit long-term. Bill had a problem and I'm sure it was because he didn't understand what the production show team did for a living. We were there to get the show from A to B, get it up on time and get the show in, get the money, check the money. He didn't have the same experience of the complexities of live shows. He was used to doing a budget for a video. We were actually dealing with hard cash at the box office.

"Michael has made a lot of people rich. They're not doing it, but they're getting twenty percent. They'd turn up, they'd be back in the dressing room with Michael half an hour before the show, during the [intermission]. You don't go near your artist [at that time]. They psych themselves up for the show, to walk on stage in front of ten or twenty thousand people. . . . You have to have some respect, grant them some space.

"People say that Michael Flatley is arrogant. Michael Flatley is arrogant, but he has to be. At the end of the day if you don't believe you are the best, you can't do that. For goodness sake, the Lord of the Dance *dates were what put Wembley P.L.C. back in the black for the first half of 1998.*

"I had a bad time with Bill Tennant in Salt Lake City, Utah. That particular day, Michael rang up and asked whether I fancied a bit of lunch. When I arrived, Bill Tennant was there. He started on me straight away. I just stood up and said, 'That's it, I'm on a plane home.'

"I went down to the venue, and Michael came down, and we went for a walk. He said, 'Look, nothing's going to happen to you, don't take it to heart. You're doing a great job. Unless you fall out with me don't worry about it.'

"Michael then took over shielding me from Bill Tennant. That happened for another few weeks, and then I went to pick Michael up for a show in Dallas, and he said, 'Bill Tennant has sent me a letter of resignation.'

"I said, 'Really?'

"He said, 'The good thing is, I've accepted it. Are you capable of booking shows, doing this, doing that?' . . .

"That was the start of getting more involved with Michael. It was the start of a great adventure for me, really. I didn't have to worry about a manager. Michael then managed himself. I could go straight to Michael and get a decision. There was not a channel to go through, and people who didn't understand [our business]. Michael totally understood the business. He's constantly checking and spots everything.

"It's like when he's dancing. On stage he never misses a trick. If there's a light out, immediately he wants to know why. The crew, the way they work. The band, how they work. The dancing. The costumes and things like that. He'd come off and go, 'Why is that like that?' and you'd say, 'Oh, we had a problem with one of the costumes.'

"Not critical. But he would want to know. Again, that's a sign of why he's done so well. Because he picks up on things and sometimes it's the attention to detail that makes it more successful. That's what his ability is. He really does get to it.

"We were on a roll doing multiple dates. We did Wembley, we did twenty-eight days and broke the record, which is still not beaten.

"It's astonishing the sheer volume of people—millions—that have seen the show live. A top artist would do three-quarters of a million to a million copies of a video. Michael in his first video did nearly seven million. One point one million CDs. Incredible. When we were out there touring, nearly every day there was an award won by Michael. It never stopped. It still never stops. He's still going full speed."

Act Four

Feet of Flames

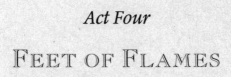

You ain't heard nothin' yet!

The Jazz Singer

Chapter Thirty-three

Material Guy

Sex is part of Nature, and I go along with Nature.

Marilyn Monroe

One hundred million pounds!

That was the projected earnings of *Lord of the Dance*. Suddenly, I was in charge of a global business. I liked it!

I also enjoyed my new lifestyle. I particularly liked the view from my penthouse suite in the Lanesborough, my favorite London hotel.

Still, I felt that by this point, I'd spent far too much of my life in hotels and on the road. I'd had some fabulous trips–some with Kelley and some alone–long stays in the Caribbean and Malibu, time in the south of France and the South Pacific's Bora Bora. With my company, I'd made the Down Under tour, traveled across England and Ireland, toured the States.

But now I was looking for a home.

Everywhere I went I wanted to put down roots. I would see properties and immediately want to buy them. I'd find myself jumping into a helicopter to go scout a potential mansion or beachfront property. I wasn't just looking for another luxury purchase, though. I really needed a home.

Because of the way my dance career was shaping up, I was searching for a home in London and a property in Ireland. With my good friend and financial adviser Stephen Marks I visited many properties in Belgravia, Knightsbridge, and Holland Park, but I saw nothing that appealed to me. Some of the fancy places were so small that you had to open your window to change your shirt.

One day, we were scheduled to see a home in the Regent's Canal area, a lovely London neighborhood known for its gracious nineteenth-century homes and its network of canals, which had lent it its nickname—"Little Venice." We approached one huge house that sat behind white stucco walls. Something about the place drew me immediately—I could picture ladies strolling the garden with parasols and hoop skirts—and I said, "Oh my God, please let it be that one that we're going to see—please be that, please be that one." I'd never had such a strong feeling for a house before.

Sure enough, the driver stopped at the house, an early Victorian place known as Park Place Villas. Without even getting out of the car—let alone asking the price—I shouted, "I'll take it!" That was it. That was the one.

Stephen looked at me doubtfully. "Are you sure, Michael? You haven't even been inside."

I've always been a man for falling in love at first sight. I said, "Yes, let's go in, right now, and ask what they'll take for it."

Frankly, the place was a disaster. No one had spent a penny on it in nearly forty years. What's more, the current owner was a theatrical costume designer who also rented out costumes, so the whole place was full of king's robes and fantastical gowns.

Eventually, we learned that the owner was in negotiations with two big stars. By rights, I shouldn't even have been shown the house. But by this point I knew how to get what I wanted. I upped the asking price by half a million pounds and said I would take it.

I'd've thought that would do it. But the seller told me that the other bidders would doubtless match my price. To sell me the place then and there, he wanted a quarter-million pounds on top of the half-million I'd already offered.

I hesitated for just a moment. But I knew that not only was I buying my dream home, I was making a good investment. "Sold!" I said, and breathed a sigh of relief. Finally, I had a place of my own. And as it happened, the place doubled in value almost overnight!

In my opinion, I've got one of the nicest homes in London. First, it's got a fascinating history: It once belonged to famed performer Lillie Langtry, who used it to entertain Edward VII. Then, it's well located—just eleven minutes from my front door to the Knightsbridge branch of Harrods, the famous department store. Yet the house is also secluded, well hidden behind a high wall—a warm, inviting, and yet elegant place, where I could entertain anyone from my pint-drinking buddies to members of the Royal Family.

In the Sunday Times, *London, on March 14, 2004, Zoe Brennan reported on Park Place Villas: "The sumptuous crimson ground-floor dining room opens off the hall, with full-length windows on two sides of the room. Next door, the sitting room is decorated in muted colours, with plush sage carpet and cream walls. Grand murals of cherubs pulling back the night sky decorate the ceilings of the master bedroom and principal bedroom on the first floor, while the guest bedroom is in tranquil blues and golds. The artwork is by Tony Raymond, whose creations also adorn the ceilings of the new* Queen Mary 2 *cruise liner.*

"An imposing landing separates the living and sleeping areas of Flatley's home. One landing is big enough for an office space complete with library. Numerous balconies allow the dancer to enjoy a morning coffee outside when the weather allows.

"Flatley did not want an entirely formal abode, however. The ground-floor kitchen area has a diner-style booth where he eats breakfast, looking out through a lush conservatory to the manicured gardens beyond. His team of chefs uses the special Fourneaux de France stove brought over from France to cater for him and his friends.

"Downstairs, Flatley's mahogany-panelled den could come straight out of a gentleman's club, complete with a well-stocked bar and false bookcases that open at the touch of a button to reveal an enormous wide-screen television. Here he entertains, or relaxes when he comes back from tour. Next door, the original 19th-century basement has been extended to include a sizeable underlit swimming pool surrounded by a classical mural featuring pagodas and peacocks. Another bar and a spa bath complete the scene. Flatley keeps fit in the adjacent gym, decorated with signed photos of his boxing heroes. His own awards and trophies litter the house. A sun bed is mainly for the use of guests, as Flatley's own tan is acquired in the Caribbean.

"Staff quarters on the top floor of the property house Flatley's team of butlers and maids, as well as his wardrobe and costume collection–while hundreds of pairs of dance shoes and rows of immaculately laundered shirts are displayed in a mirrored dressing room."

Park Place Villas was built in 1840, but there was nothing Victorian about the parties I threw there. Often, our evenings would end with the guests and me in the underlighted swimming pool, the glow of the watery lights illuminating the classical mural that decorates the pool area. At the formal affairs, many evening gowns and tuxedos were soaked in the wee hours of the morning when the happy guests leapt into the pool. At the more informal parties, it got a little wilder.

Still, entertaining at home was more pleasant and less threatening than just meeting up with strangers on the road. I've been shadowed–stalked I suppose–by some infatuated women, and they are not easy to deal with. I've been flattered to have so many women think of me as sexy, and the majority of my fans have always been fine–absolute gems. But the ones who become obsessed–well, frankly, they don't make much sense. I've been accused of some crazy things but it's always been false and I've got past it.

* * *

Areleen Ni Bhaoill: "After a performance Michael would be standing there nearly naked and sweating. The girls would be all around him, maybe wearing little, breathing heavily and sweating. It was a nightly recipe for sex. They would hang around his dressing room waiting to be noticed or maybe more. Sometimes it got a little wild, but it was all for fun, nobody took it too seriously."

Martin Flitton: "One opening night we were out for a party with the show and Michael was with two models. . . . Later, Michael asks me for my phone and gives me his in exchange. He's given the blonde his phone number but didn't want to be bothered. I thought, 'He should be so lucky,' and I forgot about it.

"Much later, I'm back in my hotel room. The phone goes. It's the blonde. The call's not for me!

"The girls were always after Michael. It was a constant thing. During a tour in South Africa he had a party for about fifty people in our hotel in Sun City. Michael got in the Jacuzzi and within seconds there were about twenty girls in there with him. It went on until about 6 a.m. They had a lot of fun–let off steam. They all worked furiously hard and this was a way to relax.

"Sex was part of Michael's life on the road–

"There were always a lot of offstage opportunities for sex. There were always lots of women around. At the shows there would be fifteen thousand screaming people in the audience, and the front row usually was packed with gorgeous girls. Some of them would turn up backstage chatting to Michael.

"During the run at Wembley there were a couple of girls who would turn up every night. They would get in his car with him and just enjoy themselves. They'd both get in the car and disappear from view. Every night of the run.

"In California he even had sex at 170 mph. He was on a freeway roaring along in his Ferrari with this beautiful girl–and the speed must have gone to her head.

"She got excited, and the more excited she got, the more his foot went down on the accelerator. It was his 355GT, and that can hit about 190 mph but before he got there the cops were flagging him down.

"He was just lucky it was an open road and the highway patrolmen realized what the girl was up to. Still, he ended up in court, but they let him off.

"Michael and sex–it's part of his way of life. I've always said about Michael's reputation for having sex two or three times a day that you have to remember that he operates on a nine-day week."

Gerry Ryan at the Four Seasons Hotel, Dublin, in May 2004: "The party after the Wembley show was worthy of Errol Flynn."

Then there are the women who are attracted by anyone whose name appears on the lists of "the world's richest people" printed by newspapers and magazines. It's ironic, but I actually pay quite a bit of money to keep my name *off* those lists, so as not to encourage anyone who might be attracted by that sort of thing. I'm not complaining, but it's definitely one of the prices of success that you don't always know who's interested in you and who's just after your money.

Money is a funny thing. In some ways, of course, I was thrilled to have more of it. After all, I'd spent many sleepless nights waiting for my overnight success.

On the other hand, I knew very early on that money means nothing if you can't spend it or give it away. What else are you going to do with it? So I view money not as an end in itself, but as a measuring stick of what I've done and what my art has brought me.

Not that I don't like money–I do, and I love to live the way I do. But what's priceless to me–truly–is the look on people's faces after a show, or after I've helped them financially, after I've been able to give someone something they deserve but couldn't afford. Although that look costs money, you can't buy it.

* * *

In late 1997, Forbes *reported that Michael Flatley had earned $54 million in 1996, which made him the twenty-fifth richest entertainer in the world. Mel Gibson and John Travolta earned a few million more, while Kevin Costner, Michael Douglas, and U2 earned a bit less.*

George Dominguez, the manager of the lounge and bar at the Lanesborough Hotel, said in November 2004: "Mr. Flatley is the ultimate gentleman. He treats everyone as if they have been a friend for life. He's quick-witted and there's always a joke and a smile. And the ladies love him–every time he walks in, all their eyes are on him. And with them he is a gentleman too. All the staff are so glad when he comes to stay–he treats the hotel like his home. He's comfortable here and we are always comfortable with him.

"I always have a joke with him and he always has the time even if he has flown from the other side of the world, which is usually the case. . . ."

On September 27, 2005, Guru, a veteran room-service waiter at the St. Regis Hotel in New York City, said: "I have been serving Michael Flatley for ten years. He has grown over the years but never changed. I've dealt with millionaires, billionaires, most of my working life here and never met anyone like Mr. Flatley. He is always busy but he takes time to speak to me, ask about my wife and two sons.

"With most of them I lay out the table, say 'have a nice day,' and that's that. But he shows a genuine interest in you. He is a real person, a real showman, and has a real heart. He has a special thing in his character and is very much a gentleman.

"And he always has energy. I hope he never loses that energy–it is inspiring in his shows and in his life."

Martin Flitton: "With Michael if you're loyal, he's loyal. He educated me along the way about many things.

"I'm not a drinker–if someone spent fifteen pounds on a bottle of wine, I'd think that was over the top. I'd go into restaurants with Michael, and the wine would cost him two to three thousand pounds a bottle.

"He was not trying to show off. He did appreciate the wine, and I'd sit there with my glass and he would explain the vintage and all the background to me. He'd take the dancers to places where they could never, ever afford to go. He always enjoys sharing these good things. I reckon he must have spent over a million pounds on jewellery and dresses for Lisa. Some of the gowns he bought in Beauchamp Place in Knightsbridge cost £30,000 each. He'd buy her three or four at a time."

Chapter Thirty-four

Up Against the Law

Truth is rarely pure, and never simple.

Oscar Wilde, *The Importance of Being Earnest*

I knew little about British law. It wouldn't have mattered if I'd been an expert, though. Nothing could have prepared me for Court 60 of London's Royal Courts of Justice, where I faced a five-week trial for alleged breach of contract, following a huge suit from John Reid.

I was an accused man surrounded by bewigged barristers. And stared at through half-moon glasses by a judge who seemed bemused by the tales of the show-business world.

I knew I was in the right. But did right matter when it came to a trial? I was so upset that I basically stopped sleeping. However, I'd built a flotation tank at Park Place Villas. So every morning about five o'clock, I'd walk downstairs in the dark, throw off my robe, and fling myself into the salt water. Floating there, breathing deeply, I'd marshal the focus I'd need to get through the day ahead. I'd visualize the end result I wanted. And I'd focus on the truth.

The truth was little help, however, in fighting my way through the gauntlet of photographers that swarmed around the entrance to the courtroom. Opposing counsel suddenly decided to put me in the witness box first. I wasn't expecting to testify that early in the trial. Nor was I prepared for the barrister's opening gambit.

"Mr. Flatley?"

"Yes?"

"Open up binder 37a, turn to page 295, paragraph 6. The sentence is marked out there."

A young woman had to help me find the binder from a huge library on several shelves. Then I actually had to read the damn thing. I'm not a good reader at the best of times, and under stress–which I certainly was!–I can become slightly dyslexic. I had to keep looking at the same sentence, again and again and again.

Reid's barrister kept asking, "Mr. Flatley, are you ready?"

"Not yet."

Five seconds later, "Mr. Flatley, surely you have read it by now?"

"Can you give me just a second?"

The barrister was constantly torturing me because I couldn't read fast enough for him. But I wanted to be sure of every word.

I kept saying to the judge, "Your Honor, please!"

The judge would correct me. "Not 'your honor.' 'My lord.' "

Then I'd look at the judge, and Reid's lawyer would bark, "Don't look at him, look at me!"

It was a bit of a sparring session. It took me four days to get my feet under me. That day, just outside the courtroom, a passing barrister threw me a real curve ball. "Mr. Flatley, isn't it fair to say that most dancers are gay?"

And suddenly, I knew what to say. "I don't know," I replied calmly. "You tell me, you're the one wearing a wig and a gown."

Suddenly I knew somehow I could win this.

Day five got even more tense. I did feel that the opposing counsel was starting to lose his way in the fog. After all, this was an enormously complicated case–but I actually did understand all the facts and figures that were being thrown around. I knew the numbers backwards and forwards, because this was my business, and I'd always kept control of it. Plus, I was working feverishly each night, trying to prepare.

But the questions kept coming and it was dizzying. And whenever the barrister asked me to read a sentence aloud, I had to keep going over and over it because I hadn't slept and I was loaded with stress. To make matters worse, the journalists in the front row were all whispering while I was trying to read. And I could feel the eyes of the whole court upon me–all those guys in wigs and bad humor. Nobody was there to support me–not Kelley, not Beata, and I had no friends in London. I felt totally alone.

Finally, Reid's barrister said, "Mr. Flatley, is it fair to say you're an uneducated man? You never did go to college. You barely made it out of high school, shall we say?"

I couldn't believe it. With all my lawyers, all the money, the £350,000 I had advanced to my own barrister, why did I feel like I still the one who had to outsmart the opposition? It was like being a schoolboy again and having to fight my way out of trouble just to get to class.

When my testimony ended and court had finished for the day, I stalked angrily to the barristers' room, where all my lawyers were huddled together, talking about Lord knows what. I could feel my hand shaking a little bit. "You know what," I said, breathless with anger, "you're all full of shit. I don't trust you. I want my money back. You're not going to win this case. I'll win it myself."

I knew I had been unfair and the criticism was wrong but as I got into the car I was still steaming. Martin Flitton was by my side as we drove up to the Lanesborough Hotel. I kept going over and over what I'd said in court that day.

At nine o'clock the following morning, Harvey Goldsmith got on the stand and gave damning testimony against John Reid.

That night my barrister called me at Park Place Villas. "They want to settle," he told me.

I knew it!

"What do you want me to do?" my barrister asked.

I remember looking in the mirror at myself. I'm a street fighter, I thought. I have to fight. But this time, I'd already won.

"Is that all? Hell," I said, "give him the cash. And give him a kiss from me." It was worth it just to not have to go back to court.

Officially, I made a statement: "The amount Mr. Reid will receive after agreeing to pay his own substantial legal costs in their entirety is a small fraction of the original amount being claimed."

And John Reid made his statement: "The serious allegations which Michael Flatley made against me have been withdrawn and a substantial payment made. Naturally, I am pleased to put this behind me. It's a real shame that so much time, money and effort has been wasted in this process of getting to the point which we could have reached two years ago."

I slept better than he did that night.

John Reid was reported in London's Daily Mail *as saying, "I wouldn't manage again if Elvis and Jesus came back."*

Martin Flitton: "When the barrister asked Michael about being an uneducated man, I could see Michael wanted to jump the rails and give the lawyer a punch. I could see his mind at work. As I recall it, Michael found his answer and told the barrister, 'I'm an uneducated man.'

"The lawyer told him, 'Yes, yes, I believe we've established that.'

"Michael asked him, 'Do you consider John Reid an uneducated man, an ignorant man?'

" 'No.'

" 'What about the barrister behind you, is he an ignorant man?'

" 'No.'

" 'What about Keith Schilling, my lawyer, is he an ignorant man?"

" 'No, what's your point?'

"Michael told him with a smile, 'Did it ever occur to you that all these men work for me?'

"Even the journalists had to applaud that. Michael finally got the hang of it and started to eat the guy alive. When he'd finished it was obvious he'd won.

"The whole John Reid business affected Michael but he got through it and he delivered on stage every night he was on. It probably did have a bit of an effect on him, but who's been the winner? At the end of the day, Michael always said to me, 'John Reid served his purpose. Bill Tennant served his purpose, that was worth the deal.' They didn't get enough money between them to buy Michael's favorite wine. The way he looks at it is, 'Well, it cost me this.' But he got the return he wanted in both cases. He was the winner in that he got his result. . . .

"What Michael finally paid them was only a day's pay for him."

Chapter Thirty-five

Feet of Flames

For years, I've had a recurring dream—my worst nightmare. I'm on my deathbed, and I suddenly think of something else I wanted to do. I've lived my whole life to keep that dream from coming true.

So when the time came to think about cutting back my performance schedule, that dream was very much on my mind. Dancing had been my way of life for so long. I'm never so alive as when I'm dancing, never so in touch with the spiritual forces of the universe, the universal energy that sustains us all.

But the punishing pace at which I'd been performing had taken its toll. As early as 1995—before *Riverdance*—doctors had suggested that I think about retiring. I was used to the pain—like a bricklayer having a bad back. It's part of the job, and part of how I was brought up, to think that aches and pains would take care of themselves.

And there was no doubt that I was paying a price for the years of self-inflicted punishment. At night, my legs shake involuntarily as the nerves try to relax into sleep. The shaking can be so violent that it shocks me awake. In the mornings, my legs are always sore, and it can take me a minute or two to straighten them. Sure, when I warm up, I can get past the pain, and when I get going, I'm absolutely fine—I can dance as well as ever. But I was beginning to understand that if I continued to perform at the same grueling daily pace, I might be facing far more severe medical problems in the future.

Kelley Byrne: "No one had done Irish dancing professionally, competitions every weekend. With Irish dancing we land with straight legs, whereas with ballet and other forms you bend your knees. Doctors and physios always say, 'Oh, that bloody Irish dancing.' . . .

"You can't keep going forever. . . . He can't even walk first thing in the mornings. He has to struggle around for a while to really loosen his legs up.

"He can't walk, but he can dance. It's amazing. He has to bathe with extra salts. The pain would be there every day. There was the bath of ice after the show, he'd stick his head in a bucket of ice and there were always these extra salts in the bath. There never seemed to be enough salts. And he would sit in the bath in pain. He was constantly in pain. . . .

"It wouldn't surprise me if Michael ended up in a wheelchair. You just don't know. What he's done has never been done before. He's in agony. He always was. He doesn't complain. He's just so focused on what he's doing at that time."

I also had to face the fact that I wasn't the only person affected by my health. After our huge success in America, Australia, Europe, and the U.K., it became obvious I could produce different versions of the show, with several companies playing simultaneously in various locations. Most of the time, a show was going on somewhere in the world, with a permanent troupe in Las Vegas. Its first home was at the "New York, New York" hotel and casino; we later moved to the Venetian. Suddenly, I had a global enterprise that employed hundreds of dancers, musicians, technicians, and other staff. What would happen to them if I became disabled?

In addition, the whole business of running the company was demanding. I had to be here, there, and everywhere. I actually took flying lessons to see if I could get myself around more easily, but there was never time for me to learn properly. My schedule moved so quickly, it was more efficient to travel by private jet.

The decision to leave the stage—or at least to drastically cut back on my appearances—was one of the hardest in my life. In the end, what decided me was knowing that, when I'm on stage, I don't hold back—I can't. And I make sure that no one in any of my troupes holds back, either. I've been to hundreds of my shows—I've danced in more than a thousand of them—and I've never been to one that did not get a full standing ovation. I feel endlessly proud of that, for it tells me everything I need to know about the dancers, the show, and the people backstage who put the shows on night after night. You don't get that kind of response from a grudging company, a company full of backbiting and bad feeling, a company marked by resentment and time-serving. To get that kind of love and acclaim from an audience, everybody has to be doing their job to perfection—night after night after night. You need technical skill, artistic dedication, and, frankly, a positive attitude, in which the people at the top make every attempt to consider every single person involved in the show, everyone's feelings and needs and contribution. In the end, no matter how much people know the name of Michael Flatley, all my shows are a collective effort, and every single person working on them helps to create that marvelous audience response.

No matter what's happened to me, I've always been clear about the need to put out that positive energy. Why hurt when you can praise? Yes, I've been betrayed many times but I'm not vindictive. I learned very early in my life not to be that way at all. There is no value in it whatsoever.

And my reward is that remarkable response from the audience, which tells me that the good energy is there, the love of the dance and the commitment of the company. That energy doesn't lie—it can't. It always tells the truth.

Now the same instincts that had always led me toward that energy were telling me that it was time to slow up with my dancing. No matter how tough I was mentally, I was born into a human body just like the rest of us. That body could only take so much. It wasn't an option to ever hold back on stage. So I'd have to say farewell, or at least, so long.

Still, being me, I wasn't just going to slink quietly away. No, I was going out with a fanfare, something extra-special. If I had to bow out of *Lord of the Dance*, I decided, I would create an entirely new version of the show.

The idea was born on a walk through London's Hyde Park with Martin Flitton, who'd come on as tour manager for *Lord of the Dance*. I pointed out that in the four years since the Eurovision Song Contest, I'd appeared in three sell-out *Lord of the Dance* shows at the Royal Dublin Society arena as a farewell to Ireland and they'd all gone spectacularly well. How could I top that?

"Right," said Martin. "So, where do we go from here? We're not going to start robbing banks, surely?"

Maybe it was being in Hyde Park that gave me the idea. "What about an open-air event?" I speculated. "With big screens, so that every seat in the house truly is the best seat. We've been doing that in arenas around the world. Why not go for bigger and better?"

Martin thought for a minute. "If you can come up with a show big enough," he said, "I think I could get Hyde Park."

"Okay," I replied. "If you can get Hyde Park, I can do the show."

Seven days later, Martin told me, "You're on." He'd managed to arrange a presentation in Hyde Park's historic Route of Kings. All I had to do was provide what I'd promised—a show that would go down in history as the greatest dance spectacular on earth. Be careful what you wish for!

After I got over the shock of the mammoth task I'd just brought upon myself, I began to learn a valuable lesson: *Nothing succeeds likes excess.* You can always go further, always do more. What we were going to present was a turbocharged, remarkable, spectacular version of *Lord of the Dance.* I decided to call it *Feet of Flames.*

There had to be new songs and dances—I doubled the number of dancers and then doubled that again. I ended up with nearly one hundred dancers performing on several stage levels to give them creative space and the perfect setup for a truly grand finale.

To accommodate all the action I had buzzing in my head, we needed the stage to be as wide as a soccer pitch and with huge sidescreens. The technical arrangements were intricate as well, including twenty-three cameras to videotape the show. We needed new costumes, a new lighting design, new this, new that—maybe we were using *Lord of the Dance* as our starting point, but as far as I could see, we were entering entirely new territory. As the project grew, we kept restaging and changing ideas. The final stage was 180 feet wide.

I also knew we needed a new dance solo—something raw and effective. The solo came to me on July 16, 1998—my fortieth birthday. I went to the studio at 8 a.m., and worked for my usual dozen hours. I was exhausted. But when I had finished, I knew I had the centerpiece of the show.

This dance was to show the naked truth—the Michael Flatley who was pure dancer. No other dancers should share the stage with me, I decided. No frills or fancy effects. Not even any music. I would give myself nowhere to run, nowhere to hide. By now, I thought, I was strong enough to be true to myself and to the audience.

The lack of music wasn't just to keep it simple. It's because, when I rehearse in the studio, long after the others have gone, I make my own music, and have done since I was a little boy. It's like being alone in my dad's garage.

Sometimes we're afraid to show people what we do on our own. For this farewell show, I was going to come clean. Here, I'd say, look. This solo was exactly the type of work I enjoy the most. It's me alone with my dancing, me alone with whatever guides me through the steps. And indeed, whenever I performed that solo, I'd get this strange tingle, as though the dance itself was dancing *me*.

On July 25, 1998, we had a sell-out audience of 50,000 people for our Hyde Park show. Most of the show was a high-energy extravaganza. But I wanted to give the audience a moment to reflect–and maybe I wanted a moment to reflect, myself. So I included a flute solo that my mother dearly liked.

I could never have known how much that decision would mean to me. As I played, I took a split second to look into the audience–and amidst the thousands of spectators, I picked out my mother.

She was crying.

I knew then that she understood what my work was about. Finally, she understood. I just wish she knew how to share her feelings.

Such a private moment–in such a public setting. But that's performing, isn't it? You take your most private feelings, your deepest secrets, your most hidden self. And you give it all to the audience.

So when I got to the *Feet of Flames* solo, I let the dance have its way with me. As I finished the part I'd choreographed, the audience was clapping. I couldn't help it–I started dancing again. They were demanding more, and I was in God's hands. I was inventing steps, right there on the stage, the steps accelerating, until the solo explodes–and vanishes.

What or who made me dance these extra steps?

I don't know the answer and I probably never will. But I put everything I believe in into that solo. And the audience cheered. Why not? They were as much a part of it as I was.

Dance critic Ismene Brown reviewed the show in London's Daily Telegraph, *on July 27, 1998: "Any difference between [Michael Flatley] and God is entirely unintended. . . . [There was] a single encore for Flatley called 'Feet of Flames' and very brilliant it was."*

* * *

Dancer Sarah Clark danced the lead role on tour with Michael Flatley in Feet of Flames. *She said in London in October 2004: "I got on very well with Michael. When I first joined the troupe I was kind of in awe because he had been this figure that I strived all my life to emulate: 'Wow, wouldn't it be amazing to dance on stage with Michael Flatley?' Then suddenly, I was! It was a bit surreal at first and I suppose it took me a while to . . . get to know Michael and be able to feel comfortable approaching him, just because he had achieved so much. He was this figure that everybody kind of aspired to be like.*

"We were able to converse about things and we had common interests about certain things, which was nice. It's nice to be able to get on with your boss.

"We did have great parties and it was a lot of fun, because it was like one big family. Michael is a very sociable person. When we were in London, Michael had just bought his house in Little Venice, and he invited the original cast and the lead dancers over to his house. . . . It was very civilized and we had a meal. It was really nice to have that opportunity to spend time with him and it was quite an intimate group.

"He was a good boss to have. He expected your best all the time but that was from someone who was so talented and such a perfectionist and who was so hard on himself, it's only right that we should be expected to do one hundred and ten percent every night. During rehearsals, yes, it was hard work, but it was always a learning experience. . . . Work was work, and then afterwards, Michael would be your buddy and be your friend and you'd sit in the bar with him and whatever . . . you could get on. . . .

"There were so many highlights with the show, but I think Feet of Flames *in Hyde Park was extra special. There was a perfect buildup and then a perfect evening."*

Chapter Thirty-six

The French Connection

I'd like him to teach me to dance although that might be a little dangerous.
He's an intriguing man. And he looks so good.

Catherine Deneuve
in Monte Carlo, August 2003

"If you're looking for the jewel in the crown, you've got to go to the top."

The French real-estate agent and I were having coffee at the harbor at Villefranche-sur-Mer. I'd always considered Southern California a pale copy of the south of France, so I was looking in the very nicest parts of the French Riviera. By this point, I'd seen twenty-two houses, each with its good points, but none that was perfect for me. I was beginning to get a bit fed up.

"Look up," the agent insisted. "At the very top of that mountain. If you can find something up there, it's out of this world."

I was skeptical. "It's not Cap-Ferrat," I said doubtfully. Cap-Ferrat was considered one of the most desirable locations.

The man shook his head in that French way and smiled. "No. You will have to see to believe what I say. I will show you a house. It's much better than what you have seen so far! Much sweeter."

He drove me up the hill and sure enough, the higher I got, the more I loved it. There was no noise, the air was clearer than down below, and the neighborhood was fascinating. And the drive itself was a spin of hairpins toward the clouds. I loved the sense of adventure!

After we'd passed a security checkpoint, we came up a drive and stopped at a very nondescript stone wall. There was no grand entrance to this property. There was only a hole in the wall, which led to a tiny elevator, which whooshed directly up through the rock.

I felt as though I were in an early James Bond movie. But our journey wasn't over. We came out of the elevator and climbed up a set of very steep stone stairs. And there was one of Nature's great prizes spread out before me all the way to the horizon: a view of the Riviera coast and the mesmerizing light that had tempted Matisse and Picasso. Before I even entered the house, I told the agent, "I'll take it."

The agent was stunned. He'd just wanted to give me an idea of the mountaintop. He hadn't even considered trying to sell me this particular house.

Of course, the place was an absolute disaster, worse than the Park Place Villas I'd bought in London. When we entered, I felt like a burglar in a derelict house.

I walked out to the swimming pool and there was a broken old table in the corner where the owner was sitting. I looked at the view behind him, the breathtaking vistas over Saint-Jean-Cap-Ferrat and Nice. "Oh, yeah," I thought. "That'll work. This is the most glamorous thing I've ever seen."

The owner and I worked out a deal right then and there. On the drive down the mountain, the real-estate agent said, "I've shown thirty people this house, and they all turned around and walked away. They just didn't have the vision."

Villa la Masquerade is now remarkable enough to attempt to match the view. Tina Turner lives around the corner, I can see Elton

John's place from my property, and Bill Gates's property is close, too—a big, yellow mansion that once belonged to King Leopold of Belgium. Monte Carlo is just a few moments away, and the private-jet facility at Nice Airport is one of the most efficient in the world. I'd found a hefty chunk of paradise.

Chapter Thirty-seven

Rock Bottom

The *Riverdance* fight, the John Reid fight, the Bill Tennant fight, my divorce, the pressures of touring, and my relationship with Kelley were all taking their toll. To say that I was drinking to excess—even in Irish terms—would be the understatement of a lifetime.

I knew I had to end it with Kelley—I'd tried a dozen times to break up with her already, but each time I'd gone back. It was intense, passionate, and utterly insane. I felt addicted, and I told myself I needed a cure—something to make me kick the Kelley habit.

Throughout that whole period of separating from Kelley, I was depressed. I'd get hammered for two weeks at a time, drinking every day from noon until 6 p.m. with all my friends. Then I'd take four or five temazepam, 20 milligrams each, to put myself to sleep. And in the morning, I'd be sipping Berocca and a glass of vitamin C to try and temper the hangover.

My relationship with Kelley seemed to be a focal point for all of the intensity, passion, and love in my life. The idea of leaving her seemed to set off literal withdrawal symptoms. I've never been addicted to heroin—thank God—but I can't help thinking that it would be easier to break a heroin habit than my Kelley addiction.

Then one day I met the woman who would help me rebuild my tattered love life As these things often do, the meeting happened in a roundabout way.

I was in Dublin to appear on *The Late, Late Show*, a major Irish talk show. My old friend, the host Gay Byrne, had retired and been replaced by a new man, Pat Kenny.

The show began, my turn came, and I sat down to grand applause. Pat Kenny turned to me and with a huge grin he asked me about the one thing I didn't want to discuss, "Michael, who are you dating these days? Tell us about your private life."

You can't imagine how mad I was. Somehow, I found a way of weaseling out of the question without mentioning Kelley's name. It was hard enough breaking up without bringing millions of TV viewers in on the act, let alone the effect on Kelley herself.

I came out of the interview and went toward the greenroom—the backstage hospitality area—where there was the usual crowd of people waiting to have a drink with me. I just didn't feel up to socializing, though I knew there was no escape. But I stopped in the middle of the hallway, taking a moment alone, and, as I'd done so many times in my life, I made a wish:

"Please, God, send me a new girl. Anything to get me out from under Kelley's spell. Please. Help me."

I headed for the greenroom, still seething with anger about Pat's intrusive question. But then someone else said, "Come on, Michael, come to Lillie's Bordello for one drink. Just one drink—come on."

I didn't want to, but I couldn't quite muster the energy to get out of it. Dave Egan, Lillie's owner and now one of my greatest friends, was part of the greenroom crowd. As a good friend he wanted to get me settled down with a drink as fast as possible. He steered me toward the club's front door, saying, "Let's go in and have a talk."

I said, "We never go in the front door!" That way we avoid the crowds and Dave knew that. Nevertheless, for some reason, we walked in through the front, and of course, we were instantly mobbed with people.

Then I saw the most perfect figure I had ever seen in my life, and my anger disappeared. It was a young woman named Lisa Murphy. I instantly invited her and her friends to join me in the VIP area.

Lisa was terrific and we hit it off right away. She was quiet and sensible and totally warm-hearted. Could she be the one who would help me get over Kelley?

Lisa and I started dating, very slow and casual, but I knew from the first there was something special there. One evening, Lisa was supposed to meet me in the bar at the Westbury Hotel. I was waiting for her down there, looking forward to our date, when my mobile phone rang.

It was Kelley. By this point, I hadn't seen her for a few months. I suppose we were officially broken up, but such things never meant anything to Kelley. She'd always made it clear that she was never going to let me go.

"I'm out with my girlfriends," she said, "and we're right down the street at Davy Byrne's Pub." I had to smile, thinking of Kelley at the famous Dublin pub where James Joyce used to drink.

"That's great," I said lamely. "I hope you're having a nice time." Having Kelley call when I was thinking about Lisa almost made me feel guilty. Plus, I couldn't help feeling nervous. Whenever I heard from Kelley, she always found a way of roping me back into the relationship. Now that I'd met someone else I was really interested in, would Kelley still have the same power over me? I feared she would.

"Yeah," she said. "But Michael, I want to see you."

"Kel, this is not a good idea. It's over between us."

"Come on," she insisted. "I'm only a few seconds away. Can't I come and see you?"

"Kelley. No. I'm going to be dating another girl now. This is wrong. Don't start the fires again."

As always, Kelley was determined. Half of me loved it and half of me was terrified. I didn't know what to say. A few minutes later, she made a grand entrance into the bar.

She was a vision, all right: tight blue jeans, a black leather coat I'd bought her at Susannah in Beverly Hills, her auburn hair blazing just like a mountain of fire, her blue eyes burning with the effect of a few pints. Kelley was blessed with a magnificent female physique and her breasts were bursting out of her low-cut sweater.

"I'm your girl and you know it," she whispered in my ear. "We'll always be together till the day we die."

I felt myself beginning to melt.

"We're like Samson and Delilah," she murmured, and indeed, I felt my strength draining away at her very touch. I could just take her up to my room, I thought. I could just carry her up.

But somehow I got the strength to say, "Kelley. No means no. No more anything. I'm sorry. No. I can't."

"Why not?" Kelley demanded. Her blue eyes flashed.

"You're not the girl for me," I lied. "You and I are totally different. You love the things I hate. You hate the things I love. I make you laugh, and you make me cry." All very true!

By now, Lisa had arrived in the hotel lobby, along with Dave Egan, who was to be joining Lisa and me for a drink before we went off to dinner by ourselves. I could see her from where I sat—and I'm sure she could see me, too, but she was too much of a lady to come and join us.

"None of that matters," Kelley insisted loudly, oblivious to anyone who might be listening. "We belong together."

"No," I said desperately. "Kelley, what can I say that could possibly get through to you? It's over."

As usual, Kelley didn't cry—she got mad. She stormed out of the hotel lobby, into the pouring rain.

I looked after Kelley, and I looked at Lisa, and then I looked after Kelley again. I stood there, paralyzed, while the previous five years raced through my head and thoughts of the next five years tried to crowd out the past.

Something clicked. I couldn't hold back any longer. My brain turned off and my heart took charge.

I ran down the stairs and into the street, bundling a bunch of pound notes into the doorman's hand. "Follow me," I told him. "I don't care what you're supposed to be doing, you've got to be my bodyguard right now."

We ran down Grafton Street in the pouring rain through droves of people. I was running as fast as I could, the doorman stumbling along behind me in full uniform, his coat flapping in the wind as he struggled to avoid the spreading puddles.

We ran all the way down Grafton Street, and I couldn't find Kelley anywhere. We ran and ran and ran, all the way to Trinity College. There was a taxi rank, crowded with angry people in the downpour, and there was Kelley, halfway up the line.

I caught sight of an old lady selling flowers. "How much for the whole bunch?" I asked her. Everybody was looking at me but I didn't care.

The flower woman was all a-fluster. She stared at me and said nothing. I gave her a fifty and said, "I'll take it." I grabbed the flowers and went over to Kelley, pulling her out of the line. Then I dropped the flowers and I kissed her, right there in front of Trinity College, in full view of several dozen people waiting for taxis in the pouring rain.

That kiss must have lasted an eternity. We didn't come up for air. And that was the last time I ever kissed Kelley Byrne.

I can honestly say there was a time I would have traded every other memory I have for that one kiss. I would have traded all my money, all my houses, all my talent, all my friends, my family, even my dancing—all for that one kiss.

As I put her in her taxi, my face was soaking wet and it wasn't the rain. My heart was bleeding. But I let her go.

Kelley Byrne: "Suddenly, [after Lord of the Dance*] he had all this money and it was so new to him. But it was horrible, because he was famous, because he was rich. We'd be out together and girls would be literally standing beside him and girls would hand him their phone numbers. It was just unbelievable what happens when you're famous. I'm just not into that at all and I don't agree with it. I used to say to him, 'I just wish you were poor, and ugly.'*

"We could have lived happily ever after. That really screwed everything up. We already been together about two years when Lord of the Dance *happened, I guess. I don't exactly know when we started thinking, 'Oh, right, we'll be together forever.'*

"He's very sensitive. If he was poor and we lived in a little cottage, it'd be great.

"A woman actually pulled up in a car beside us in Beverly Hills and she was talking over me to Michael: 'Nice car.' She was really flirting. I hated this, and we were totally at odds over it. I could still be with him now if I had let him do what he wanted and if I was into money, but I am not. Sometimes he's on the phone to me when I'm going to work, telling me he's going to Barbados. I could have all that, but I wasn't willing to turn a blind eye, and I think some people are. I think, for us, that wasn't a good thing. [But] I had a great time, a great life.

"I think we'll always be good friends and we'll be able to go out for a drink together and he can bring his girlfriend and I can bring my boyfriend. But it was his success that ruined what we had. He's always had to pay a price all his life with the personal always at war with the professional life. For us, as a couple, it would have been better if he'd not gone on to create Lord of the Dance.

". . . He'd come home, and every night he'd be wrecked and he would sit in a bath of ice. We'd have nice holidays, but on tour it wasn't easy working and living with the same people. You've no life of your own

outside of that. I had five years of living out of a suitcase and I'm not putting it down at all, but it wasn't all plain sailing. When we finished, I found it such a novelty to go to work from nine to five.

"Once, we lived in Malibu Colony, right on the beach next door to Tom Hanks. I used to email all my friends: 'Oh my God, you've no idea. I'm looking at Tom Hanks on the beach right now.' But we were never happier than going to a little pub on Lincoln Boulevard in Santa Monica where we'd have a chat and a pint in the quiet. In Malibu, more often than not we'd stay in and have dinner or even get pizza and watch videos.

"Oh, yes, the temptation. People would hand him their phone numbers and stuff. It's very hard to say 'No' when they're all gorgeous women. People throw themselves at him. It happened to him later in life but it's probably every man's dream to have women throw themselves at him. Maybe that's his weakness. Women.

"I love him and he's my best friend. I blame the sudden fame, the money. I blame . . . I don't blame the women. He's the one who has to say 'No'–but I know it would be hard to say. . . .

"[Being with Michael] was the best experience of a lifetime. I don't look on things as a bad experience, I've learned my lesson. It was good fun. And we're still good friends. That says a lot about Michael."

In the end, Lisa saved me. I didn't want to drink when I was with Lisa. I felt I could trust her, that I could count on her not to be fiery or to disrupt my life. I became friendly with her parents, Des and Eileen, and I visited their family home in Ballinteer in south Dublin.

Ours was never love at first sight. Our relationship developed slowly, an on-again, off-again relationship that I felt was all the more true and close for taking so long to find its way.

Lisa is a sweet, genuine, loving little girl with a big heart and a bright smile. She has such a beautiful disposition. Mainly, we could laugh and have fun. We laughed and laughed for days at a time.

Before I knew it, I didn't need sleepers or beer. I was blooming again. The sun was shining! I had my heart back, and it was finally whole once more.

We met in September, and soon thereafter, we went to the Imperial Ball at the Imperial Palace in Vienna. We kissed at midnight, and I knew the magic was there. I was so happy. Three months later, I went to Graff Jewellers in London and bought Lisa a ten-carat D flawless engagement ring. I knew I had loved Lisa but as soon as I proposed I realized I wasn't ready to be married again. I broke it off after a few days. She understood and we continued to have a fantastic time together.

Lisa Murphy: "We first met in Dublin. It was in Lillie's Bordello. I was nervous. I was introduced and said, 'Hello, how are you. Nice to meet you. . . .'

"My sister Kyra and my friend Miriam sat on one side, and myself and Michael on the other. I was so nervous. I couldn't even sit back on the chair; I sat up straight at the front of the chair. Poor Michael was trying to have a conversation with me, and all my answers were one word, yes or no. I couldn't even talk to him. I remember he went to the powder room and my sister kicked me under the table and said, 'You look so ridiculous. For God's sake, I can't believe how you're acting, have a drink, do something. You look ridiculous.' She told me to relax. I couldn't.

"That was a Friday night. Anyhow the next night I was home and just pottering around upstairs, and it was about five o'clock in the evening and my sister comes running up the stairs, 'Michael's on the phone!'

"I said, 'Michael who?'

"She said, 'Michael. The gentleman that we met last night.'

"I was so nervous. He said that he would love to take me for dinner. He was sorry for the late call but my phone had been engaged. That was because my sister had been on the phone telling everybody about the night before. I said I would meet him at the restaurant.

"My mother and father had to give me a Valium to calm me down. I couldn't get ready.

"I went into the restaurant, and I met him, and we went for dinner. It was lovely. . . . He invited me back to his hotel, the Westbury Hotel, and I said I was going to go back home. He said to just come back and have a drink with him. So I went back anyway, and we spent the whole night talking. We ended up falling asleep about five in the morning and then he was flying to Castlehyde [Michael's Irish estate]. He asked me to go with him, and I said, 'Oh, absolutely not. I have to go. My parents will be waiting for me. I've got work on Monday morning.' . . .

"It was a pleasure and privilege to share Michael's life–at every level. We laughed all the time. It was always fun. We made love day and night. He's the sexiest man in the world. He's a classy, sexy guy–there's no taking away from that. He also displays such perceptivity. He believes in the good things in life and in people. He always wants to see the positive side. . . .

"And, yes, he's sexy. That's very important. We enjoyed a wonderful sex life. For me, it was very fulfilling. Deeply sexual. We always had a very intense time–when we weren't making love two or three times a day we were thinking about it. It was very much part of our lives together. It was totally natural for me to appear naked in front of Michael no matter what the time or the place. I never caught him when he wasn't ready. He was always the most enthusiastic man. . . .

"I know I'll always love him throughout my life. He's brought me so much joy and happiness. We were so very close. Michael has said to me, 'Lisa, if I'm a vegetable in a hospital and I can't talk and I can't see, you must end it for me.'

"I said, 'Michael, I could not physically do that.' I would look after him until he passed over, but I could not take that plug out. I would mind him until the day I die, from the bottom of my soul, because I love him so much. I wouldn't be able to end it for him. It wouldn't be in my heart.

"We've been around the world together–I've sat in the jungle for twelve hours at a time, being eaten to death by huge insects, just to be close to him. I'd support him anytime, anywhere.

"You know how people say they would go to the end of the earth for someone? I would–for Michael.

"And he would do that for his family and friends, for the people he loves. He's so loyal. And generous. In the past year he's given away seven cars that I know about. And there's all the charity work he does, and no one hears about. He's a doer–he gets things done and doesn't just talk about it.

"And he's not a boastful person–he's quite hidden about a lot of things. He's very grounded and people feel comfortable around him. He's been so true to his own family. And to my family–treated them like his own. If Michael loves you, he's never going to totally leave your life–he'll always be there for you."

Chapter Thirty-eight

King of the Castle

Michael Flatley has a lifestyle to envy.

HUGH HEFNER, May 2004

I WAS ABOUT TO LAUNCH *Feet of Flames* on a world tour. We had a list of tour dates in former Eastern bloc countries where the show had never played, so potential audiences in places like Budapest and Moscow weren't aware of the type of work that we were doing. At the same time, it was difficult to create a splash with the new show because *Lord of the Dance* had broken so many records and made such an impact worldwide. How could I top that?

I would walk on water.

We staged a press conference in Germany at the bottom of the Burg Satzvey near Cologne. It was all very dramatic. I appeared suddenly on the lovely lake, set afire by clever and very safe special effects. I then appeared to walk on water–that is, I tiptoed across a neatly constructed and skillfully disguised platform. The newspapers had me rising "from the depths of a fiery lake."

Of course, someone wanted to know if I'd intended any sort of hidden message. No, I told the reporter, I was only sending myself up. If only the tour had been as simple as that walk! In fact, our millennium show offered more risks–and perhaps, also, more rewards.

Our plan was to entertain around one million fans in five countries in one hundred days. I'd changed the show almost entirely, with new costumes and set as well as a deeper, more developed story line. With a well-known, successful show, you have to be very careful. People want to see the best of what you've done, but they also want to see something new. I couldn't change too much, so I decided to make what we had bigger and better. For me, though, the center of our success was always that "Feet of Flames" solo. I had grown into it, and the audiences seemed to love it, too. So I left that pretty much alone.

All my decisions paid off. The Budapest debut was a sensation. We played to more than one hundred thousand people and they went crazy for us. I could tell the confidence of the dancers had reached a new peak. The tour was an enormous high for all of us that continued through Belgium, Austria, the Netherlands, Switzerland, and at the legendary Waldbühne in Berlin.

Financially, the tour was also a high. As always, I paid close attention to that aspect of my business. I knew exactly how much was being earned from merchandising and video sales, how many seats we sold–and how many in advance, at special prices–as well as what the action was on the Web sites. That paid off, too. During the German tours we came out with millions of pounds cash.

Yet we never let the success go to our heads. One promoter looked at me and said, "You're so young and the show is so great."

"Thank you," I replied.

Then he looked at Martin Flitton and his big leather bag. Martin was the very picture of an Englishman on a seaside holiday–in a shirt and flannel trousers and shoes, but no socks.

"You march into our country, our town, and you don't even wear socks!" the promoter marveled. "You don't go to parties, and there's no big entourage. You don't even have the bodyguards. And then you take all this cash like two cowboys."

He had it right. On the performing side, I'm dedicated to delivering the best I can. On the business side, I'm into results. We go in quietly. We extract as much cash as humanly possible. Then we get out of town. The minute a show sells out, we pull the advertising. It surprises some people but I'm not into vanity advertising. If we've already sold all the tickets, why keep telling people we're around? We can come back sooner if we're not overexposed.

Our last European stop was Stormont Castle in Belfast where for so many years political debate had raged over "The Troubles." But none of that mattered to me. As far as I'm concerned, Ireland–north and south, it's all the one. And I dearly wanted to give Ireland our best. In fact, I canceled half a dozen European dates so we would be able to perform in Belfast during the millennium.

Belfast in turn welcomed me and my company. I was only the third performer, after Pavarotti and Sir Elton John, to be granted permission to appear in the grounds of Stormont Castle. And when we finished our show, more than fifteen thousand fans cheered us on. A wonderful end to the old millennium–and an exciting beginning for the new one.

By now, I'd settled into a relationship with Lisa Murphy, in a lifestyle that included the world's penthouse suites; Park Place Villas in London's "Little Venice"; the Villa Masquerade on the French Riviera; and a rather broken-down old pile in Ireland, the late Georgian home known as Castlehyde.

It had been my dream to live full-time in Ireland, and I'd either looked at or been told about almost every property available in the country. As with my previous real-estate searches, nothing I'd seen seemed right.

Then one day I was flying over the area around Cork by helicopter and I caught sight of Castlehyde, the ancestral home of Ireland's first president, Douglas Hyde.

The castle had been built in 1760 and extended forty-one years later. In its day, it had been a jewel, a treasured hospitality point, on Ireland's aristocratic High Road. Winston Churchill and Fred Astaire had been regular visitors to this lovely place, which was set in some 150 acres on the banks of the River Blackwater in north Cork. The castle was a gem, to be sure, but two and a half centuries had taken their toll. At a glance, the place was a mess, but with foresight and imagination, the possibilities were endless.

The asking price was steep, and the money needed to restore Castlehyde to its former glory was at least ten times more. For starters, there was water damage to the roof, and to the basement area where the foundations had subsided after more than one hundred years of water seepage. The main walls were out of sync, leaning at some points as dramatically as the Tower of Pisa. The general opinion was that this was a hopeless property, the very definition of a money pit. When I asked a builder about renovation work, he suggested that it would be more humane for all concerned to simply demolish the four-story structure.

Of course, I bought it. I've never regretted buying Castlehyde but, at moments, in the small hours, I have sometimes wondered if I'd be in the castle or at the gate when the work was finally complete!

Meanwhile, *Lord of the Dance* and *Feet of Flames* were dancing around the globe–and I was dancing with them. My enthusiasm for dancing was always–and probably always will be–in conflict with how long I could physically carry on delivering top-class performances. I decided that at the end of the American *Feet of Flames* tour in Dallas in July 2001, I would officially walk out of the spotlight.

Nevertheless, the touring shows were entitled *Michael Flatley's Lord of the Dance* and *Michael Flatley's Feet of Flames*. Even though I wasn't on the stage, I was still hands-on, the creative director as well as the guy in charge of all the business decisions.

By now I was watching over three touring troupes plus the permanent Las Vegas-based show. It was my name out there and I never wanted it to be taken in vain. Happily, quality control had been in place for a long time.

Marie Duffy personally took all the auditions for me, and she's the most wonderful and fairest person I know. Marie is like my twin sister—one of my dearest friends. I love her. She shares my high standards—and my open mind. We take all levels, sizes, colors, and shapes. And we don't necessarily take who you'd expect. I've worked with some of the greatest world champions in Irish dance history but they weren't made for the stage. They just didn't have that kind of performance in their hearts. They didn't love to be there.

Then I've worked with other kids, dancers who never really got to the medal rounds in Irish dance competition but who desperately wanted to be on stage. I never had to tell them to smile for the audience—they came to life in the spotlights and simply glowed.

My most fulfilling task these days is to display the marvelous talent of my dancers for all the world to see. It's a system that works: the *Guinness Book of World Records* has recognized me as the world's highest-paid dancer, earning $1.6 million U.S. per week. And *Lord of the Dance* has consistently topped international ticket sales.

I'm proud of my success, of my Irish heritage, and of my American citizenship. As an American, I consider that there's no greater honor than to meet the President, and I am proud to have shaken hands with three of them: President Ronald Reagan, President Bill Clinton, and President George H. W. Bush.

It was a great honor to receive the Irish-American Lifetime Achievement Award in 2001 from President Clinton at the Plaza Hotel in New York. I'd gotten a similar award from his wife, Hillary.

I believe in sharing the wealth, so I decided to bring Martin Flitton in on the action. Martin is a great buddy. He's always looked after me with the best of intentions. We've had wild times, arguments, crazy times but always fun. What a great guy. I love him, and I knew he'd love to meet the President.

Although Martin was with me in New York, he didn't know about the ceremony. So at the last moment I told Martin that I was off to visit with Bill Clinton–did he want to come along?

He thought I was joking, but he dutifully got dressed up and came with me.

I know he's still got that photograph of him and Bill Clinton somewhere!

Martin Flitton: "Michael designed the business books in such a way that he could understand them. There's probably some big business bigshot who would say it's all wrong, but it worked for him. His shows made more money than the Rolling Stones–because we did it this way. It was all business. One German promoter said he had pop stars who demanded ten beautiful girls, three bodyguards, and white couches and Oriental furniture in the dressing room. They demanded this suite and that luxury.

"I swear, few people in show business would go into Michael's dressing room. He'd take the one that was left over. He's never been about any of that other stuff.

"Me? I never wear suits. It's always jeans and T-shirts. Michael knows that. We were in New York and he said, 'You need to go and get a suit.'

"I could usually do the jacket and tie route, but he wanted me to have a suit and I got suspicious. Then I almost panicked, for Michael ran down to the shops and bought me a suit and I got dressed up.

" 'You look a right proper gent,' he said. And the suit fitted perfectly. What I didn't know is that he'd had one of the assistants get my measurements and had a tailor fix me up a suit.

"The next day he announces we're going on a trip and he told me, 'Be ready, wear your suit.'

"So I get ready, put the suit on, and the car is outside. He asks me if I want to meet the President. I thought he was taking the piss. We get in the car and again he says, 'Do you want to meet the President?'

"And off we go and meet the President.

"And all the time he's with Bill Clinton he's looking over at me and smiling. . . ."

Stephen Marks: "Michael really does manage himself. He's happy for people to help him in various things, but Michael has gone past, as a lot of artists do, having the need to have a manager to tell them what to do and how to do it. He's gone past that level and I think he doesn't need his hand held. With Michael you can't ever sit and relax.

"He's not one of these people you can say 'Everything's fine and going along nicely today.' It's just not that sort of environment. There are always things. Don't catch your breath! Don't!

"Every year there's something, the John Reid and the Bill Tennant situations . . . divorces and all sorts of issues have arisen over the years. I've said, 'We've got a lot to do now but don't worry, it'll all calm down soon.'

"But with Michael it's double-speed, it doesn't really calm down. There's always things happening.

"Michael's memory is the thing that everybody underestimates. Michael never forgets anything. Ever. If I give him figures, or if I quote him something, three or four years later, he can quote me exactly what it was. His memory is like an elephant. That's why you shouldn't bullshit or mislead him because he will come back and say, 'You said such and such . . .'.

"You learn very quickly. He's difficult, he's demanding, he has great vision; very warm, very generous. People always ask me what he's really like as a person, and everybody is going to have a different relationship with him. Michael is genuine. I think he has his faults but deep down, for me, he's a fantastic person. He likes nice things.

"The key to Michael is to be honest and tell him the truth. He's not going to want to hear it from everybody. He's got to have all the other

ideas–that's what makes him an artist. Michael is good in that he wants to know where he is. He never, ever wants to go back to where he came from. Never. He never wants to go back to his life or what it was. Maybe that's why he doesn't want to live in America. He doesn't want to be a part of it. He had a hard upbringing. It might look like an easy life, but it's not. There's always a lot to deal with. . . ."

Chapter Thirty-nine

Trouble Spots

Michael is a genius at what he does. To survive and prosper for five years on the Las Vegas Strip, one of the most competitive places in the world? That says something about the man and his determination.

TOM JONES, Las Vegas, October 12, 2003

BY NOW, the media had dubbed me "the billion-dollar dancer" in recognition of all the money my shows had made. We profited at home and abroad: With our permanent troupe at the Venetian Hotel, we got our share of the more than forty million annual visitors to Las Vegas. And by the twenty-first century, our show had premiered in Japan, Lebanon, Bulgaria, Russia, South America, and Africa, as well as doing sell-out business throughout Western Europe, Australia, and the United States.

As my reputation grew, my troupe and I continued to be invited to appear at all sorts of special events, from a Christmas run at Euro Disney, and annual appearances at Disney's Epcot Center in Orlando, to five evenings in Beirut at the ancient Roman site of Baalbek, where followers once gathered to worship Jupiter, Venus, and Mercury.

On the first night in Lebanon, such a troubled part of the world, there was a full moon and I was close to tears. I was so moved to see these Irish dancers receiving a huge ovation from thousands of Lebanese fans. It brought home to me how close and small the world can be if we allow it to be so.

I was very aware of security in Beirut, as well. All over the world I've had bodyguards for both crowd control and protection against overzealous fans. My insurance demands that I employ the best security during my tours and for personal appearances–and a good thing, too, or tragedy might have ensued at several points.

I think at one time the FBI, Interpol, and the British authorities all had alerts out over threats or other security problems I was facing. It's one of the cruel prices of fame. After all, the nature of what I do is to attract fans, which then makes it hard to discourage the obsessive ones.

One of my most terrifying experiences occurred at the Villa Masquerade, at a time when Lisa was staying with me. Earlier that evening, we'd had dinner at the Louis XV restaurant in Monaco's Hotel du Paris. Now Lisa was sound asleep with me in the second-floor master bedroom suite.

As usual, I was only half asleep. Suddenly I heard someone banging on a downstairs window. Was the intruder actually in my house? I waited silently in the dark, Lisa sleeping peacefully by my side. I could feel my heart pounding. Could I be wrong?

Then I heard the unmistakable click of my bedroom door. I slowly sat up in bed, and by the light of the full moon I could see a big shadow of a bald-headed man. He silently stuck his head in through the door of my bedroom.

My heart was hammering and I could feel the hairs going up on the back of my neck. But I simply waited.

A moment later, the big head had come so close that I could see the whites of his eyes as he stared directly at me. "Get the hell out of my house!" I yelled at him.

He took a step towards the bed. I thought he was going to come after Lisa.

I jumped out of bed and went toward him. Thank God, he ran. But I'm sure he didn't come in unprepared. He could have killed me. He was certainly bigger than I was. I was screaming at the top of my lungs. I thought it must have taken at least two people to get the man to the second-floor window. Then I heard Lisa shouting at me, "Michael, Michael, wake up! You're having a nightmare!"

All she could see was me standing there naked. She was half awake and petrified, and she imagined I was sleepwalking.

"Lisa, call the police," I said as I looked for my shoes, wondering if I should go after the bastard. "I'm going to chase him."

As I headed for the door, I heard the chair outside my room move and then some hurried steps. He'd been waiting right there to jump me. I took a deep breath and went running into the hall. He was gone–and I was shaking.

It was only then that I wondered if the intruders had been armed, if they had guns or knives. They didn't seem to have taken anything. I wondered what they'd wanted.

Finally, the cops arrived. They found that these intruders had broken in at the upstairs window to the second bedroom using a very sophisticated tool. They'd removed the lock with one bang–the sound I heard.

Lisa couldn't believe her eyes. There were wood shavings all over the other bedroom's floor, and the lock was gone. She'd really thought I'd been dreaming.

"This is not good news," the police inspector said to me with typical French understatement.

"Well, obviously it's not good news," I snapped. "They could have killed us."

"Yes, they could. The big problem is they didn't take your wallet, which was downstairs. They didn't take all that cash sitting on your bureau right outside your bedroom or that black American Express card."

I'm one of the few people in the world lucky enough to have a black Amex card. It's special because it has no limit. I was hugely relieved that it hadn't been stolen. But the officer had the opposite reaction.

"They didn't take your cufflinks or your watch," the man went on. "Or the diamonds. They left them all on the little table. They didn't take anything. They didn't take any of the art on the walls."

He looked at me. I got the message. He added, "Monsieur Flatley, doesn't it strike you as strange that they went straight for your bedroom, the only closed door in your house?" They knew where we slept, he said, adding, "They've been watching you."

I said they could have wanted a party with Lisa but the inspector said, "Don't be ridiculous. It's nothing to do with women. Women are easy to find." He told me a billionaire had been murdered at a villa in the area in the previous month–and three weeks before the killing there had been a break-in.

"They came in and took a look at where he slept, saw him in his bedroom and left. Later, they came back and shot him. It was some very bad business."

What he said was horrifying, but it had the effect of making me even more vigilant about my security. I was determined to take precautions and get on with life. I thought it would be disgraceful to react to thugs in any other way. But I had to prove that theory to myself in St. Petersburg, when MI5 called Martin Flitton to say they'd intercepted a Russian death threat that had been made against me. It wasn't safe, the authorities told me, and I was strongly advised to leave.

But I couldn't bring myself to run and hide. What would my life be if I behaved that way? I stayed an extra day. As it turned out, I got off easy compared to what my friends suffered in Moscow.

Lord of the Dance had had a fantastic reception in Moscow, as in St. Petersburg. The Russians had been instantly mad about *Lord of the Dance,* and there's even an Irish dancing school in Moscow because of it–the Iridian school, founded by Igor Denisov, the only one of its kind in Russia. Igor was inspired by a video of the show, and he was clearly onto something: he never has fewer than a hundred pupils.

Along with my dancers, I met a lot of the children in the school as well as Igor, who'd learned all my dance routines. We got very friendly with them. The next time I heard of Igor and his students, they were among the hundreds of hostages held in a Moscow theater by a group of Chechen rebels. The suicide squad threatened to shoot all the hostages one by one unless Russian troops were pulled out of Chechnya. Igor had taken the kids to see a show at the theater when the rebels marched in and took them captive.

The crisis became even more personal for me when one of my friends, Rita Nekrasova, who worked for the Russian promoters of *Lord of the Dance,* began acting as a negotiator between the rebels and the authorities in Moscow. Rita had been involved with all my trips to Russia and had handled all the local press inquiries. Now, trapped in the theater, she was in the midst of a nightmare. I heard the news when I was in Las Vegas, where there was nothing I could do but wait and pray like everybody else.

I kept monitoring reports from Moscow, but the news was never good. Russian military hawks were trying to talk President Vladimir Putin into sending troops into the theater regardless of the "inevitable" casualties. One report I read had Major General Viktor Karpukhin arguing, "The bandits won't surrender. They must be mercilessly eliminated."

On October 26, 2002, more than 120 hostages–as well as all forty-one Chechen militants–were killed when Russian special forces stormed the theater. Deputy Interior Minister Vladimir Vasilyev said that Russia would grieve with the relatives of the civilians who died, but stressed that 750 people–including all the children held captive–had been rescued alive. I was greatly relieved to hear that Rita had gotten out safely with the rest. But it was a scary three days; as the minister said, everyone in the theater could have been killed if the mines laid by the rebels had exploded.

The tragic events made me even more aware that as the boss of a business with dancers touring the globe, I always had to be on top of world events. It's one thing for me to go barreling into danger, but I insist that every safety precaution is taken for every man and woman–on stage and off–who tours with my shows.

Chapter Forty

Show Business

THE SMARTEST THING I ever did was to listen to my brain and not my heart about *Lord of the Dance.* I knew that *Feet of Flames* could not go on the road without me, because of the solo I'd created that only I could do. But *Michael Flatley's Lord of the Dance* could certainly fly without me. And although my heart wanted to keep me center stage forever, I knew my body couldn't take the abuse.

Maybe, I thought, it was time for me to give up another central position, that of sole owner of my enterprise. Perhaps it was time to consider making my business, Unicorn Entertainment, a public company.

I was advised that Unicorn was a powerful worldwide brand with resiliency in the marketplace, enormous cash flow, and room to expand. If I floated the company on the stock market, I was told, it would be valued at around £250 million. Sales of the stock would fund my business developments: an exclusive, top-of-the-market brand expansion into themed restaurants and pubs, dance studios, and possibly an Irish-themed hotel-casino in Las Vegas.

But the tragedy of 9/11 had sown economic doubts. By the end of U.K. financial year 2002, I decided against going public, even as I pursued my casino dreams.

One day the news hit the *Las Vegas Sun* that I'd bought some land on the Strip. That night I was in New York, staying at my favorite hotel, the St. Regis. I'd been out for the evening having dinner with a few friends. It was quite late on a winter's night when I walked back to the hotel, and the lobby was almost empty.

I got the key to my room and wandered happily over to the elevator. I stepped in and, seemingly from nowhere, two guys followed me. Their overcoat collars were turned up and their hats were pulled low over their faces.

I pressed the button for the penthouse floor and the two men said nothing. They didn't try to call for another floor. They didn't press any button. They simply stood on either side of me, staring directly at me. Silence. I couldn't see their faces but they were so close, I could practically feel their breath.

We reached my floor and the doors whooshed open. My heart was in my throat.

I got out and heard the doors close behind me. I looked around and saw from the elevator light that the car wasn't moving. My mouth was dry, and my heart was pounding. Finally, after what seemed like an eternity, the elevator light began to move down to the lobby.

I will probably never know who those guys were.

David Chesnoff is one of the top attorneys in Nevada and is in legal partnership with Oscar Goodman, the mayor of Las Vegas. In March 2004, he spoke about the impact of Michael Flatley and Lord of the Dance *on Las Vegas: "I've been here twenty-five years, so I've seen the change in Las Vegas from a kind of limited entertainment capital of the world to the more cosmopolitan place that it has become—and Michael Flatley has been a big part of that. He brought something that they had not seen before here in Las Vegas. It was more cultural than just entertainment, which was important.*

"He is very respected. The show is a huge success, I know from my own experience of people coming to visit. It's one of the first things they ask me if I can help them get tickets to. If you live in a place like Las Vegas long enough, you become a concierge no matter what your profession is!

"In that respect Michael Flatley has been a very big part of the change of Las Vegas to a place where there is diversified entertainment, not just showgirls and risqué comics. Pavarotti is here. Lord of the Dance *and Elton John are here. There's Celine. All big, class acts.*

"Every year there is something exciting that happens in town that's never been here before, and I think Michael contributed to that. He is . . . part of the expansion of Las Vegas into a real world entertainment center. That's his impact."

Chapter Forty-one

Don't Catch Your Breath

Michael Flatley has done us a great honour by appearing.
He said he would help, and he has, and I will always be grateful.

Prince Albert of Monaco, August 2003

When the telephone rang, I was looking out across calm, clear blue waters from the deck of a luxury yacht gently idling, like me, in the dock of St. Barts. I was sipping a cup of strong French coffee and thinking that life was sweet. After ten years of dreams and hard work, I'd finally made it.

It was January 6, 2003, and with Lisa—now my fiancée—I had enjoyed the New Year celebrations in Vienna before we took the jet to the Caribbean.

Lisa was across from me now, wearing nothing but sun cream, lipstick, and a pair of high heels. She smiled with her radiant red lips, picked up a cushion, and began heading toward me with bad intentions in her eyes.

The phone rang a third time. Lisa looked at me with her big blue eyes as if to say, "Don't answer."

But I couldn't ignore the insistent sound, and I took the call. It was Stephen Marks, my business adviser, calling from London.

"Michael, they want you to dance in St. Petersburg at the opening ceremony for the G8 and European Union summits in May. And Prince Albert has called and asked personally if you could come and perform at his annual Red Cross Ball in Monaco."

I stared out to sea, thinking. Both requests were huge honors but I hadn't danced in public for almost two years. I was enjoying my retirement.

Lisa knelt in front of me, a beautiful distracting presence, "Michael," she said softly. "Is everything okay?"

Stephen was still on the phone. "Michael! Are you still there?"

"Michael," Lisa repeated. "What is it?"

My mind was already buzzing with possibilities. The Warlords routine from *Lord of the Dance* would be perfect for St. Petersburg but what about Monaco?

"Michael," Stephen said. "Hello! Are you going to do it?"

"I'll do it," I said.

Then I looked at Lisa. The dance could wait.

Lisa Murphy talked about Michael in February 2004: "I know Michael so well. We spent twenty-four/seven together. We've spent so much quality time together; we've been dating for four and a half years now.

"There are couples that go away for two weeks' holidays and they're dying to get home, to get back to their friends and reality because they're sick of their partner after two weeks. With me and Michael, we can't get enough of each other. I have to be honest, I eat, sleep, drink, think Michael Flatley. I love him so much. At the end of the day, no matter who approached me, if he was the biggest male model in the history of the world, if he was the biggest movie star in the history of the world, that came up to chat me up, they would have absolutely minus zero chance of even having a conversation with me, never mind an intimate encounter. Because if I'm with somebody . . . when I love, I love from the soul: there is nothing could tempt me.

"To this day, I have never lost one ounce of love for him. . . . I have never loved another man like I love Michael."

St. Petersburg, that historic Russian city, was celebrating its three-hundredth anniversary in May 2003, as well as hosting the G8 and European Union summits.

Russia's President Vladimir Putin, President George W. Bush, Prime Minister Tony Blair, Ireland's Bertie Ahern, President Chirac of France, and Germany's Chancellor Schroeder were among the dignitaries gathered for the events including the opening ceremony where we appeared. Being invited was a thrill and a great honor, and I'd hand-picked eighteen dancers from all of our troupes for our performance at the Konstantinovsky Palace.

None of us will ever forget such a landmark event. I received warm wishes from President Bush and Tony Blair and Vladimir Putin, and I was proud to dance for and represent our taisoch, Bertie Ahern.

And of course, everybody cheered! It appeared that people everywhere regarded *Lord of the Dance* as an ambassador and a brand name for goodwill worldwide.

A few months later we presented the show at the Red Cross Ball, which was held in August 2003 in Monte Carlo. It was one of the world's most prestigious charity events, a fanfare of an evening that included Prince Albert, Princess Caroline, and Prince Rainier, who was particularly intrigued by the history of *Lord of the Dance*. Shirley Bassey sang "Diamonds Are Forever," and we were congratulated by Roger Moore–a former UNICEF ambassador in real life, an ex–James Bond on the silver screen. The French actress Catherine Deneuve was equally kind and asked one of my guests how she could arrange to take dance lessons from me.

Such events were fulfilling for me as a creator-producer, for they gave me a view from the other side of the stage, showing me what could be achieved by careful planning and good intentions.

This feeling was reinforced in September 2003 when I visited South Africa to see various aid projects run by the Nelson Mandela Children's Fund and World Vision. I was fortunate to spend time in Soweto, visiting children who were suffering from AIDS.

Mr. Mandela graciously cleared his diary for the afternoon, so that we could get to know each other. He was a wonderful man. But I felt that it was I who had benefited most from that humbling visit. Millions have been moved by his positive attitude–and I was no exception.

Chapter Forty-two

Alive-Alive-Oh!

"If a man has greatness of mind, and the breadth of vision to contemplate all time and all reality, can he regard human life as a thing of any great consequence?"

"No, he cannot."

"So, he won't think death anything to be afraid of?"

"No."

Plato

"Mr. Flatley, you have cancer."

I'd been in Las Vegas celebrating our company's five-year anniversary there. I'd gone to the usual whirl of business meetings—the Irish-themed casino was still in the works—but I'd made time to jet down to Los Angeles in October 2003 for my regular medical checkup.

I'd been in terrific health, except for the usual problems with my legs, but the doctors became concerned about a mole on the left side of my face. To my astonishment, they wanted to test it immediately. They left me with a neat scar running down from just beside my left ear, and then twenty-four hours later, they gave me the news: malignant melanoma. It was very serious. They went on to operate again, removing three more inches of my face. The scar grew.

Finding out that you've got cancer gives you great pause no matter how positive you are. Your life and your future–or your possible lack of it–fly across your vision. What could I do? I didn't want to sit around Las Vegas and mope. I didn't want to lie down and cry, to crumble and cancel all future engagements. Stop feeling sorry for yourself, I told myself. Get up. Fight back!

So I telephoned my parents and my brother Pat and told them the news, and then I went on with my regular schedule. Later that month, I called a friend in London from my mobile on the tarmac at Las Vegas's McCarran Airport. He thought I was about to fly into London and said, "Well, at least you'll be out of the sun."

"No," I said. "I'm on my way to Barbados."

I don't know whether it was a half-laugh or a groan I heard–I had to switch off my mobile for the takeoff.

Cancer? On the flight I thought of my great friend big Chris Roche. After a phenomenally brave fight the man who was literally a giant of Irish showbusiness–he was big man, 6 feet 4 inches tall–had died from the disease on December 6, 2002. Chris was a fabulous public relations man and my *Lord of the Dance* promoter Jim Aiken and I asked him to join our team.

We became great friends and had enormous fun together. His wife Geraldine is one of the nicest and most loyal friends I have and she may well be the best PR person in the business. A couple of weeks before Chris died we organized a reception for him at the Four Seasons Hotel in Dublin. He was so thin and grievously ill but what an entrance he made in his pinstriped suit and big grin.

The gathering was to celebrate Chris's company signing a worldwide agreement with me and also a tribute to his life from all his friends, an expression of all the affection we had for him. He worked the room liked he always did, provoking laughter and our admiration at his courage and dignity.

As I reflected on Chris's memory, I thought there was no fear in death if you could face it like that.

A few hours later, I was sitting in a swimming pool in the Caribbean, holding a packet of Bird's-Eye frozen peas against the stitches in my face and sipping from a bottle of cold Tiger beer. I thought to myself, "It's all proof that I'm alive."

I'll admit it freely: I do love life. Every minute of it. The good and the bad. I've always lived every day like it's my last and I will till the day God calls me.

Thanks be, the doctors caught the problem early on, and I'm in great health now. But a scare like that makes you even more aware you need to live every moment while you can. So while I was in Barbados I made another survey of some sea-frontage land that I wanted to buy on the west coast of the island.

The land was on the ocean between Speightstown and the Sandy Lane Hotel, behind an area the locals call Billionaires' Row. I've traveled all over the world and Barbados is still one of the most special places I've ever found. I have great friends there and very fond memories. I guess it helps a little that the Irish lads own most of the island. And I love walking on the beach. One of life's great pleasures and it's free for everyone.

Still, I knew it would take a huge amount of money to build again. But I thought this would be my Castlehyde in the sun. Paradise Found. So I bought the place. What the hell! Why not?

After all, you only live nine times.

Isn't life great?

Geraldine Roche, whose husband Chris was Michael Flatley's publicist, said on January 26, 2006: "Michael and Chris came together at Diggs Lane in March 1996 when Lord of the Dance *was in rehearsals. Over the next eight years they would forge an enduring friendship and working relationship. Michael and Chris were always positive about life. They embraced it and lived it to the full. But most of all they shared a wicked sense of humor and a love of laughter.*

"Then on March 15, 2002 our world collapsed when Chris was

diagnosed with gastro-oesophageal cancer. Over the next eight months Michael was Chris's life line to normality and work. They hatched plans together, shared confidences and stories. At key moments Michael would be quietly there for Chris and for me. On yet another dark day my mobile rang and it was Michael phoning from New York. I told him things were not good and I cried.

" 'Ger, listen to me, it is midday there so let me hop on Concorde to London and then into Dublin. I'll see you at 8.30 p.m. at the clinic.'

"Bang on 8.30 he arrived laden with presents for Chris and they both hugged. Michael came back the following day and the day after that. Then in November Michael appointed Chris as his worldwide publicist and they announced it at a party at the Four Seasons in Dublin. It was one of Chris's proudest moments and for days afterwards he could talk of little else. Chris died on December 6, 2002.

"I will never forget Michael for the wonderful and magical moments he gave Chris when he most needed them. He quietly stood by him and he has done the same for me. Michael is at once ordinary and extraordinary. As his publicist over the past three years I have come to know him as a great artist and friend. He is the sum total of two parts; a true artist and performer driven to push the boundaries with dedication and skill. The other part is the private person who is witty, roguish and full of fun."

Derry Ann Morgan, February 2004: "One life and so much to do, that's Michael. Really, he has only one life and yet he needs fifty."

In 2005, Thomas Trautman had been Michael Flatley's private secretary and "lifestyle manager" for more than three years. He joined Michael after his previous employer, Gianni Versace, was shot to death in front of him when the two of them were staying at the Versace home in Miami. Michael says of him: "I've been blessed over the years with great assistants, wonderful people like Sharon Ashley and Emma Pitcher. A great addition to my team has been my private secretary and valet Thomas Trautman. He's got great dignity and integrity, is loyal and extremely efficient. Over the past five years we've become great friends and he's a hell of a golfer. Thomas is like my American Express card–I don't leave home without him."

Trautman talked about his relationship to Michael during 2003 and 2004 in London, Dublin, Las Vegas, Los Angeles, New York, Chicago, Barbados, Monte Carlo, Villefranche-sur-Mer, and St. Tropez: "They called me for an interview at Park Place Villas in London. I had no idea who my prospective employer was until I got there; you have to go with no preconceived ideas.

"I walked in, and there were six, seven, eight bankers sitting in the dining room, waiting, waiting, and waiting and he had all the time for me.

"Perfect gentleman. Elegantly dressed. Not dressed like an entertainer or a dancer. We had a great long chat, and I left feeling very confident.

"I realize now why all those bankers were waiting, for Mr. Flatley was changing the structure and plans for the company. Yet he kept them waiting for me. Some days later I got a call from the headhunters: 'Can you go to Barbados on Monday?'

"This is on the Friday night. He had guests arriving two days after I arrived, and a week later he threw a cocktail party for about eighty people.

"He's extremely driven, which is great. He's always thinking and doing and doing and thinking. He expects it of everyone else. It's a lot of work. It's a twenty-four/seven day.

"His last words each night are: 'I'll try not to call you.'

"All my friends love to hear where I am because it's an exciting job. We were driving back from Monaco during the World Cup and he said, 'Let's go see Ireland play Spain on Sunday night in South Korea.' Done. Saturday morning, get up, get on the plane, go to Paris, switch planes, get into South Korea. Check in. Two hours before the game starts, go to the Irish FA [Football Association], get the tickets, get to the match. Perfect–and Mr. Flatley takes the Irish team out for drinks. It worked."

* * *

Frank Gillespie is the owner of the famous Blackthorn pub in South Boston, where Michael Flatley first met him in 1991 during a tour with the Chieftains. They met again in South Korea when Ireland was playing Spain in the second round of the World Cup. Frank was in Dublin in November 2004 when he recalled: "I saw Michael at the game and we arranged to meet up afterwards to catch up. I went back to Seoul with him in his limousine, and we stopped at the Westin Chosun Hotel where the Irish squad were headquartered.

"While we were having a drink, the physio Mick Byrne arrived and invited us up to eat with the official party. Mick was keen that the players should meet Michael.

"After that they took over Michael's limo and transported the players to a nearby Irish bar. There were Damien Duff and Jason McAteer and Robbie Keane pushing their heads out of the sun roof. We went on to a nightclub and then it was 7 a.m.

"Where to go? Michael had the answer. We all went back to his place–a fantastic suite at the Ritz Carlton Hotel. He was hospitality itself–drinks and eats just kept arriving and arriving. The players were relaxed as never before. Michael then played a few traditional tunes on his flute–he's a champ with the flute.

"The players were still upset at going out of the tournament on a penalty shootout. Michael told them they couldn't leave until they felt better. He gave them an inspirational talking to. He explained the setbacks were similar to those he had experienced–you get knocks in life.

"He told them they might feel down–but what about the achievement of getting so far in the World Cup finals? What about just playing in the World Cup?

"The more Michael talked the more the boys' spirits were raised. They were all sitting around him, like a group of schoolchildren listening to the teacher. And that's what he was for them–an inspirational teacher. He had matured so much, this man I'd first met when he really didn't have

the price of a pint. His circumstances have changed–but not the man. He's down-to-earth and all class, a class act."

Damien Duff's mentor, Pat Devlin said in October 2004: "Damien was bowled over and inspired by Michael. All the team were."

Thomas Trautman: "Then, 'While we're here [in Seoul], we've come this far, let's go to Tokyo and see England play Brazil.'

"Two days later: It works. [Although it would seem to be impossible to get the tickets, somehow, we get them.] Somebody knows somebody. Somebody always knows somebody. Sometimes that can take a while. There are times when Michael wants something, and he wants it right now. You can't say, 'It won't happen right now.'

"As you keep going forward in anything, you have the right connection. I'm not Superman. I make mistakes, but we have not really had rows. He'll tell me off but not tell me off. He'll point it out, and if I'm wrong, I'll admit it. We spend so much time together, but he's the boss. There's a line. I know where that line is. I know when it can be crossed. When it shouldn't be crossed. It's understood. Not many people have that close a relationship with their boss anywhere.

"The Americans have a term for me called 'lifestyle manager.' Others call it 'private secretary,' 'valet,' 'gentleman's gentleman'–it's all of the above. It's a very undefined . . . role.

"We use bodyguards, but invariably they don't even speak English and I've got to babysit them. They're supposed to be looking after us, but if we have to spend twenty minutes explaining where we're going and how long for, it's difficult. It's easier without them, but sometimes you obviously have to have them. In Russia, in Kiev, and in places like Beirut, we definitely have bodyguards. And at major events. I'd never considered kidnapping and I don't know whether he has. The break-in at the Villa Masquerade scared him. And there was a threat against him in St. Petersburg. He didn't want to leave. He told me, 'I'm not going to go

early for this.' He was not going to bow down to it. So we stayed the extra day.

"Mr. Flatley is recognized by a lot of people. It's fascinating to walk down certain streets in London or wherever we are in the world, and suddenly people look. He's a very good people person as well. That's just the way he is. He's extremely personable to everyone. He will take the oldest lady or the youngest girl, and he gives them the warmest hug. You can see the smile on their face. I've seen other celebrities who you would absolutely have no chance with at all. They have no charisma.

"He could survive on a desert island on his own. He is perfectly self-sufficient. I'm there to make him able to do more, to use all the time available. The one thing he could not live without on a desert island would be his mobile phone! That phone is the one thing that makes me want to break our employer-employee understanding and complain. And that's only when he answers it on the golf course. Just at the vital putt."

Act Five

CELTIC TIGER

. . . the jessamine and geraniums and cactuses as Gibraltar as a girl where I was a Flower of the mountain yes when I put the rose in my hair like an Andalusian girl used or shall I wear a red yes and how he kissed me under the Moorish wall an I thought well as well him as another and then I asked him with my eyes to ask again yes and then he asked me would I yes to say yes my mountain flower and first I put my arms around him yes and drew him down to me so he could feel my breasts all perfumed yes and his heart was going like mad and yes I said yes I will Yes.

JAMES JOYCE, *Ulysses*

Chapter Forty-three

Irish to the Core

He's done a massive amount to promote Ireland.

Bono, Dublin, February 2004

My parents are Irish. So were their parents, and all of my ancestors, going back thousands of years. I may have been born away from home. But if you take all these thousands of years as opposed to the years I've been alive, which do you think is going to win?

So I'm very Irish. Ireland is the closest thing to my heart. There are an estimated eighty-four million people of Irish descent living outside of Ireland. There's four million in Ireland. We're all Irish. We should all stick together.

Part of my love for Ireland is expressed at Castlehyde, where the River Blackwater flows slowly at the bottom of the garden. To me, that river is a symbol of the life I want to establish at Castlehyde—unhurried, rich with memory, fragrant with the past.

The history books call Castlehyde one of the finest examples of Georgian architecture in Ireland. But when I bought the house, I wasn't just acquiring a famous building. Even in the derelict state in which I bought it, the house—and the narrative it tells—remind me that Ireland is part of my past but also the lodestar of my destiny. Yes, I was born in America, and I worked hard and I got lucky. But no matter where I was or what I accomplished, the most important thing in my life was always to be Irish. I said that when I had nothing, and I'm still saying it now. So to own such an important part of Irish history is one of the pinnacles of my life.

My deep feeling for Castlehyde and its story made it even more painful when the local planning authorities repeatedly put up obstacles to my plans for restoration. I was spending millions to make Castlehyde the great, grand house it had been designed to be–yet there was delay upon delay as we dealt with planners.

Let me tell you, it wasn't an easy situation. I watched money vanish, soaked up by the damp basements and crumbling plasterwork; lavished on ruined roofs and leaning walls; invested in new foundations, plumbing and heating systems; and spent on restoring every window in the house to its original splendid specifications. I saw cash disappear into a financial abyss, into the so-called invisible expense of planning applications and appeals. I saw my good humor tested when everything I was trying to do for the best was simply shoved back at me.

I'd been told that without the kind of work I was financing, Castlehyde would have fallen to pieces within a few years. What I've done with the help of teams of craft workers is not simply renovate the house but reengineer it. If you think of Castlehyde as a puzzle, I put the pieces together again. Each brick, roof beam, wall panel, win-dow sash, and slate was dismantled and numbered, reconditioned and restored, reassembled and put back exactly where it began.

I'm a perfectionist, and I know there are a lot of people who took advantage of this. As the local joke goes, "They came on bicycles and left in Mercedes-Benzes."

It was all worth it. I started it–I finished it.

Frankly, ninety percent of what I did was for my parents. They left Ireland with nothing, and yet they love it so much.

I love Ireland, too, and I wanted to express that love through my restoration of Castlehyde. But that sort of loving care can't be achieved by simply throwing money around: you need expert advice and craft workers. I'm not sure that the planning authorities understood this. I never asked for any favors during the work on Castlehyde, only to be treated fairly and in the end I was. Often, as my frustration with them grew, I wondered why I bothered. Then my roots took over. Had not the Irish been fighting bureaucracy for centuries?

Sometimes I thought the board would have made less of a fuss if I'd allowed this priceless piece of history to collapse from neglect. Instead, I spent millions saving a national treasure–protecting the character and integrity of the house all the while. While the house itself cost me 4 million euros, I must have spent ten times that on the restoration, sparing no expense to be accurate and respectful of the architecture and history that the place embodied.

But I found some comfort in what the historian Pat Bartley told me: "When this is finished, it will be like a little bit of the eighteenth century brought back to life." And it is.

As always, the Irish people cheered me on. They stood by me. Cork County Council became *very* supportive. And the rest relented. Maybe it just took a while before they could see how much I loved Ireland. After all, it's how I was brought up.

Michael Flatley, Senior: "We're awful proud of him, to tell you the truth. Awful proud of him.

"It's fantastic what Michael has achieved and part of what makes him so fascinating is that he made it on his own and in a short period of time. He didn't need forty years or parents before him with money.

"He was awful bright, no matter what he did. Maybe it was a combination of both of us. He just went out there and got on with it. That's why we're so proud of him. It's all guts.

"I'd like to see him get married, though. I'd like to see him settle down. He's not a kitten anymore."

* * *

Eilish Flatley: "I think you either have it or you don't. I don't know how we ever got such a smart kid at all, to tell you the truth, where he came from.

"The good thing, though, is what Michael has done for Irish dancing: he made it a viable, an acceptable thing for people to do, where, before Michael, it was all done behind closed doors. It was almost like something to be ashamed of.

"He made it the in thing to do, and it has been extended and brought up and developed and it makes money for people. Finally, it's an acceptable form of entertainment.

"We have a lot of respect for him for keeping his faith and going on and doing it and accomplishing it. We're very happy that he did. Like I say, we don't know where he came from in our family. We're awful lucky, thank God. We are really blessed with the children. You don't find people like that in America anymore. We have a few friends who have nice children. We also have a few who don't have such nice children.

"Michael is the furthest away, but he has to be. His world is not our world. It's a beautiful world and it's very fancy and high-class and demanding. It's so nice for him, we see him once in a while, but it's over there and it's his world, and our world is really a quieter one."

Michael Flatley, Senior: "He really is a down-to-earth kind of a guy. I remember we were in Dublin, and Michael was a really big name, and we were having dinner, and the waitress come over and she shook hands with Michael.

"I couldn't believe that he would shake hands with a little girl like her. She said to Michael, 'We have footballers here, Irish footballers, who wouldn't even talk to me apart from to order. That's how big they think they are, and here you are, known all over the world and you put your hand out and shake hands.'

"It's the way it should be. You make a lot more friends that way. You can never have enough friends."

* * *

I have to share one more story with you about my dad, and I guess this is the place to do it. My father and brother had heard of the Concorde for years, and they were mightily impressed that I regularly flew on that supersonic jet. So one day I bought them two tickets on the Concorde so they could come and visit me in style.

When they arrived, I asked them how it went. "Oh, great, great, Mickey," my father said. "Look, the girls on the plane gave me bags of champagne to take home!" I've always loved British Airways—they're my favorite airline, and this was just the kind of service we'd come to expect from them.

"Oh, Dad," I said now, teasing him, "you must've been chatting up the girls again!"

"Sure, they're lovely girls," he told me, and that seemed to be the end of that.

But then, a few months later, I was on the Concorde myself. There are only a few flight attendants who fly it regularly, and because I take it so often, they all know me.

"Oh, Mr. Flatley," they said, "you have the nicest father!"

"I know," I said.

"Do you know," they told me, "he was crying on the way over."

Now that surprised me. My father is a warm-hearted man, but I hadn't often seen him cry. That he'd show so much emotion to a lot of strangers struck me very much indeed.

"Yes," they went on, "he said to us, 'When I was a little boy, I had to leave school in the fourth grade. I went everywhere in my bare feet, or by ass and cart. And to think, that in one lifetime, I've moved from bare feet and ass-and-cart to flying on the Concorde.'

"Then he said, 'When we were young and poor, my wife and I had to move to America, just to make a living. Isn't it ironic that my son had to go to Ireland to make his?' "

* * *

Niamh O'Brien, a dancer in the permanent Las Vegas troupe: "Michael . . . was there from the start. He was the one that had pressed us to keep going and told us we could be the best. . . . It was really tough but at the same time you knew what was coming out of it. We knew it could be huge.

"He's brought Irish dancing to the world. Places where there is no Irish dance. Germany, France, Switzerland, anywhere. It just wasn't heard of. Now there's Irish dance schools all over there. In Japan. All over Asia there's Irish dance schools popping up and all because they've seen Lord of the Dance *and the videos.*

"There are people who never danced before, and they've learned the steps off the video. They can't tell you what they do, but they can do the steps, or near enough.

"It's unbelievable, the amount of interest people have taken in Irish dancing. People didn't know it existed. Even in America where there was Irish dancing anyway.

"Before, we never used our hands. Michael brought that in. It's given us as entertainers more freedom.

"Michael's been so good to us as well. Any time he comes out here, he always praises everybody, and he's good like that. He will give you corrections and stuff, but he'll always tell everyone how good they're doing. He's very, very generous. If he thinks we're not being treated right, he's the first one to say 'sort it out.'

"We go out and we sign autographs and stuff after the show. So many people will come up to you and say, 'You are the only show we've come to see here in Vegas. You're the only one we've wanted to see.' That kind of spurs you on. The reactions seem to be the same everywhere."

So let me take you on a tour of my private palace. After all, not many people have had the chance! And you'll probably get to meet my friend Pat Bartley. He's an expert on the area and like an uncle to me. He's affectionately known as Uncle Pat by all, and is one of my closest and dearest friends in the world. I've devoured books on

Irish history but Pat can always surprise me with something new about Castlehyde.

Castlehyde has fourteen bedrooms (down from twenty-nine), an entire first-floor master suite, two climate-controlled wine cellars, a Roman spa, a twenty-seat private cinema, an African safari room, a Jameson-designed whiskey room, a three-story three-thousand-volume library, a music room, a gym, various reception rooms, and a reinforced-steel eight-bay garage for my collection of Ferraris, BMWs, and Rolls-Royces. As the garage is near the cliffs, we had to use steel with a toughened concrete roof to truly protect the vehicles, including my Rolls-Royce Phantom, which is such a monster we had to redesign the garage to house it properly.

I love the library, which features a painted ceiling mural and hand-carved American walnut shelves. It's in the library that I've housed my favorite works by my beloved James Joyce. The last lines of his *Ulysses* are the most moving words I have ever read. I am continually looking for memorabilia about Joyce and all his work, and it is my dream that one day Castlehyde will house one of the world's most magnificent literary collections, with the Joyce archive as its centerpiece.

At auction at Sotheby's in London on a sunny July 8, 2004, I managed to dominate the bids for the thirty items once owned by Joyce's brother, Stanislaus. The collection was offered for sale by the family of Stanislaus's daughter-in-law, Jeanette, who hoped to raise four hundred and fifty thousand pounds but instead realized more than seven hundred and twenty thousand pounds. Peter Inston bid for me and, among other prizes, carried off Joyce's trademark gold glasses and his prized cigarette case. I also bought a bronze medal awarded to Joyce in 1904 at the Feis Ceo singing competition, engraved "Tenor Solo James A. Joyce 1904." And now, visitors to my home can hear Joyce's voice, for I also bought from Sotheby's a recording of Joyce reading from the Aeolus episode of *Ulysses,* the only recording Joyce ever made of his great novel. The 1924 Paris recording is one of only thirty copies and is signed and inscribed by him. Presumably, it is Stanislaus's copy that we now have at Castlehyde. I am so glad that I was able to help keep these items in Ireland.

Come with me now to the front door of my castle, where you can see parkland rolling from the front of the house down to the River Blackwater–once known as the Irish Rhine because of the castles and grand houses along its banks. If you walk around the back of the house, you'll see grounds that run to the ruin of the thirteenth-century Condon Castle atop a cliff face so menacing yet so romantic that Daphne du Maurier could have conjured it up.

My entranceway leads to a stone cantilevered staircase and includes eighteenth-century marble fireplaces that can still be used. Notice as well the twenty-first-century gadgets, including the computer-controlled electric conveyor belt coat rack, and the centralized, computer-controlled, audiovisual system offering satellite television and classical and popular music throughout Castlehyde. All the cloakrooms are climate controlled and for a grand party I can open all the main ground-floor hallways and create one giant dining room stretching the entire length of the house.

Look up and around, and you'll see that all of my home's original plaster cornices and murals were restored by specialists in giltwork. Come with me into the soundproof music room, which looks over the Blackwater valley, and take a moment to appreciate the Steinway grand, the concert harp, and my collection of flutes. Yes, we're a long way from Q and F on 79th Street!

The entire first floor is my domain: a suite with a butler's chamber, an Italian-style bedroom with four-poster bed and hand-crafted silk hangings; matching bathrooms and dressing rooms off the bedroom. I had the eighteenth-century baths raised on a special dais to allow a view of the Blackwater River. I know that space is the great luxury, so I appreciate that my entire wardrobe can be stored in the changing room. When the seasons change, we move one set of clothes into the basement storage room and bring up another set of garments. And from my floor I have a doorway that opens onto the balcony of the two-level library.

The guest bedrooms are upstairs. I've tried to give them a link to either the house or to my own special interests. There's the China room, the American Presidents room, the French room, the Napoleon room, the Venetian room, and the Beecher-Wrixon room, which shows off the yachting exploits of Castlehyde's former owners. Each bedroom has its own specially-designed wallpaper or hangings and its own marble bathroom.

The basement is where the fun and action are. The African Safari room has canvas-lined walls to give the right atmosphere for playing billiards, drinking whiskey, or smoking Cuban cigars. For my thirstier guests, the Jameson-designed whiskey room runs along the corridor, complete with four giant casks of Irish whiskey and cabinets lined with my favorite rare malts and distillations. I have two wine cellars, red and white, with a special climate-control system. The Chateau Latours and Margauxs are stored by the case.

I have a twenty-seat cinema that can be turned into a dance rehearsal hall. I've also got a Roman spa, including a massage room with heated floor, a relaxation room, steam room, sauna, saltwater flotation tank, showers, mechanical massage room, hair salon, and a high-tech gym. I believe we've thought of something for everybody. If anyone arrives with kids, we've got a children's dormitory with plasma television screen and computer games.

Still, I don't know how any newcomers will find time to watch television or play games. There's so much to show, and I'll be taking them on this tour. . . . Welcome to Castlehyde!

Peter Inston, the interior designer who worked with Michael on his homes in London and France as well as on Castlehyde, said: "Castlehyde was restored to bring it back to its former glory . . . [and] so that it could once again be lived in and enjoyed. This isn't a museum. It's a family home.

"Nevertheless, I don't think any private individual has ever undertaken a restoration project of this scale or cost. I've never seen anyone take such a hands-on interest in restoring a property as Michael has. Everything in this house is original. We've saved absolutely everything we could. We've repaired and restored the original floors, windows, ceilings and slates. In the basement we even stripped out the original bricks, numbered them, repaired the flood damage, and then replaced the bricks exactly as they were.

"With the basement located at the foot of the cliffs and prone to flooding, which is aggravated by the nearby river, the entire substructure had to be waterproofed. That waterproofing program cost almost twenty percent of the original purchase price of the house.

"The library with its collection of classic first-edition Irish books is really exciting and one of the stars of the house. And there's the art collection and the furniture collection . . . it's marvelous what Michael has achieved with Castlehyde."

Historian Pat Bartley said at Castlehyde estate on January 17, 2006: "Now the work at this great house is coming to an end there is great hope for the future. I knew the house and grounds in the year 2000 and to see them now is almost unbelievable. When Michael Flatley moved here the house was derelict and the grounds were a wilderness. Now, it is a sight to behold. The splendor of it is breathtaking; the 800-year-old Norman castle still stands guarding this historical place and Michael; the peacocks and pheasants strut around the river and woodland walks and the lawns and avenues.

"There are very people who could have achieved this. It's like Michael dancing or a bird flying. I always think of Virgil who said: 'They can because they think they can.'

"Michael's put the love and perfection he puts into his shows into the house, turned it into a masterpiece. But it's his home too where his

family and friends come and stay. There many bumps along the way, just like his life, but he never gave up on turning Castlehyde into a great house again. I am so fond of Michael–and admire what he has achieved here."

Chapter Forty-four

Responsibility

I am the Lord of the Dance, said he.

SYDNEY CARTER, "Lord of the Dance," 1963

MY BUSINESS RESPONSIBILITIES continued to grow. Chief among my new projects were my plans for the Las Vegas casino and ideas for a new show. In June 2004, I attended some heavyweight meetings in America–only to receive some devastating news when I returned to London. The merchandising executive on tour with *Lord of the Dance* in South Africa had been murdered.

Darryl Kempster was only thirty-seven years old. He was killed on the steps of the Parktonian Hotel in the business district of Johannesburg, shot three times as some of my dancers watched from the foyer of the hotel. The theater was just next door, but the dancers had been escorted back. Darryl had returned on his own, and the police told me he'd been followed by two men, one of whom had shot him, the other who'd run off with his laptop computer bag. What an absolute waste of a good life. They couldn't even have known for sure what was in his bag.

I was jetlagged, angry at the waste of life, and frightened for my troupe and everyone else in South Africa. I jumped straight into the shower, changed my suit, packed a little carrier bag, and caught the next flight to Johannesburg. It was a long, worrying flight, for I had to consider all the implications if I canceled the rest of the tour. After all, I had thirty-five dancers and a crew of fourteen people in Johannesburg. What if I was exposing them to danger?

I was flying into a dangerous situation. So I brought along one of my regular bodyguards, the tall, striking Priscilla, who offers a great deal of knowledge, experience, good humor, and a nine-millimeter automatic pistol in her shoulder holster.

With Priscilla's help, I would be able to arrange twenty-four-hour security for everybody and to get a swift appraisal of the situation on the ground. I had to know—really know—the gravity of the threat to all our personnel.

When I met the dancers, many of them were in tears. They had not slept. They were traumatized and fearful. Some of them just wanted to go home, and I understood that. I hadn't slept in days myself. But I was the boss, the father figure, the one to take care of them. I take care of my people.

It was all very emotional. I hugged them and told them no one had to stay. I explained I could bring in another troupe if the show went on. And in fact, I put nine of the dancers on a flight to London that night, at their request. Then I took everybody else to dinner, where at least they could all start to deal emotionally with Darryl's shooting.

I can't describe how terrible I felt. I was responsible for my dancers and my company—and now one of them was dead. And I knew that if another were to die in the same way, I would feel—and be—even more responsible.

Meanwhile, I was on the phone to London to ensure that everything possible was being done to keep Darryl's family informed and to keep the concerned relatives of all the *Lord of the Dance* company as up to date about events as we could. The relatives were encouraging me to cancel my show, as publicly as possible, so as not to expose any more of their children to what they saw as a dangerous country.

I knew if I did that, all the other big European and American touring shows would pull out of South Africa as well. Did I want to be responsible for that? And indeed, when I met with the British High Commission in Johannesburg, as well as the local authorities and the concert promoters, they all made a solid case for me not to cancel the tour. In fact, they begged me to stay, for the sake of the South African economy.

So I held a press conference, at which I was as diplomatic as possible, weighing my personal feelings about the violence and Darryl's death against the ongoing good of the local people and the economy on which they depended for their livelihood. It took a great deal of soul searching, but with the support of the troupe I think I made the correct move when we decided to keep performing there.

The security issues seemed all the more urgent because I had a troupe about to debut in Israel in August 2004. But we moved forward without incident. Darryl's death has left its mark, though. I continue to be grateful for every day a troupe of mine spends abroad without another tragedy to mar the triumphs.

Meanwhile, I was arranging to sell Park Place Villas, my little palace in London. It had been a good, wise investment, but I was barely spending forty days a year there, and it didn't make sense to hang on to such a wonderful house for so little time, not when some worthy family could be enjoying this dream home.

I had a few bad moments when I returned from South Africa to make my final farewells. Finding the house littered with packing cases, I couldn't believe what I had done. A friend told me to buy it back–and I certainly thought about it, for it was only as the house was going from me that I realized how many important memories it held for me.

Still, it was time to move on. I sat on the balcony on my last day there, sipping my coffee and watching the boats sailing by on the canal, the people walking by, the girls in their summer dresses looking beautiful. I was sorry I hadn't taken the time to just sit there and do that more often. I cried. I felt very emotional after that trip to Africa. Was I working my whole life away?

I promised myself I would take time in the future. Meanwhile, it was time to celebrate my birthday. Sometimes I like to spend that special day alone, to contemplate and to reflect. This was one of those years. So I went to Villa Masquerade, where I gave thanks for life and the strength to enjoy it.

Chapter Forty-five

Celtic Tiger: The Show

Ireland has come of age in the past few years and I can tell you that
Michael Flatley had a big part to play in that. The country has thrust
through into the twenty-first century economically and in art and culture.
Michael went full circle. He came home and people didn't understand that
his dancing was something new and wonderful—it took him to see it.
I was at Eurovision and the place erupted. What a marvel it was.
My wife Kathleen went to the National School in Sligo with his father
before he emigrated to Chicago. We looked forward to Michael
making the grade and, oh gosh, did he make the grade.
Not just in Ireland but around the world.

Albert Reynolds,
former Taoiseach of Ireland, January 31, 2006

Celtic Tiger opened with a roar at Madison Square Garden in New York City on September 27, 2005. We got five standing ovations and I received some of the best reviews of my career.

I created the show as a celebration of Ireland, all her people and her heroes, as well as a tribute to my 45 million fellow Irish Americans. It gave me great joy. And pain.

There were so many people again in my life saying it couldn't work. They knew what I had been through but insisted: "It can't be done, it can't be done." According to them it was impossible: "Flatley, you're past your sell-by date. It's a day late and a dollar short." The message was clear: "You're forty-seven. It's twelve years since we did *Riverdance* and even Ireland doesn't want to see any more of this stuff."

It was like going full circle back to *Lord of the Dance*. Still, after all these years, they didn't believe. I knew I could do it. As the saying goes, "I am not as good as I once was, but I am as good once as I ever was." All my lessons of the past were well learned and I never needed that experience more than on the North American leg of *Celtic Tiger*. The shows were not selling as well as I had hoped. I didn't know if it was the marketing or the advertising or what. And people lined up to say: "Flatley, you're finished." "It's too late." "It didn't work." "We told you so."

I told them I would do it on my own in Europe and they said: "Flatley, it's going to be worse in Europe."

I took over the marketing. We sold out at The Point in Dublin in eight minutes. Throughout the UK and the rest of Europe we sold fabulously well.

For me personally the show was incredibly demanding. Getting my body back in shape took a lot longer than it had in the past. It's much more difficult, much more strenuous and I had to be so careful about injuries. Yes, I was forty-seven when I created the show. The next-oldest dancer in my troupe was twenty-three. The others called him "Grandpa." I hate to think what they said about me.

I was running at 6 a.m., driving out from London to Shepperton Studios where we were rehearsing and often not going back until 10 p.m., doing my business phone calls in the car. I was passionate and so were the dancers; they were gems. We all worked so very, very hard, pumping our hearts and soul into it.

People ask me why I took on the challenge of such a show but it's who I am and what I do. It's been there since I was a little boy. It's the same thing that's been there for ever.

I love to perform and I could not find anyone who could do my Al Capone solo in *Celtic Tiger*. As I created that number I realized I had to be the lead role myself. I had a mental block about the solo. I just couldn't create, just couldn't do it. I left it to the last second. I had to absolutely force myself to do it; I was backed into a corner, there was no time left. The dancers had gone, tired out, and I went to work on the solo with just the echoes of the rehearsal hall. It just came. It was remarkable.

Celtic Tiger was a challenge in so many ways. First and foremost it had to be an entertainment. I had grown up with the story of Ireland and its people and of the Irish in America. There are huge restraints trying to tell such a massive story in theatrical terms. It's not like a movie. Yet, the constraints worked for me. I had to tell the story fast and keep the audiences with me and entertained.

I devoured books on Irish history, especially on the Famine, and *Celtic Tiger* juggled itself together in my mind. I know some of it is controversial. But it's the truth as I see it and so often the truth is what gets people arguing.

The show also gave me a chance to fulfil a promise I'd made long ago to myself. Paul Harrington was the guy who'd won the Eurovision Song Contest the year "Riverdance" appeared at the interval. Because "Riverdance" had created such a stir, Paul never got the acclaim he deserved, so I vowed to right the balance. I found him playing piano in a tiny Dublin pub. In *Celtic Tiger* he's center stage singing several gorgeous numbers, among them, "Four Green Fields," one of my favorite Irish songs.

Most important to me, though, is the final dance number of *Celtic Tiger*. With a chorus line of dancers I perform to "I'm a Yankee Doodle Dandy," written by the great Irish-American composer George M. Cohan and made famous by the great Irish-American actor Jimmy Cagney. By ending my show with this grand patriotic tribute,

I was able to bring together all the best elements of my heritage from both sides of the Atlantic. It's a heritage I'll always be proud of—and one I'm delighted to share with every creed and kind all around the world.

Peter Aiken of Aiken Promotions who staged Lord of the Dance *and* Feet of Flames *in Ireland also presented* Celtic Tiger. *Tickets for the show at The Point Theatre in April, 2006, sold out within eight minutes of going on sale. He said in Dublin in December, 2005: "I was stunned when I saw* Celtic Tiger *because I wasn't expecting it. I thought it would be an extension of* Lord of the Dance *and* Feet of Flames. *I had it around my head that it was a trilogy sort of thing. But this is a very original, really good theatrical dance show. It has the best sound, the lights, the best production. If you look at the standard of production, it's awesome. It would blow you away. The production of it was second to none. He hasn't spared a shilling on it.*

"It wasn't hard to know it was a great show—people gave it a standing ovation. I was stunned by some of the stuff that happened in it and it never drags. This is entertainment A+. The best thing about the show is him. And I'm the most heterosexual A+ man in Ireland. It's him. He just has that personality."

On September 27, 2005, the Wall Street Journal *called the show "flat out fun" and "a heady mix of Irish and other dance styles and music often breathtaking in conception, execution and sheer cheek. Michael Flatley's* Celtic Tiger *finished in a shower of sparks and Irish-American pride, capped by a chorus line dancing to 'Yankee Doodle Dandy'. George M. Cohan and James Cagney would have beamed at Mr Flatley's talent, still brash and brilliant."*

Joan Acocella in The New Yorker *magazine on October 24, 2005, wrote: "In 1999, Michael Flatley launched a new production by rising from the depths of a fiery lake in the grounds of a German castle. In his current show,* Celtic Tiger, *he merely danced onto the stage–accompanied by maybe forty or fifty other clattering tappers and a gigantic video projection of what appeared to be sunrise over Stonehenge–in a backless Roman-gladiator outfit. The crowd would no doubt have preferred a burning lake, but it roared anyway, and with reason. Flatley is an extraordinary dancer. He has clocked thirty-five taps per second. I don't know how that's possible, but suffice it to say he's fast. More important is his musicality. Flatley can't walk, can't turn his head, except in relation to the beat. He is also a natural charm-boy: happy onstage, at home in his body."*

Gerry Kelly, host of The Kelly Show *on UTV in Ulster for seventeen years, said in Belfast on January 25, 2006: "I first saw Michael years ago performing in Cork, this new way of Irish dancing. It was fantastic but I thought nothing more of it until Eurovision. I was there to see the technical side of it and somebody said: 'Don't miss the interval act.'*

"I heard it was Irish dancing and went, 'Right, right . . .' I was sitting two rows from the front and then Michael came on and like everybody else I was on my feet applauding. My first memory of him was as a pure fan.

"Later, I met him in Dublin when he was rehearsing Lord of the Dance. *We were doing a special show from the Opera House in Belfast and he came up with the men's line-up and did a piece which was just staggering.*

"That was the start of a great friendship. He's a very good human being. He's very good to his friends, he always treats you with dignity. He's been loyal to my show over all the years. He flew in from Germany especially to appear on my last show and wish me good luck. That was a great gesture.

"He tends to think that we did something for him early on which is a load of rubbish. He was going to be one of the great superstars with or without The Kelly Show *believe you me."*

* * *

Bill Cullen, the head of Renault Ireland, author of It's a Long Way from Penny Apples *and chairman of The Irish Youth Foundation, said on January 25, 2006: "*Celtic Tiger *is a stunning dance and musical presentation of our great Irish heritage. From the Viking invasion, through centuries of British colonialism, the Great Famine and the emigration that saw millions of Irish people leave our shores for America. Then the triumph of their return as the Celtic Tiger grew in strength.*

"Yes, Michael Flatley has shown the resilience of the Irish nation to the world, and it reflects his own personal commitment to achieving. Anyone from Ireland who sees this show will realize with pride how much a privilege it is to be Irish."

The Tanaiste (Deputy Prime Minister) of Ireland Mary Harney said on January 26, 2006: "His family were immigrants into the U.S. but he has never forgotten his roots. He's extraordinarily committed to Ireland–he's globalized Irish culture in a very permanent way. He's modernized Irish dance, made it something you can take to the world stage.

"There's a phrase from Seamus Heaney that says 'when hope and history rhymes' and I think now the economy and culture very much rhyme and he's played a big part in that.

"He's made Irish dance trendy and cool and confident among modern folk. In my job I go all over the world and in my last job I was Minister of Industry and Trade and I was in China and India, all over the place. People knew Michael Flatley who didn't even know about Ireland. He's had that impact. There's only about one thousand Irish people in Japan and he was a sell out there. It's not just where Irish people are.

"He's bought a house in Cork and never mind all his success and fame, when he's there with the local people he's one of them. There's no airs and graces, people feel very at home with him which is fantastic. Despite his extraordinary talent he's a very ordinary guy. He's super."

Encore

Whenever I think life is getting tough,
I remember it beats the freezing cold shovel.

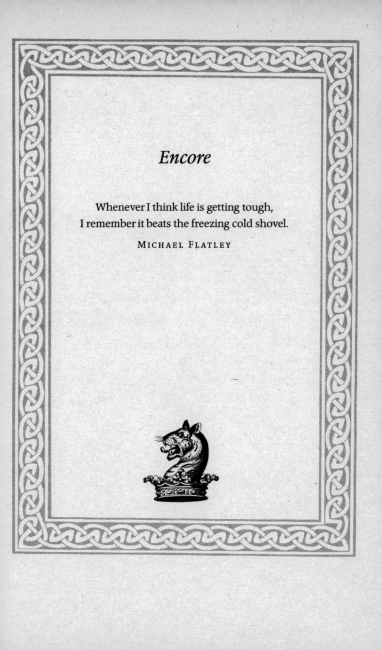

MICHAEL FLATLEY

Chapter Forty-six

A Light in the Darkness

Just as my dad is the greatest in boxing,
Michael Flatley is the greatest dancer.

MUHAMMAD ALI'S DAUGHTER RASHEDA,
Las Vegas, December 2004

IN MAY 2004, I attended a black-tie gala in New York to be presented with the Ellis Island Medal of Honor, which is given for professional and patriotic contributions to America. I couldn't believe I was getting such a meaningful award. Past recipients include Presidents George Bush, Ronald Reagan, and Bill Clinton; Prime Minister Tony Blair; Gregory Peck; Frank Sinatra; Donald Trump; Bob Hope; former New York Mayor Rudy Giuliani; and Muhammad Ali.

All the honorees marched down the aisle to the stage with the U.S. Marines on either side of us. It was beautiful.

On stage I was facing the front row of the audience where I noticed my great friend Dr. Michael Smurfit, a successful Irish businessman who was also giving a speech that night. He was receiving the Overseas Medal of Honor, which was why he was sitting in the audience and not on stage with us.

I noticed, too, that there was one empty seat a few seats down from him, directly in front of me. All the seats had the names of the person supposed to sit there written on a card taped to the back of the seat. When you're on stage, you don't really see anything for the first few minutes, especially in a situation like this, with thousands of people surrounding you. It takes a while simply to look around, get your bearings, and figure out where you are to speak.

But finally I saw the older woman in a white dress who was standing up in front of the crowd waving her arms at me. I had no idea she was trying to get my attention until the Chinese man next to me tapped me on the arm and pointed to her. I don't know how she managed to remain standing, because everybody else was already seated and the ceremony was beginning. But there she was, pointing to this chair which was right next to her and directly in front of me—reserved with a card that said "Hannah Ryan."

An empty seat for my grandmother. I couldn't believe it. Then I thought, "Well, I'm flattered that somebody knows I always leave an empty seat for my grandmother."

The ceremony went well. After I came off the stage, I asked to speak to the woman that both I and the man next to me had seen waving. Nobody had ever heard of her. Then I asked the organizers, "Who put that chair there?" They had no idea.

Suddenly I shivered. I thought, "Wow, she's here."

A few months later, I was in the St. Regis Hotel in New York. I was on the phone when suddenly the lights in my room—the chandelier above me—snapped off. Again, I shivered. "Is that you?" I asked. Then the chandelier went off in my bedroom, too, even though the bathroom and hall lights were still on. I called in the hotel butler and asked, "How come my lights just went off?"

He shook his head. "I dunno."

I asked him if they were on a timer and he said, "No."

He went right over and pressed the buttons and they came right back on. Totally bizarre.

If it wasn't such a good thing, I'd be scared, especially since it happens all the time now. The lights dim. Or the lights move. Any time that happens, I know Hannah's there.

I only hope she's proud of me. I couldn't have done it without her.

Dr. Michael Smurfit, September 2004: "Michael is somebody I am proud to call a friend. He is straightforward, honorable, and kind beyond belief. He was always going to be successful, but nobody knew just how successful he would become. We Irish are very proud of him."

Derry Ann Morgan has been present during "visits" from Michael's grandmother. She said at the Westbury Hotel in Dublin in February 2004: "Hannah was often with us. We were preparing for a show at the London Coliseum in July 1996 with Prince Charles as the special guest, and Michael was checking that an empty seat had been left at the front of the theater for his ongoing tribute to his grandmother.

"We were talking casually in the dressing room . . . [which had] a tall table lamp over on a corner table. Suddenly, as Michael made some remark, there was a crack and a bam! And a flame burst out of the lamp.

"We started to laugh, and Michael said, 'Okay, Hannah, stop, we know you're around. That's grand, we don't need any signs.'

"Little things like that would happen all the time I was with him. In Birmingham a journalist came to do an interview with Michael about his training and health, and I was there. And so was Hannah, I could very much sense Hannah.

"The girl asked me if she could wander into my room to ask me a few questions, and we left Michael. The next thing, Michael's security guy knocks at the door and said that Michael just wanted 'to let you know that the picture fell off the wall when you left the room.' Hannah was around, no doubt about it."

Writer Jan Moir interviewed Michael Flatley in Beirut where they walked down the Temple of Jupiter together. She reported in London's Daily

Telegraph *on August 5, 2002: "We carry on towards the exit when something strange happens. The lights around the site flicker and go out and we are plunged into the darkness of a Middle Eastern night.*

" 'There we go, that's my grandmother,' says Flatley, now just a voice in the blackness. . . . 'I truly believe that she and I are in contact and there is something special out there, that she watches over me.'

"With this answer, the lights go back on."

CHAPTER FORTY-SEVEN

Lady of the Dance

IN OCTOBER 2005, I had gone to the opening of Matt Malloy's pub in America. That evening, while we were kicking up a storm of music on the flutes, I turned and looked towards Lisa. I knew our relationship wasn't working out. I loved Lisa, but I was never *in* love with her. We had a nice relationship as lovers, but had come to realize that it was never going to be more than that. We had travelled the world in style, going to the best hotels and restaurants, beaches and resorts, the fashionable cities and designer stores, but marriage was just not on the cards. We had always enjoyed ourselves. Lisa was a fun girl, we had a good time together and laughed so much, but the engagement ended because our relationship was never going to be more than just fun.

When I first saw Lisa at Lillie's she was wearing a high-street dress and plastic platforms. The last few times I saw her she was wearing Armani, Gucci, Valentino and Versace, and looking a million dollars. She's come a long way and I'm very proud of her. She's made it to the top of the world. Yet, that night at Matt Malloy's pub, I made up my mind that fun girls were never going to be enough for me. I told Lisa it was all over and we were never intimate again. She asked if we could stay together until Christmas, for the sake of the families, and I agreed. It seemed the right thing to do.

Christmas came and we had a party for the dancers at Castlehyde. Niamh O'Brien walked into the room that night wearing a beautiful red dress. I saw her from across the room and something clicked. I spent the whole evening talking to her and it felt right. I didn't notice Lisa that night. In my heart I knew I loved Niamh. She clearly felt the same, but we tried to pretend it wasn't there.

When New Year's Eve came I had to ask Lisa to leave. There will always be a place in my heart for Lisa and I know we will always be friends, but as 2006 moved along I found myself sharing more and more of my heart with Niamh, and talking about life and future plans with her. I'm pleased to say that Lisa has moved on now and I understand has a lovely new boyfriend.

Niamh and I had been best friends for a long, long time, but this was different. Until that moment I'd been searching for someone real, someone substantial, a powerful woman with a great mind, who could help me make decisions. The thunderbolt had struck that evening, 21 April 2006. It was Niamh I was looking for and she'd been right next to me on stage for all these years. Perfect partners on stage, I knew we could be perfect partners in life. There's no way to explain how you know it's the right person. You just do. And you know precisely at that second. I give thanks every day that she felt the same way.

When *Celtic Tiger* was at The Point in Dublin, the scene of so many important professional moments in my life, Niamh came around to my dressing room after the show with her parents, Tom and Monica. She was wearing a navy-blue dress with white pearls and I'll never forget it as long as I live. The second she opened the door and I looked at her I knew for sure I was madly in love. Niamh O'Brien was never going to be just another girlfriend, she was always going to be my wife. That's why I asked her so quickly to marry me. I should have asked her right then.

We both remember a moment at the fifth-anniversary celebration of *Lord of the Dance* in Las Vegas, when I was kissing the dancers goodbye. Niamh came along and I said to her, 'Will you marry me, Niamh?' Was it in jest? Or did my sub-conscious know better than I knew myself? She whispered in my ear, 'If only you meant that.'

In Budapest, she was with me when we played to an enormous crowd. When the show is over the lights are so bright in my eyes that I'm blinded as soon as the stage goes dark and Bernadette Flynn or Niamh always have to come and take my hand and pull me off stage. That night it was Niamh. As she grabbed me by the hand I stopped her and pulled her back, even though the show was over and the audience were on their feet. There were enormous back lights that lit the full football stadium, all three tiers. We could see right to the back of the crowd and one hundred thousand people standing up.

I remember whispering into her ear: 'Isn't this incredible? Let's just stand here in the dark in front of all these people, who cannot see us, and feel their energy and experience this moment.'

That's the first time I ever kissed Niamh. That night. Right there on stage in front of all these people. Both of us will remember that for ever. There was something in that kiss. There had always been a chemistry between us, but we had never acted on it. We'd be dating other people and the timing was never quite right. But the woman I was meant to be with was there all the time. I know that we'd loved each other all those years, but it was never physical. Now, finally, the time was right for both of us and the true romance began.

One of the things I love about Niamh is that she is her own woman. She is a very quiet woman and highly intelligent. There are times when she shocks me with her insight. Naturally, we have similar views on some things and we have contrasting views on others, so at the very beginning, from time to time, there was a bit of an explosion. Even when we are hotly debating something it is exciting. When we're having an argument I sometimes half-smile to myself at how smart she is.

We were still going around the world with *Celtic Tiger* and after a long, exhausting, Asian tour the two of us flew out to Barbados. We had a really nice, romantic house on the beach, and Niamh did all the cooking and cleaning and really looked after me, at a time when my body was all torn to shreds from the tour.

As each day passed, what seemed to be preoccupying my mind was the thought that I couldn't let this woman go. It got to the point where I couldn't remember ever dating anyone else, I loved her so much. We'd swim in the ocean every day and stand and talk for hours in the water. This was July, and we'd only been together since May, so I kept thinking, don't rush into anything, slow down, slow down, don't ask her, but it was so hard for me to stop because it was all I wanted to do – I wanted to ask Niamh to marry me.

While we were there, we went to the Cliff restaurant, one of my favourite haunts in Barbados. As you'd expect, it's perched on a cliff, it has these magnificent torches that are lit all around the edges of the cliff. It's just the most beautiful place.

Niamh had a new white dress on and I just wanted to sit and admire her. I don't know what it was about that evening I think that it was the way that she looked so beautiful, but I just knew it was the right time. She was telling me some story, in her inimitable style, and smiling with her eyes, with that little girl's look on her face that is indescribable. I wasn't listening to a word she said. She was going on and on and I didn't hear any of it. Then it just came out: 'Will you marry me, Niamh?'

She stopped and looked at me, almost in disbelief. Half thinking, he's not been listening to a word I've said, and half thinking that I was joking. Then she just said, 'Yeah.'

For a second I thought she was going to go on with her story, but then I saw the tears, and before I knew it we were hugging and that was it. I couldn't believe I'd said it, but I was just the happiest man in the world once I had. As soon as she had said yes I knew everything else was going to be easy.

The proposal had been so spontaneous that there had been no engagement ring in my pocket. But I knew it was the right time. It had to be right, because I felt as if my heart was going to burst out of my chest. I could hardly breathe I was so in love with her.

We went home and I put on the iPod and we danced to Frank Sinatra's, 'Fly Me to the Moon', followed by Louis Armstrong's, 'Mack the Knife'. They are two of our favourite songs – we have the same taste in music. We danced all night, drinking bottle after bottle of champagne. Niamh called her dad and mom to tell them the news and we had the most beautiful, beautiful time.

I wanted her to be my wife so much and now, she is. Niamh is such a respectful and faithful person. I have always looked up to her. She knows every flaw I have, and there are plenty, but she still loves me. She'd never been married before and I never thought I'd get a second shot at it. I am so happy that it is with Niamh.

We wanted a proper Irish wedding, a traditional wedding for family and friends. We made all the decisions about the day ourselves. It was an enormous task. To begin with, we had met up with a few wedding planners. They were all great people, but the more we looked at it and thought about it, the more we realized it wasn't for us.

What they tried to do was to pitch us this idea of having a marquee on our front lawn. They were going to bring in all these specialists – one to do the tables and another guy to organize the speeches and another guy to organize when the bride would throw the flowers and another specialist to tell people to be quiet or to announce the first dance. They wanted to fly in a huge big-name rock band for the music. Niamh and I just looked at each other. Neither of us talked much after one of these meetings. We sat down in the dining room, poured the red wine and took a toast. I looked at Niamh and I said,

'Here's to us having none of that shite. And to having the wedding in our own house.'

She smiled the biggest smile I've ever seen and went, 'Yeaaaah!'

Why have your wedding in a tent when you live in a castle?

We arranged for it to be at St Patrick's, our local church, in Fermoy, County Cork, about three miles from Castlehyde, on 14 October 2006. My friend Father Aidan Troy from Belfast, where he has done so much for the peace process, agreed to celebrate the wedding with our parish priest, Father Anthony O'Brien.

Our friends came from around the world. Happily, my parents and the rest of my family could be there, as were Niamh's. She had six bridesmaids, including her sisters Aoibheann and Derval, who are also dancers and graduates of *Lord of the Dance.* My nephew Patrick Jnr., who was only five years old on the day, was the pageboy. It was a wonderful thing. His father, my brother Patrick, was my best man. The groomsmen were my wonderful friends Dave Egan, Daire Nolan, from the original *Lord of the Dance*, Ronan Hardiman, Matt Malloy and Martin Flitton.

I wanted some time alone to reflect before the ceremony started at 2 p.m., so I drove myself to the church. It was going to be hard to concentrate, for as I got closer to St Patrick's I saw the crowds blocking the way. I needed a police escort to get me into my own wedding! Talk about 'get me to the church on time' – it was nearly 2.30 p.m.

Then I started to worry about Niamh. By then I was out of the car and making my way to the entrance of the church. Still distracted by my concern for Niamh, I suddenly found myself in the church. It was packed. Our invited guests were in the centre of St Patrick's, which seemed like a flower-filled cathedral to me. All the other spaces were taken up by local well-wishers. There were so many friendly, encouraging faces. People stood up and started applauding. This was the most important standing ovation of my life.

There were my parents, at the front of the church, and my sisters.

Across the aisle I could see Niamh's mother and family. I was feeling very emotional. I gave my brother and my parents a hug.

While I was sitting there waiting for my bride, a fella walked over from the side of the church and asked for my autograph. I've never refused before and I didn't this time. He wished me well and said that he'd seen Niamh arriving at the church. (I didn't know till later that she could hardly get out of the car for the crowds.)

Then, I could hear something – it was the silence in the church. It's funny how you can 'hear' a hush. Some gasps followed and then applause. I turned around and there was Niamh. She was stunning. Absolutely radiant. The perfect bride. I had to hold back the tears. I had never seen anything so lovely in my life and I knew I was the luckiest man alive. I could see Niamh had a tear in her eye. One of the bridesmaids – they looked radiant in floor-length navy-blue dresses – handed her a tissue.

We weren't nervous, we knew this was the true day for both of us, but we were emotional. We said our wedding vows with passion.

For the wedding music, we were able to call on the best. Ronan Hardiman composed 'Angel of Mercy' for this so special day. The Chieftains, who'd witnessed me through ups and downs, were there to play on the happiest day of my life. Seamus Tansey, who'd seen me dance as a little boy in Chicago, was there, with a haunting flute solo. Niamh and I had heard soprano Sarah Barry from Fermoy singing, a wonderful talent, and invited her to perform at the wedding. The church was enchanted by her rendition of Mozart's *Ave Verum*. What a soundtrack for our wedding!

The ceremony lasted for about seventy minutes, which felt like seconds to me. There seemed to be love all around us, as well as some humour. I adored it when Father Troy told everyone, they could have married anywhere in the world but 'He shopped local.' I took that as a reference to my bride as well as St Patrick's. I wouldn't have had any other church, or any other girl.

In the closing moments of our wedding, Father Troy revealed to us that on a trip to Rome he had arranged a special blessing for us – from the Pope. He produced a parchment with the Papal seal and presented it to us. We'd enjoyed a truly traditional Catholic wedding, warm and gentle as it should be, and this was the seal on it.

Outside the crowds were waiting for us, Mr and Mrs Michael Flatley. We drove back to Castlehyde in a dream, but then we had to be prepared – we had a couple of hundred guests to entertain. As they arrived we greeted them, some, of course, reasonably formally, but for others it was lovely to be able to say, 'Meet the missus!'

The champagne and the wine, and the black stuff, flowed until the early hours. We enjoyed oysters and caviar and all the rest of a wonderful buffet. I picked up the flute and joined the boys, with Seamus Tansey and Matt Malloy. We played our hearts out.

Eventually, Niamh and I cut the cake and we had the first dance – an appropriate start to our married lives. The tune we danced to meant so much to us. It was 'Fly Me to the Moon', the same song we had danced to on the night I proposed.

On 23 October 2006, Mrs Michael Flatley, the former Niamh O'Brien, said: "I've married the man that I love and for me that's all that will ever matter. I always loved Michael and I always respected and admired him. It's great to have married my best friend. I care for him passionately as he does for me. Our love was always there but it took time. This is the highlight of my life, a dream come true.

"It's a wonderful thing that happened. That what was meant to be happened. Our wedding day could not have been more perfect. I wasn't nervous. I just wanted to get into the church and see him waiting at the bottom of the aisle for me. I wanted to be married to him and that was all that mattered. There were no nerves. As we kneeled together in the church I could only look at him, and he at me.

"It was a special thing between us. It was lovely to share the wedding with everybody but it was for us. It was for me and Michael."

Among the many celebrity and political guests at the wedding was Mary Harney who said during the Castlehyde reception: "It was a fabulous service, very emotional and very well done and I'm really happy for the couple."

One newspaper fashion editor, one of scores of journalists sent to report on the wedding, said: "The lace trimmed bridal gown by Manuel Mota was simple but gorgeous, set off by that spectacular pearl necklace. Now, that necklace was romantic – Michael gave it to Niamh that morning of the wedding. I reckon it cost him £200,000 but it looked fantastic – just like the bride."

Former Taoiseach Albert Reynolds, whose wife, Kathleen, went to school with Michael Flatley Snr., said: "From start till finish, it was a great service. The bride looked gorgeous, absolutely stunning, and it was wonderful to be there for such a love match."

Father Troy said: "Niamh was very emotional coming up the aisle and had a tear in her eye. It was a display of her overwhelming happiness at marrying the man she loves. They are a couple who God always meant to be together."

Celebrity driver Mick Devine, who drove Niamh to the church in a £500,000 Rolls-Royce Phantom, a gift from her husband, said: "It was absolute mayhem. I've done loads of celebrity weddings but they were nothing in comparison. We could hardly make it through the crowds. When we got there they were all talking about Michael's arrival and how the crowds were grabbing and kissing him."

Chapter Forty-eight

The Never-Ending Dream

What's past is prologue.

SHAKESPEARE, *The Tempest*

SO HERE I AM, back on the porch of Castlehyde, staring once again into the depths of the Blackwater River. So many of my dreams have come true. So many more are left to envision. Wonderfully, now I will be chasing them with my true love by my side.

I've experienced some passionate love and fabulous romances, but nothing like this. I feel blessed, even more so that I am about to become a father. Shortly after our wedding, we told our families that Niamh was pregnant. I can't think of any other way to spell happiness. We're overjoyed, and have all the more reason to look to the future, as a family, to make all our dreams come true.

I truly believe that the best is yet to come. As I look towards the horizon, to hopefully my next century or so, I feel that everything that's happened has somehow been just a tune-up, preparation for the main event. Yes, I've finally learned how to protect myself and how to run my business. But what I love most in myself is the artist deep down in me, the little boy who taps me on the shoulder when I'm thinking about a business deal and whispers, "Can we go out and play?"

As I reflect, I see that indeed, the same fights keep occuring again and again. Me, with my dreams and visions, up against those who say the odds are too great, the obstacles too daunting, the difficulties too overwhelming.

At the end of the day I made it because I believed in myself. In spite of all the begrudgers and the nay-sayers, in spite of those who would steal from me and those who would hurt me, life is wonderful, both the good and the bad. If you believe in yourself and you follow your dreams then nothing is impossible.

Index